DATE DUE

MILITARY MUSIC
of the American Revolution

MILITARY MUSIC
of the American Revolution

by Raoul F. Camus

The University of
North Carolina Press
Chapel Hill

This book has been published with the aid of a grant from the Sonneck Memorial Fund administered by the Music Division in the Library of Congress.
The University of North Carolina Press wishes also to acknowledge the financial assistance of the U.S. Army Center of Military History in making this publication possible, part of its support of the American Revolution Bicentennial.

Musical Examples by Helen M. Jenner

Library of Congress Cataloging in Publication Data

Camus, Raoul F
  Military music of the American Revolution.

  Bibliography: p.
  Includes index.
  1. Military music, American–History and criticism. 2. Bands (Music)–United States.
  3. United States–History–Revolution, 1775–
1783 –Songs and music–History and criticism.
  1. Title
ML1311.C35   785'.06'71   75-38947
ISBN 0-8078-1263-3

CONTENTS

ILLUSTRATIONS

MUSICAL EXAMPLES

PREFACE

From its first appearance in prehistoric times, military music has served as a necessary and indispensable part of warfare. So ingrained is the concept of military music that musical instruments have gained military symbolism. The drums of a British battalion, for example, are second in importance and significance only to the actual colors of the battalion and receive the same respect and veneration. An emblazoned drum on a recruiting poster in colonial or even Civil War America added dignity and respect to the call to arms. Contemporary journal entries indicate that recruiting parties in colonial times literally paraded with drums, and the act of enlisting (or reenlisting) was called "following the drum." This traditional symbolism also appears in works completely devoid of musical content but with musical titles, such as General Maxwell D. Taylor's *The Uncertain Trumpet* and Thomas J. Fleming's *Beat the Last Drum*.

In spite of the ubiquitousness of military music, very little seems to be known about its traditions and heritage. For many years it was believed that bands and band music were nonexistent in the Revolutionary period and that bands were not authorized in the regular army of the United States until 1834. Some tradition must have stemmed from the previous century, however, because of the tremendous vitality of the band movement in the nineteenth century. By 1825 the band movement, civilian and military, had become an indigenous part of the emerging American culture. While, in Europe, band music has always been known as *musique militaire*, in America it stemmed primarily from the militia, or civilian-military associations. Richard Franko Goldman pointed out that the existence of so many college bands in uniform is a strong reminder of this militia tradition.[1] Uniformed bands of musicians were, and still are, available for hire for any patriotic, educational, or civic function. At a time when symphony orchestras were not generally available as in Europe, military and militia bands were serving the musical needs of the new nation. It has been said that more Americans heard orchestral music in band transcriptions than in their original form. In these bands the young student could learn and gain experience. Victor Herbert wrote that "the important part that military bands have taken in the development of musical knowledge in America can not be overstated."[2] In 1907, Oscar Sonneck pleaded that the educational influence of military band music "should not be underestimated in a future comprehensive history of music in America."[3] I hope that this work will help to provide an understanding of the military music of our early history and will instill a feeling of pride in this important American heritage.

It would be difficult to name all the persons who helped to develop this study, but my debt to some of them must be acknowledged. Roger P. Phelps and William P. Sears of New York University devoted much time and patience to guiding the work through its stage as part of a doctoral dissertation. John Moon, retired senior Drum Major of the British Brigade of Guards and Household Drummer to Her Majesty the Queen, presently Drum Major and Musick Master at Colonial Williamsburg, read the work as it progressed and provided great encouragement, insight, and many factual details.

Of the many librarians and archivists who helped in locating sources upon which this research was based, Elizabeth E. Roth, Keeper of Prints, New York Public Library, deserves special mention for her kindness and generosity. Sara Dunlap Jackson and Elmer O. Parker were considerate and painstaking guides through the many treasures of the National Archives, an institution whose wealth is matched only by the friendliness and courtesy of its employees. Stetson Conn and Detmar Finke provided many important leads in locating primary sources and unhesitatingly opened their files in the Office of the Chief of Military History to many interesting items. R. G. Hollies-Smith of the Parker Gallery, London, was most kind in locating some of the rare prints used as illustrations, and Alexander H. King of the British Museum provided copies of many items unavailable in America. William Lichtenwanger of the Library of Congress and Harold L. Peterson, chief curator, National Park Service, gave constant encouragement, enthusiasm for the subject, and prodding comments to get the work completed. R. John Specht, friend, colleague, and choir director, read the draft and provided a nonmilitary perspective.

Finally, as conventional as it may sound, mention must be made of the long suffering and endurance of my wife, Amy Edith Camus, a musician, music educator, and mother, who subjugated her many activities to the completion of this work.

MILITARY MUSIC
of the American Revolution

1. EUROPEAN TRADITIONS

For a number of years it has been generally believed that the first United States army band was authorized in 1834. This misconception is due to a number of factors, not the least of which is a lack of understanding of the European traditions of the eighteenth century. In order to understand the military music of the American Revolution, therefore, it is necessary to understand the function of military music and the two organizations that provided music for the military: the field music and the band of music.

THE FUNCTION OF MILITARY MUSIC

The primary mission of an army, in general terms, always has been to deter or fight wars and to render the enemy incapable of further resistance. Any military personnel not directly engaged in that mission must be considered as supportive and secondary. Musicians, as overhead personnel, have been expensive—in former times usually paid more than the basic soldier and often more elaborately dressed. That musicians have always been associated with the military bears testimony to the value of their services in spite of their additional expense. These services can be divided loosely into four interrelated activities: development of esprit de corps and morale; camp duties; ceremonial functions; and social and recreational activities.

From the earliest times, music has been used to encourage the troops and to raise their spirits both in battle and during the difficult moments before and after the conflict. The ancient Greeks used instrumental music not only to maintain orderly ranks when marching into battle, but also to accompany the singing of paeans designed to instill patriotism and devotion to duty and to encourage the soldiers to excel in feats of valor. Similar examples can be found throughout the ages.

The questions of what can make a good soldier—and how to develop these desirable qualities—have been the concern of writers for many years. Tolstoy tried to explain the force of armies in warfare as "the product of the mass multiplied by something else, an unknown x. . . . X is the spirit of the army, the greater or less desire to fight and to face dangers on the part of all the men comprising the army, which is quite apart from the question whether they are fighting under leaders of genius or not, with cudgels or with guns that fire thirty times a minute."[1] Music, and ceremony in which music is an integral part, form a significant part of this "unknown x." One of the earliest leaders to understand this relationship was Marshal Maurice Comte de Saxe (1696–1750), one of the greatest generals of his age. Military historian Alfred Vagts believes that Saxe "possessed a flair for military psychology. He knew that the drilling of men . . . could not alone guarantee the quality of the troops, that rather the '*imbécilité du coeur* was among all things in war the most important, that to which the greatest attention should be paid.' On this feeling he intended to play with regimental music; not unlike some modern employers, he wanted to apply music to make the men forget the hardships of long marches. . . . Music would make them forget the exertion as it inspires people to dance to music all night who cannot continue two hours without it."[2] Reducing the above generalizations to the level of one soldier, perhaps representative of all soldiers throughout time, a South Carolina private who heard several bands play "Pop Goes the Weasel" at the end of a public function in 1861 said, "I never heard or seen such a time before. The noise of the men was deafening. I felt at the time that I could whip a whole brigade of the enemy myself."[3] The value of military music in fostering esprit de corps and morale needs no further documentation, but undoubtedly each member of a military band can supply his own examples.

Along with the morale requirements of music, the military musician has from earliest times acted as a conveyor of signals and orders. As armies increased in size, and particularly after the development of gunpowder, it became increasingly impossible to give oral commands. The development of techniques of mass unit warfare led to the need to move large bodies of men in a systematic and orderly manner. The easiest way to keep the men moving as a unit was to maintain cadence by means of a tap on the drum. It is difficult to determine whether the drum was used first for cadenced marching or for signaling, but since they are mutually reinforcing, the drum was quickly adopted for the foot soldiers, with the trumpet being adopted for the use of the mounted troops.

As the art of warfare became more formalized, the signals assumed definite form and tradition. While the first signals seem to have been merely blasts or taps on an instrument, by the seventeenth century the various camp duties and military signals had begun to be associated with specific melodies or rhythms. In addition to the standard commands used in battle, signals such as reveille, retreat, and tattoo assumed definite form, both musical and ceremonial, and became an integral part of the soldier's daily routine. The contribution of music to this movement toward traditional ceremonies can be shown by the fact that practically no ceremonies have survived without music, while those encompassing music have continued virtually unchanged to the present.

Along with these ceremonies, armies have traditionally indulged in the spectacle of parades. The addition of music to accompany marching serves the triple purpose of keeping the cadence, of encouraging the spirit of the men while marching, and of attracting and entertaining the spectators. Whether it be the arrival of government dignitaries or of the circus, bands have always attracted crowds to the locale of the sound and have normally maintained spectator interest during otherwise tiresome activities.

Ceremonial functions normally are inseparably linked with both music and spectacle and are aimed at the development and maintenance of the esprit de corps of the troops. Music and ceremony therefore complement each other and promote the same military objectives. As Farmer put it, "Every nation takes pride in its military music because, even apart from the appeal of music and spectacle, there is the call of patriotism. In Britain—a land as indicative in this respect as any other—the ceremonial of military music is closely linked with its glorious past."[4]

As the dependence upon music increased in the strictly military sense of camp duties and ceremony, it was found that the recreational aspects of music could not be denied. The same musicians and instruments providing signals and music for marching could also provide recreation by means of open-air concerts and diversions, performances during meals, evening entertainments, sports festivals, and riding exhibitions. Not only were there recreational benefits to the troops, there was also the advantage of better public relations with the local populace who were allowed to see and hear the performances. The nobleman who wanted music for his regiment could use the same performers to provide music for his evening's entertainment, whether in the open air such as the carousels of Louis XIV, the elaborate celebrations for the peace of Aix-la-Chapelle at which Handel presented his *Fireworks Music*, or the simple band entertainment as portrayed in the supper scene of Mozart's *Don Giovanni*.

With the democratization of the army in France after the Revolution, military bands were used to provide the music of the elaborate patriotic spectacles so favored in the early days of the Republic. In remembering the great popularity of the military and civilian bands in the last decades of the nineteenth century, one can accept the fact that Kappey was not being snobbish when he wrote in 1898 that the orchestra "addressed itself to the cultivated musical intellects," while the military and brass bands appealed to the masses at large.[5]

Music, in all the various military aspects mentioned above, is primarily devoted to the spirit of the fighting man. This function of music, and a justification for the band, is retained in the present mission of American army bands, which is "to promote and maintain the morale and esprit de corps of troops by providing suitable music for military formations, formal concerts, and recreational activities."[6] The mission of the band has remained the same through the ages.

FIELD MUSIC

The manner of warfare and the formal organization of the armies that had evolved by the dawn of the eighteenth century were quite different from the hand-to-hand combat practiced by the loosely organized armies of the Middle Ages. The soldier now was required to function as a part of a team, almost as an automaton, obeying strictly whatever command was given him by his superiors and never acting independently without orders.

Military music became an integral part of the training of the soldier in the required tactics and maneuvers. There were throughout the century two distinct types of music that had their own organization, traditions, and repertoire. These existed simultaneously and by the end of the century were often combined for special occasions. These groups were the field music and the band of music.

The new infantry tactics required the men to march in step, advancing or retreating in block movements. The drum, which the Crusaders had brought back with them in several forms from the Saracens, was found admirably suited to the purpose of maintaining the cadence of the men while marching. Garrard stated in 1591 that, "according to the stroke of the drum . . . so shall they go, just and even, with a gallant and sumptuous pace; for by doing so they shall be honoured and commended of the lookers on, who shall take a wonderful delight to behold them."[7] The eminent musicologist Henry G. Farmer noted:

The drum march, pure and simple, was one of the main features of martial discipline, and every nation had its own particular national type. Gordon Rothiemay records of 1637–1638 how Scottish drummers were teaching their soldiery to distinguish between "the marches of severall nationes . . . the *Scottish Marche* . . . the *Irish Marche* . . . the *English Marche.*" This knowledge was a necessary item even in the economy of tactics. During the Thirty Years' War the Germans once used the *Scots March* so as to deceive the enemy. At Oudenarde the Allied drummers beat the French *Retraite*, which even a Vendôme could not stem.[8]

These drum marches were held to be as significant an insignia of the nation as blazonry or standards. Exactly what these drum beats or marches were is quite difficult to determine at this date, but some indication of their nature can be obtained from contemporary sources.[9]

In order to provide some melodic interest, fifes or bagpipes later were added to the drums. At certain times of the day, or for special occasions, the musicians of the whole regiment would be combined. Whether fifes and drums, or bagpipes and drums in the Highland regiments, this combination was called the field music.

France and England had two basic cadences for their marching troops: the common or ordinary step and the quickstep. An understanding of the maneuvers of the period, as well as of the music performed, must take into consideration that "march" normally meant the common step, not the quickstep. Drill manuals prior to 1759 did not specify the length of the step, nor the tempo of the cadence, but in that year the Windham plan, published in London, specified a 24-inch step at the rate of 60 per minute for the common step and 120 for the quick. By 1786 the common step had increased to 70 per minute, and in 1794 it was set at 75 with a 30-inch step. As the cadence had increased by 15 steps per minute in these thirty-five years, it is possible that the cadence prior to 1759 was even slower than 60. Since armies were trained by the noncommissioned officers who had served in the ranks, there was no need for printed directions. The Windham plan, published especially for the militia, filled the void created by the lack of experienced drill sergeants.[10]

France, until 1791 had a step of 24 inches, 70 per minute for the *pas ordinaire* and 120 per minute for the *pas redoublé* or *pas accéléré*. Prussia had but the one cadence, the *langsamer Marsch*, which was between 60 and 72 steps per minute. When German troops served with the British during the Revolution, they were required to march at the quickstep. Georg Pausch, a German commander, noted in his journal:

Jealousy was the cause of my not being allowed to drill separately any longer; and I was forced to drill at 4 o'clock in the afternoon, according to their [British] drums, which my men do not understand at all, and who, if I left them to drill alone, would be totally demoralized. Every day, to my disgust, I have to practice the [lately] introduced quick-step, which we do not have, nor do they have it in Prussia—nay, not in the world, except in the chase, with fast horses and good dogs! This is a splendid exercise for men in winter; but in the summer, when the weather is warm, it is detrimental to the health of the men. It has no good result except to make the spectators laugh.[11]

The common or ordinary step was, as its name implies, that used at all times by the marching troops. The quickstep, sometimes called *pas de manoeuvre* by the French, was used only for turning movements or for changing position, and then the cadence would immediately revert to the common step. Some idea of the limited use of this step, which is today the standard cadence for most armies, may be gained from the British *Regulations* of 1794, writing of the quickstep of only 108 per minute: "This is the pace to be used in all filings of divisions from line into column, or from column into line; and by battalion columns of manoeuvre, when independently changing position.—It may occasionally be used in the column of march of small bodies, when the route is smooth, and no obstacles occur; but in the march in line of a considerable body it is not to be required and very seldom in a column of manoeuvre; otherwise fatigue must arise to the soldier, and more time will be lost by hurry and inaccuracy, than is attempted to be gained by quickness."[12] The regulations explained that the word "march" by itself always meant the common step, and that if the quick march were meant, it must be so commanded. Any performance of the marches of the period by a modern band or orchestra must take into consideration that the slower tempo was meant, not the quickstep cadence.

The drummer was musically responsible for the everyday routines of the soldiers. He would beat the calls, perform the camp duties, and provide the cadence for the march. Available records indicate that prior to the eighteenth century, nothing musically involved was expected from the technique of the drummers. With this consideration, plus the many additional duties enumerated below, it can be readily understood that the drummers were adult soldiers who were given the drummer's position in the company as an honor, which carried with it an increase in pay. As technique improved and greater facility was expected musically from the drummers, greater flexibility and longer training time were needed to develop proficient performers. Young boys could be developed into fine drummers, since they had the physical flexibility and the amount of time needed to learn the necessary rudiments and beats. Bennett Cuthbertson, writing in 1768, recommended that boys below the age of fourteen be enlisted to train as drummers, to be instructed by the drum major. These boys were not to be paid as musicians, but as privates, until they could perform their duties "in a tolerable manner." What is significant is that these boys were to be carried as privates in addition to the regular adult drummers of the company. The romantic legends of boy drummers of the American Revolution or Civil War should not suggest that these boys of the eighteenth century in any way replaced the adult musician; rather, they served as supplements. Cuthbertson also recommended that these boys, both drummers and fifers, preferably orphans or the sons of soldiers, be fully trained as soldiers as well, for they would make excellent non-commissioned officers when adults. In addition to the length and excellence of their training, he observed that "such boys, from being bred in the Regiment from their infancy, have a natural affection and attachment to it, and are seldom induced to desert, having no other place to take shelter at."[13]

Because of his important function and long association with the ceremony of the colors, the musician was dressed differently, and usually more elaborately, from the soldier. This difference also allowed the captain to locate the drummer, his signalman, quickly in the smoke and confusion of battle. In the British army an intricate color code developed by which each regiment had a distinctive color for its uniform linings, cuffs, and lapel facings. In the clothing warrant of 1747 the drummers of royal regiments were to wear red coats faced with blue, while those of nonroyal regiments were to wear coats the color of the facing of their regiment, faced with red. Strips of regimental lace were allowed to be sewn on the drummer's coat "in such manner as the Colonel shall think fit for distinction sake." In addition to this extra lace, which can be seen on the drummers' coats in figure 8, there were also strips of material hanging loose from the back of the shoulders, ending about level with the waist. These hanging sleeves were a remnant of earlier centuries and can be seen on the drummer illustrated in figure 1. This regulation applied to the troops sent to America under General Edward Braddock in 1755, so that the colonists would have seen soldiers of the 44th Regiment of Foot uniformed in red coats with yellow facings, while their drummers wore yellow coats faced with red.[14]

The clothing regulations of 1768 continued the use of reversed facings and special lace for musicians, but eliminated the hanging sleeves. During the Revolution, when over forty British infantry regiments were stationed in America, the colonists could have seen drummers wearing coats of blue, gray, orange, white, four shades of yellow, two shades of green, two shades of buff, or royal red. Under the coat a white or buff waistcoat and matching breeches with black gaiters were worn. Red breeches and waistcoats were provided for coats of white or buff. The musicians carried a short sword with a scimitar blade and wore a black bearskin cap with a silver-plated crest of the king's cypher. The drum was painted in the color of the regimental facing, so that the shell would match the drummer's coat.

This intricate system of color codes and additional finery seemed to lose favor in the eyes of some after the turn of the century as the following entry in the standard military dictionary of that time indicates:

MUSICIANS.—It has been often asked, why the dress of the musicians, drummers, and fifers should be of so varied and motley a composition, making them appear more like harlequins and mountebanks, than military appendages? The following anecdote will explain the reason, as far at least as it regards the British service:—The musicians belonging to the English Guards formerly wore plain blue coats, so that the instant they came off duty, and frequently in the intervals between, they visited alehouses, &c, without changing their uniforms, and thus added considerably to its wear & tear. It will be here remarked, that the clothing of the musicians then fell wholly upon the colonels of regiments; no allowance being specifically made for that article by the public. It is probable, that some general officer undertook to prevent this abuse by obtaining permission to cloth the musicians &c in so fantastical a manner that they would be ashamed to exhibit themselves at public-houses, &c.[15]

This is fine fabrication of legend without substance, which did not prevent the practice of reverse colors continuing well into the nineteenth century, and drummer's lace can still be seen on the dress uniforms of British drummers.

The word "drum" had two meanings during this period. When used in orchestral context, it meant the kettledrums, but outside the orchestra it signified a military drum, that is, a snare or side drum, there being no bass drum at the time. The first true side drum was the tabor, which is clearly depicted in fourteenth-century miniatures as being rope-tensioned and having two snares. The drum of sixteenth- and seventeenth-century Europe was considerably larger than that of the early tabors or those of the eighteenth century to the present. A drum of the Elizabethan period still in existence measures 22½ by 22¾ inches, which bears out Arbeau's 1589 description of 2½ by 2½ feet, since the unit of measure was literally the size of the human foot. Bobillier described the French drum of the sixteenth century as approximately 26 inches deep by 20 inches in diameter. Two gut cords were stretched across the bottom of the drum. These snares are not discernible in the reproduced illustration of a sixteenth-century drummer in figure 1, but are visible in the original etching. The lower right hand corner of the lithograph shows the drummer's position in the ranks in close proximity to the flag or standard. A fifer has been added in Schoen's work illustrated in figure 2, and this combination of standard-bearer, fifer, and drummer appears frequently in contemporary illustrations.[16]

Drums normally were emblazoned with the arms or crests of the king or the colonel. Ffoulkes noted that "the earliest known representation of the Royal Arms on a drum" appears in a picture of the campaign of Portsmouth in 1545. This type of emblazoning, as well as the snares and type of sticks used, can be seen clearly in figure 2. By the end of the seventeenth century, French drummers wore the livery of the king or of the colonel of the regiment, and the drums were painted blue with the arms of the king or red with those of the colonel.[17]

The drum of the eighteenth century was generally smaller in size than the earlier drums described above. A drum left by a straggler of Charles Stuart's retreating army in 1745 measures 17 by 16¾ inches. Another drum of almost the same date measures 19 by 18 inches, while a battle-scarred Flemish drum which Bessaraboff describes as "a typical infantry drum" measures approximately 18 by 17½ inches. It would seem that the drums were becoming smaller toward the end of the century, for a brass drum made in 1796 measures 16¾ by 15½ inches. This is also borne out by illustrations of the period and may in part be explained by the introduction of the bass drum near the end of the century. A greater tonal difference can be achieved between the bass and snare by increasing the differences in their sizes, resulting in larger bass drums and smaller snare drums.[18]

By the Royal Warrant of 1768, British drums were made of wood, painted the color of the regiment's facing, which would also be the color of the drummer's coat. The king's cypher and crown and the number of the regiment would be painted on the shell. Illustrations that are sufficiently clear to distinguish the details indicate that the drum slings or carriages of the period were worn about the neck of the performer, rather than over the shoulder as is the current practice. This is also borne out by Farmer, who in 1904 referred to the former method as being used "in the old days." These carriages apparently were made of "scarlet cloth with worsted lace" and had two loops attached for holding the sticks when not in use. When not actually played upon, the drum was suspended over the shoulder by means of a plaited cord, or drag rope, attached to the bottom hoop. Drag ropes are still to be seen on modern marching drums, but their original use for carrying the drum seems to have been completely forgotten.[19]

In addition to their musical duties, the drummers were expected to perform other important military functions. Ralph Smith listed some of the qualifications he thought were necessary in picking fifers and drummers:

All captains must have drommes and ffifes and men to use the same, whoe shoulde be faithfull, secrette, and ingenious, of able personage to use their instruments and office, of sundrie languages; for oftentimes they bee sente to parley with their enemies, to sommon theire fforts or townes, to redeeme and conducte prysoners and dyverse other messages, which of necessitie requireth language. If such drommes and ffifes shoulde fortune to fall into the handes of the enemies, noe guifte nor force shoulde cause them to disclose any secrettes that they knowe. They must ofte practice theire instruments, teache the companye the soundes of the marche, allarum, approache, assaulte, battaile, retreate, skirmishe, or any other callinge that of necessitie shoulde be knowen. They muste be obediente to the commandemente of theyre captaine and ensigne, when as they shall commande them to comme, goe, or stande, or sounde their retreate, or other callinge. Many things else belonge to their office, as in dyverse places of this treatise shal be saide.[20]

The drummer seems to have absorbed the medieval position of herald, which partly explains the high esteem held for these performers, as well as the custom of dressing them in elaborate uniforms.

Additional duties of drummers not mentioned by Smith were added in the eighteenth century. One was the execution of court-martial sentences. This involved the actual task of lashing guilty soldiers, as well as the ceremonial function of drumming miscreants out of the service. Another duty was performed by the musicians of the company on guard. The drummer had to take care of the guardroom and "keep it clean, attend to the fire and candles, and be responsible for every article in it." Francis Grose, in his humorous, tongue-in-cheek *Advice to the Officers of the British Army* (1783) suggested to the drummer that he "never sweep the guard-room till the guard is just going to be relieved; the unsettled dust will prove to the relieving officer that you have not omitted that part of your duty."[21]

In case of battle, the drummers were expected to remain with their companies, continuing to give the signals of the drum as required, normally marching immediately behind the advancing line. Following the battle, the drummer was expected to stay with his company to assist the wounded.[22]

When companies acted independently, their one or two drummers were under the direct command of the captain. As the number of drummers increased with the formation of regiments, and as ceremonial functions assumed more importance, someone to supervise and command these musicians had to be designated. The early history of the drum major, as this person came to be called, is amply described by Farmer.[23]

By the beginning of the eighteenth century, both France and Germany had authorized the position of drum major, but Britain did not do so until the end of that century except in the Guards and Royal Artillery. Nevertheless, one of the drummers, appointed by the colonel, performed the duties of that position and received some extra pay from the officers of the regiment, as well as stoppages from the pay of the boys he taught. The drum majors universally "should be men whose regularity, sobriety, good conduct, and honesty can most strictly be depended upon; that are most remarkably clean and neat in their dress; that have an approved ear and taste for music, and a good method of teaching, without speaking harshly to the youth, or hurrying them on too fast." In addition, they must "take particular care that those under their command are properly and uniformly dressed, as they are to be answerable for their good appearance; nor are they ever to over-look any neglects or irregularities committed by them. They must be very circumspect and exact in keeping their instruments of music in order, and that they practice three times a week under their respective masters."[24]

The drummers were part of the company, and the drum major had control over them only when combined or when functioning in a musical duty. The guard company's drummer would remain at the guardhouse, beating all daily signals and commands as required. Those drummers and fifers not on guard duty were to gather under the command of the drum major and beat the ceremonies or calls for reveille, troop, retreat, and tattoo. On these four occasions the drum major had control over the musicians and could dispense with his own playing; he could carry the traditional staff which had become the symbol of his office. The Honorable Artillery Company of London has a staff dating from 1671, and French illustrations of the next century depict drum majors with elegant batons similar to the gentleman's walking stick or *batons* of that period. Baton signals were already being regulated in France by the ordinances of 1754 and 1764. The shape of the staff seemed to have depended upon the wishes of the drum major or perhaps the officers who purchased it. Some carried the halberd, the traditional symbol of rank of the sergeant, as can be seen from Ffoulkes' statement that the last halberd known to have been carried in the British army was that of a drum major who used it until 1880, almost ninety years after their order into disuse by attrition. Since the drum major was not an officer, he would not have carried a spontoon, a practice in some modern "Revolutionary" units.[25]

The British *Manual Exercise as Ordered by His Majesty in 1764*, used as a basis for the colonial forces until the adoption of von Steuben's *Regulations*, does not mention a drum major by title and in the formation of the regiment calls for the drummers to be equally divided on the two flanks. When passing in review, the drummers are equally divided among, and marching directly behind, each of the four divisions of troops. Farmer commented that in time of war the drum major gave up his staff and took the drum, but this does not explain the *Manual* of 1764, at which time Britain was finally at peace after the Seven Years' War. The Prussian *Regulations* of 1759 also required the drum major to perform on his instrument. The French *Ordonnance* of 1753 does not mention the drum major, so he presumably was required to play. Since Cuthbertson (1768) recommended that the drum major's ebony sticks be tipped with silver, "it being part of the Foppery to be allowed in his appointments, for no other purpose, but merely shew," it can be assumed that the practice was quite recent in that the drum major still carried sticks, but no longer used them for their intended purpose. This was only a recommendation, however, and may not have been practiced generally, for the drum major of the 25th Foot was performing on the cymbals in 1777. Farmer noted that the *Rudiments of War* of that same year included the statement that the drum major is "always that person who beats the best drum," but he believed that "in time of war" should be added. Because Britain was at that time involved in the American Revolution, Farmer's addendum may or may not have been taken for granted. At any rate, British military illustrations do not depict the use of a drum major with staff until the end of the eighteenth century, considerably after the American Revolution. Since von Steuben's *Regulations* specifically positioned the drum and fife majors in the rear of the right division with the drummers and fifers equally divided on the flanks (see figure 13), it would have been ludicrous for the drum major to have carried a staff instead of the drum. One must therefore assume that the drum majors of the American army were performing drummers at least until the early nineteenth century.[26]

In addition to his musical and teaching duties, the British drum major was expected to act as the regimental postman, a practice which continued into the nineteenth century. Of more importance to the regiment was his responsibility for the execution of punishment against court-martialed soldiers. He was required to supervise the drummers as they lashed the bare backs of those soldiers found guilty of petty crimes and was even responsible that "no cat has more than nine tails" when used as an instrument of punishment.[27]

The uniform of the drum major was more elaborate than that of the drummer, usually on a level with that of the noncommissioned officers. In 1745, for example, a drum major's coat was prepared for fifty shillings, which would have been the equivalent of two months' pay for the private soldier. Later in the century uniforms became even more elaborate by the addition of epaulettes, silver or gold lace, and sashes. Cuthbertson admonished, "It should never be objected to a Drum-major that he is too great a coxcomb: such an appearance is rather to be encouraged, provided it does not exceed the bounds of proper respect to his superiors; his dress and appointments should all tend to promote that character, as it is absolutely necessary for him to strut, and think himself a man of consequence, when marching at the head of his drummers."[28]

At the same time that the drum was being introduced into the foot companies of Europe, it was accompanied by the fife for melodic interest. The Swiss infantry of the sixteenth century had its drum and fife, as did the Swabian infantry of Maximilian. Jean le Maire de Belges, in 1507, made reference to the specific military use of the fife and drum. Farmer believed that this instrument, like the drum, also was borrowed from the Saracens. Whether this claim can be substantiated is not relevant to the topic at hand, since under any circumstance fifes were adopted by European armies in the sixteenth century. Virdung (1511) mentioned it as a martial instrument of the Germans, and this is substantiated by Macqueron in 1527. François I authorized two drums and two fifes per company of a thousand men for the French army in 1534. Citizens of London mustered to the sound of the drum and fife in 1539, and an illustration of the siege of Boulogne by Henry VIII in 1544 shows fifers and drummers before the flag. Henry also used the fifers and drummers in his procession from Calais in the same campaign. Binet's *Essay* of 1646 mentioned a drum and fife as being part of foot companies of France. England already had them as a part of the regular troops on campaign at St. Quentin in 1557. The fife was considered as important to the unit as the drum, and the performers were equally respected. With the advent of the oboe into the foot companies, however, the fife seemingly was forgotten, and it fell into oblivion in the British army by the late seventeenth century. France and Germany did maintain the tradition, and England restored the fife to the foot regiments near the middle of the eighteenth century.[29]

Fifes of the sixteenth and early seventeenth centuries were one-piece wooden cylindrical flutes with mouth and six finger holes. The instrument was the same as that often referred to as "transverse flute." They seem to have been playable either to the right or the left of the player's face, according to taste or custom. While not standardized, they seem to have been, on the basis of the few examples extant, just under 24 inches long, and sounding the primary scale of D. The sound seems to have been quite different from the modern flute, for Shakespeare wrote of "the vile squealing of the wry-necked fife." Eight years later the same poet referred to

> The spirit-stirring drum, the ear-piercing fife,
> The royal banner, and all quality,
> Pride, pomp, and circumstance of glorious war![30]

Whether the "vile squealing" and "ear-piercing" descriptions are prejudice, poetic license, or accurate description of the sound of the instrument, is hard to determine at this date, but Shakespeare's characterizations would seem to be accurate, since with a ratio of one fife per company of a hundred men, a soft flute never would have been heard.

The music that these fifers played is mainly a matter of conjecture. Arbeau (1589) stated that the fifer could improvise anything he wished as long as he kept time with the drum, but he quoted several melodies for the fife. The Artillery Company of London exercised in 1638 to three specific airs for the fife which have been preserved, and Markham (1622) wrote of the drums and fifes sounding the calls together. Add to that the popular melodies played by the fifers in the seventeenth century which are still performed today, such as *Lilliburlero*, and it would seem that Arbeau's period of improvisation was not very extensive. Most likely each of the drum beats would have had a specific fife tune associated with it. The Earl of Arundel and Surrey's *Lawes and Ordinances of Warre* (1639), as noted by Farmer, directed that "every souldier shall diligently observe and learne the distinct and different *sounds* of Drums, Fifes, and Trumpets, that he may know to answer and obey each of them in time of service." The word "sounds," even to this day in English usage, means "to give a call to arms, battle, etc." The inclusion of "sounds" for the fife is significant in the above quotation, as then improvisation would be out of the question. Until a tutor or other manual such as those published for the fife in the middle of the eighteenth century is located, however, the music that the fifers performed at the earlier period must remain a matter of conjecture.[31]

When fifers were reintroduced into the British army around the year 1745, it was by means of a young Hanoverian who was given by his colonel to his British counterpart. The fife had not disappeared from France and Germany as it had in England, and the fact that the impetus for this renaissance came from a young man is significant. While the fifers of the earlier period always seem to have been men, from this point forward young boys predominated. Cuthbertson's recommendations regarding the enlistment of young boys to learn drumming are also applicable to fifing, except that the age limitation had been replaced by the statement, "As their duty is not very laborious, it matters not how young they are taken, when strong enough to fill the Fife, without endangering their constitutions."[32] Healthy boys of nine or ten could be trained as fifers, and this would explain the many diminutive fifers accompanying full-grown drummers in contemporary illustrations.

Only the grenadier companies were officially allowed fifers in British regiments. Composed of the "tallest and briskest" men, the grenadier companies were considered elite troops and took the position of honor to the right of the battalion. There being but one grenadier company per battalion of ten companies, that meant a ratio of two fifers for twenty drummers. The Prussian *Regulations* of 1759 allowed three drummers per company, but still only two fifers for the grenadiers. This may sound out of proportion, but the grenadier fifers and drummers always marched with their own company, while the foot companies had their drummers massed on the flanks. Thus only the grenadiers would have the benefit of the fife melodies, the others having to remain content with the cadence of the drums alone. Understandably, the others wished to have the same, and Farmer noted that "in the 1750s and 1760s, despite regulations, most regiments had from four to six fifers and twice as many drummers" in their field music. It would be logical to assume that the young boys, after having learned the fife, would be taught the drum as soon as they were physically able to handle it. In this manner the musicians of the companies, when gathered together for the daily camp duties, would be able to provide a balanced ensemble.[33]

Regulations continued to authorize two fifers for the grenadier company only, as shown by the establishment of the Buffs (3d Foot) in 1759. When George III raised the foot regiments serving in North America from ten to twelve companies in 1775, he authorized only two fifers and twenty-four drummers, or two drummers per company, with the fifers for the one grenadier company. When additional regiments were raised in 1778 to serve in America, the organization remained the same as before. Since contemporary accounts refer only to "the fifes and drums" without enumerating the specific number, it is difficult to establish the exact ratio, but there must have been more than two because the position of fife major is referred to in orders, and in one case a fife major gave concerts in America. Such a position would be unnecessary if there were but two performers. In addition, the number of fife manuals published in this period indicates a wider market than the small number of fifers officially authorized.[34]

The fife major, when authorized, was responsible for the instruction, discipline, and welfare of the fifers, just as the drum major had responsibility for the drummers. The drum major, being the senior of the two, had the final responsibility for the whole group. Cuthbertson recommended that the fife major be chosen with as great care as the drum major and even recommended that they both be tried out for six months in their duties before confirming them in "such respectable offices." The fife major was an actual performer. He was never expected to march before the fifes and drums, even if there were no drum major. His place was in the ranks with the fifers, and he chose the melodies to be played against the beatings chosen by the drum major.

The fifers and fife major were dressed in the same manner as the drummers. In addition to the scimitar-bladed musician's sword, they had a wood or brass fife case emblazoned with the arms of their regiment hanging by their side. A detail from a Hogarth lithograph, reproduced as figure 3, clearly illustrates the engraved brass case with its little lock and fife belt. His sword hangs by his side, but no sword belt is visible. The fife belt seems to be the traditional scarlet cloth.

When the Scottish Highland regiments were raised in the British army, they brought with them their own national martial instrument, the bagpipe. Turner (1683) noted that the piper was paid by the captain of the company, as he was not authorized by regulations, but pipers were later authorized for the Highland regiments in place of the fifers. The 42d Foot officially had a piper with its grenadier company when stationed in the American colonies in 1759, and an entry appeared in the regimental orders appointing him pipe major. Another of the same surname, possibly a brother, was carried in the ranks as a private, but upon the promotion of the other to pipe major was "to be on the posting of a Drum and to be subsisted accordingly."[35] Since the pipe major was only drawing the pay of a drummer, or twopence per day more than the private, the piper was making the same salary as the pipe major. What is significant is that there was a piper at all in any other company than the grenadier and that a pipe major was appointed. If there were but two, there would be no need for the major. The position and function of the pipe major was similar to that of the fife major, since these regiments also had their drummers and drum major.

While there have been many forms of bagpipes in existence since antiquity, the Highland pipe has been adopted as the primary martial instrument of the Scots and Irish. With the exception of the third drone added around 1700, the instrument has not changed basically since the early fifteenth century. The instrument consists of a sheepskin bag with a blowpipe, a chanter, and two or three drones. The chanter consists of a conical wooden tube with seven open finger holes and a double reed, with a range of g' to a''. The two drones consist of a tenor tuned to a and a bass drone tuned one octave lower. The third drone would be an additional tenor normally doubling the a, but occasionally tuned to sound the fifth (e'). An engraving by Engelbrecht, figure 4, portrays a piper of the mid-eighteenth century with a two-drone instrument, which was most likely the type used by the Highland regiments stationed in America before and during the Revolution.[36]

Because the chanter is never silent, a melodic technique involving many grace notes peculiar to the instrument developed. To what extent this gracing was practiced in the eighteenth century, particularly by military pipers, is unknown at this date, since practically all the music was traditional.[37]

While the foot troops had their fifers and drummers, the mounted troops had their trumpeters. The mode of battle and the vigors of the campaign, the small size of the troop of thirty to fifty men, and the requirement of being a skilled horseman normally precluded boys from serving as trumpeters. Because of the small number needed and the glamor associated with serving in the horse regiments, it is probable that the trumpeters were performers before enlisting and were not trained in the service as were the fifers and drummers. The simplicity of the calls, as well as the small number to be learned, did not prevent a private from learning if he wished to advance to the position of trumpeter.

The trumpet had not changed significantly since the sixteenth century. It was a cylindrical tube made of brass, sometimes silver, usually with two rings attached to which an emblazoned banner would be tied. The standard trumpet was in D, with a sounding length of over seven feet, reduced to 27 inches by the double fold in the tubing. The range of the instrument was the same as the hunting horn, that is, the natural harmonic series. While the same trumpeter may have been called upon to play the higher harmonics in concert performances, the normal military use of the instrument usually involved the third to the ninth or tenth partial.[38]

The music that the trumpeters played, usually accompanied by tonic-dominant tones in the kettledrums, consisted primarily of fanfares and flourishes. Those assigned to field duty also were required to know the various signals associated with the camp duties. At first the instruments seem to have been used merely to sound blasts which were understood by previously determined agreements, such as at the battle of Arsuf (1191) where "it had been resolved by common consent that the sounding of six trumpets in three different parts of the army should be a signal for a charge."[39] Another example is given by Jean Froissart, who included the following instructions in 1338: "At the first sound of the trumpet one dressed, at the second one armed oneself, and at the third sound one mounted on horseback and departed."[40] By 1622, however, Markham listed and described six calls for the use of the horse troops, which indicates that by that date the trumpet had been fully adopted for use by the cavalry and that signals were no longer vague blasts of extemporaneous character, but specific melodic calls with definite meaning. These stages of development are important to remember, however, for when the bugle horn was introduced during the Revolution it was used as in the first stage of the trumpet.

The British regulations of 1768 did not specify the dress of the trumpeter, except to say that he would not have hanging sleeves. He wore a hat, with a feather the color of his coat, instead of the helmet worn by the private. The 4th Dragoon trumpeters were permitted to have "Moorish Turbans" instead of hats, but this can be explained by the fact that since at least 1755 the musicians were blacks. For arms the trumpeters had two pistols and the scimitar worn by the foot musicians. The brass trumpet had a banner or tabard suspended from it, upon which was the king's cypher and crown with the number of the regiment under it, similar to the emblazoning of the snare drum. In addition, there was attached a crimson cord mixed with the facing color.[41]

The trumpet major was in all respects similar to the drum major of the foot regiments, except that he was always a performer. He was responsible for the welfare and discipline of the trumpeters and, of course, their instruction, since even a professional trumpeter would have to be taught the various sounds and signals. Later in the century the trumpeter was required to learn the bugle horn and its special calls.

BANDS OF MUSIC

The tradition of open-air music is an old and important one. During the Middle Ages and the Renaissance the town waits or *Stadtpfeifer* supplied the most common types of musical entertainment. The musicians who performed in these groups had gone through apprenticeship and formal training and usually could perform professionally on many different instruments. A woodwind player especially was required to know not only the varieties of one instrument, but the other instruments of the family. Carse stated that the woodwind player of the eighteenth century was fully capable on the oboe, flute, clarinet, and probably also bassoon. The performer also was required to double on the string instruments to form orchestral ensembles. This requirement has not completely died out even today. The British Royal Marines still require their bandsmen to double on string instruments. The German *Luftwaffe* band was able to perform also as an orchestra, the men being double-handed. Advertisements for musicians for the American army in the

1920s often preferred, or offered rapid advancement to, men doubling on strings. In the eighteenth century almost every musician was also a composer, and Carse observed that "most of them turned out musical works in an unceasing stream."[42]

The officers of eighteenth-century European armies, being primarily of the nobility, were accustomed to musical entertainments and did not wish to forego this pleasure while in service. Since the only musicians authorized in the regiments were the drummers and fifers, the officers, at their own expense, often hired professional musicians, clothed them in uniform, and had them serve as the regimental "musick." These men had not taken the king's shilling, the sign of enlistment, and generally refused to cede their civilian status. Existing side by side with the field music, these bands were primarily used for the entertainment of the officers, such as providing music during meals and for dances and social activities, including serenading. As the century progressed, however, more and more military activities were included. By the 1770s "no military ceremonial would have been considered complete without the 'Music' i. e., the Band, not only as an accompaniment to the 'Salute', but for the spectacular march past in slow and quick time."[43]

In an effort to reduce the amount of money paid by the officers for the maintenance of their band, some regiments required their musicians to enlist as privates (not as musicians, that is, drummers), and the difference between the private's pay and that contracted would be given to them from the officer's band fund. The British Third Guards apparently commenced this practice in 1749, but some regiments were still sustaining bands privately in 1824 when the War Office required all bandsmen to be enlisted.[44]

The British army of the eighteenth century had the curious practice of carrying noneffectives on the muster roll and pay list. These were fictitious names merely to draw the pay and subsistence allowance for some particular purpose, of which the support of the band was one. Other "contingent men" included three per company for the captain's own fund, two "widow's men" per company to raise a fund for the support of the soldiers' widows, and other miscellaneous funds such as for recruiting, agent's fee, and the colonel's allowance. The Royal Artillery, for example, had nine such dummies for the support of the band in 1772. In 1784 these contingency funds were abolished and an allowance substituted. Apparently the allowance was smaller than the funds gained from the former method, as the following letter of battalion commander Colonel Stephen Kemble to his commanding officer implies:

Dear Sir,

The Allowance for Contingent Charges to the several Regiments of Foot is so very inadequate to the Expenses incurred, . . . that I do not know, after repeatedly considering the Matter, how to provide for the following Extra but absolutely necessary and customary charges Regiments are liable to:

Viz.		Per Muster		
To the Serjt. Major, One Shilling per day		£	3	1s
Qr. Master Serjt., sixpence	"		1	10s. 6d.
Regimental Clerk, One Shilling	"		3	1s
Masters of the Band, sixpence	"		1	10s. 6d.
Nine Musicians at 2 per day	"		4	11s. 6d.
		£	13	14s. 6d.

During the War Establishment, 4 Corporals per Company were allowed; the extra pay of one went towards paying the Musicians and others, as also one Contingent Man per Company. . . . But it is impossible for us to make the above Provision in our present situation, and my ideas suggest no other mode of providing for these Contingencies, but by getting them admitted as charges on the Non-Effective fund, Which it may be in your power to get done. Will you therefore my dear General, consult with the Agent on the Subject; . . . but, should it not be favorable, the band of Music must be laid aside, for it will not be in our power to support them. . . .

The Extra pay of one Corporal and one Contingent Man per Company, as mentioned above, is communicated to you in confidence, and only expressed now to show former ways and means for a fund, but not possible to be put in practice at this time. [45]

Colonel Kemble's letter clearly implies that this was the normal manner of obtaining extra pay for the band for all regiments, not just his own, in the period before and during the American Revolution.

The famous "Articles of Agreement" of 1762 whereby musicians were contracted to serve in the Royal Artillery band illustrates how these musicians were obtained. According to these articles, musicians were to be hired by an agent in Germany to serve with the regiment while stationed there and then return with it to England. There were to be eight in number, specifically two trumpets, two french horns, two bassoons, and four oboes or clarinets. The enumeration of ten instruments for eight players has not been sufficiently resolved and may be a copyist's error in changing "2" to "4" or may be explained by the ability of the performers to play more than one instrument. The instruments were to be provided by the regiment, but maintained by the musicians. In addition, the musicians had to be capable of playing violoncello, bass, violin, and flute, "as other common instruments."

This double-handedness, the ability to play both a string and a wind instrument, is a very important consideration for understanding references to a band's performances, for no distinction in name would normally be made when a band played outdoors on wind instruments, or indoors on string and wind instruments, yet the musical differences would be quite striking. The articles also included the statement that "the musicians will be looked upon as actual soldiers," and they must "also behave them according to the articles of war." Farmer noted that if they actually had been enlisted, no articles would have been needed, and he therefore assumed they maintained their civilian status. Of interest also is the stipulation that the musicians were to perform at the wish of the commanding officer as often as he might desire without further gratification, but if any other officer wished them to perform, he must pay extra for that entertainment. This is not quite as unfair to the other officers as it may seem. Aware of their financial support of the band, the officers might have felt individually able to command it to play at any time, an inconsiderate situation as there were more than thirty officers. The commanding officer would normally be responsible for the coordination of all regimental activities and could therefore be expected to provide the band.[46]

Since the officers supported the musicians, they had a free hand in determining the uniform used and "gave them the most showy dress possible so as to give the greatest *éclat* to the regiment. The tendency was to dress them in coats of the facing colour or white elaborately laced and tasselled." The musicians would then be wearing the same coats as the drummers and fifers, but would not have the additional drummer's lace. The lacing referred to is the normal trimming, common to all uniform coats of the period. The only weapons they had were swords, and since these were provided from the colonel's private purse, they were of different designs as choice or expense dictated. The musicians in France and Prussia were dressed in the same uniform as the drummers and fifers, except for the special lace. Prussia allowed the musicians noncommissioned officers' hats and white sword knots, but no other distinctions.[47]

Considering their special civilian status, it was extremely important that one of the musicians be given responsibility for the others. These men placed in charge of the band were most commonly called "music master," but also "master of the band," "music major," or "master musician." The word "major" is an adjective denoting a superior position in a specific class and had become traditional in the military as, for example, sergeant major. Comment has been made on the adoption of the titles of drum, fife, and pipe major, but no such standardization took place with regard to the "greater" musician. This may in part be explained by the civilian status of the latter as opposed to the military status of the former, major being used primarily to denote military rank. In regiments where the bandsmen were enlisted, including the master, there would have been no objection to the term "music major," but its use seems to have been quite infrequent. Even though each regiment had a music master, later bandmaster, not until the middle of the nineteenth century was provision made in the British Army Estimates for this position. Simes insisted that "the best proficient in music and otherwise capable of directing, is to be appointed to act as master of the band, under whose immediate care and inspection the rest are to be placed, and he must be answerable for their clean and uniform appearance." One of the duties required of all the others placed in charge of musical groups was not required of the music master: the ability to teach. He was to direct competent musicians, not to instruct boys or soldiers in becoming musicians. The master was a performing musician, frequently on the oboe, clarinet, or horn, and he led the band with his instrument. Some idea of what was required from this man can be gathered from the advertisement placed in the *Daily Advertiser*, January 1774, when the Royal Artillery was looking for a master: "WANTED, immediately, a Person qualified as a Master Musician to a Military Band of Musick, who is a perfect Master of the French Horn, and performs on other wind instruments, as Great encouragement will be given. None need apply who is not a perfect Master, and can be well recommended as a Person of Great sobriety and good character."[48] The position was filled four months later so musicians with these qualifications must have been relatively difficult to find. In recognition of his position, his uniform would usually differ slightly from those of the musicians; it might have gold or silver lace instead of cloth, a cocked hat instead of helmet or cap, and it would be of better quality and workmanship.

Three periods of development can be seen in the band of music of the eighteenth century, and each is quite distinct in its concept. To lump the three together into one generalization causes much confusion, particularly with regard to interpreting the compositions that were written for each stage. As with all cultural periods, it is impossible to state precise dates for the end of one and the beginning of another, but each dominated a part of that century. In the early period the hautboys carried on the tradition inherited from the middle of the previous century. From the middle of the eighteenth century to the last two decades is generally referred to as the time of the *Harmoniemusik*, which was absorbed and almost engulfed throughout Europe by the third stage, Janissary music.

From the time of its introduction into European armies before the middle of the seventeenth century, "hautboy" did not necessarily refer merely to the player of the oboe, but to the military musicians in general, as distinct from the drummers and fifers. This broader meaning is used here to include early military musical combinations, or bands of music, the oboe itself, and the bassoon.

Fortescue wrote of two important relics of the Crusades, the first being the adoption of a cloth cross over the armor, each nation adopting a different color, which eventually developed into the military uniform. He noted:

> The second relic is the military band, which, there seems little doubt, was copied from the Saracens. In their armies trumpets and drums, the latter decidedly an Oriental instrument, were used to indicate a rallying-point; for though at ordinary times the standards sufficed to show men the places of their leaders, yet in the dust of battle these were often hidden from sight; and it was therefore the rule to gather the minstrels (such was the English term) around the standards, and bid them blow and beat strenuously and unceasingly during the action. The silence of the band was taken as a proof that a battalion had been broken and that the colours were in danger; and the fashion lasted so long that even in the seventeenth century the bandsmen in all pictures of battles are depicted drawn up at a safe distance and energetically playing.[49]

European leaders seem quickly to have adopted this practice. One reads, for example, of the battle of Halidon Hill in 1333 where Edward III of England was victorious over the Scots. According to the ancient chronicler, "This was do with merry sowne, With pipes trumpes and tabers thereto, And loud clariones thei blew also." Later in the engagement "the Englishe mynstrelles beaten their tabers and blewen their trompes, and pipers pipende loude and made a great schowte upon the Skottes."[50]

Musical units apparently did not exist in the various military organizations from that time until the Restoration, however, so the Halidon Hill minstrels may have been part of the royal entourage, rather than musicians in the army regiments. But the practice of outdoor music was not lost; it continued in the town waits and in the royal bands of music in England, France, and other European countries. These groups usually were comprised of shawms, curtalls, sackbuts, cornets, and recorders, the shawm being the principal instrument. Farmer stated that the shawm, like the drum, was taken from the Saracens.[51]

By 1643 the oboe had been introduced into the French army, and by 1665 the *mousquetaires* had three oboes and five drums to each company. In 1672 the practice was extended to the dragoon regiments, and by 1677 a fourth oboist and a sixth drummer were added. Jean-Baptiste Lully (1632–87), for many years *surintendant de la musique* to Louis XIV, arranged many compositions for the French units in the combination of descant, alto, tenor, and bass. The descant and alto parts were performed on the oboe, the tenor part on the oboe or tenor oboe (modern english horn), and the bass part on a bass oboe or bassoon. The four parts, playing together, were called "hautboys," a term which stood for the musicians as well as for the musical combination.[52]

Since Louis XIV set the standards for the age, other monarchs emulated this practice. The year 1678 marked the introduction of hautboys into the British military service, when six were authorized for the regiment of Horse Grenadiers. Charles II had been a refugee in France before his restoration to the throne in 1660. He often made secret negotiations with Louis XIV and must certainly have been familiar with the state of the French army, including its musical practices. The French form of the improved oboe had arrived in England just four years prior to Charles's authorization. The introduction may have been coincidental, but by a warrant of 1684–85, Charles, in the last year of his reign, authorized "twelve oboes in the king's regiments of Foot Guards in London, and that a fictitious name should be borne on the strength of each of the other companies quartered in the country with a view to granting these musicians higher pay."[53]

The warrant of 1684–85 may have been only an authorization for a larger number than normally accepted, or for the official authorization of extra pay, for the practice seems to have been common prior to that date. The *London Gazette* of 27–31 May 1686 presented "An Account of the Solemnity observed at the Proclaiming our Dread Sovereign King James II in the City of Madras on the Coast of Choromandell in the East Indies the 13th day of August, 1685, by Order of the East-India Company," in which "12 English Trumpets with Silk Banners, and Six Hoe-Boys, all in Red Coats, playing by turns all the way" are featured. While the East India Company was not a part of the military establishment, it did have troops for its protection, and these red-coated hautboys may very likely have been part of the troops stationed at that post. As travel was slow, the distant outposts of the empire would not have had the same practices immediately after their introduction in London. Further, *An Abridgement of the English*

Military Discipline, published in London in 1685, directed "the Ho-boys to be on the Right of the Drums, which are on the Right of the Battalion, ranged in the same rank with them." This same abridgement stated that in preparation for battle the hautboys were to join with the colors. It would not seem plausible to enter these instructions into a manual for foot troops if only the Foot Guards in London had these instruments, so presumably the regiments of the line had them some years prior to the date of 1690 ascribed to them by Farmer. Most likely, all the regiments were at full complement by the end of the century, for on 22 March 1693/94 John Mawgridge, His Majesty's drum major general, issued a warrant "to presse or cause to be impressed from time to time such numbers of Drums, Fifes and Hoboyes as shall be necessary for His Majesty's Service either by sea or land."[54]

In order to help musicians in this new type of military music, method books were published, such as John Banister's *The Sprightly Companion* in 1695, which has been called the "earliest surviving English tutor for the oboe." Just two years later Thomas Crosse was more specific when he published a volume entitled *Military Musick; or the Art of Playing on the Haut-bois, Explained and Made Familiar to the Meanest Capacity by Compendious and Easy Directions, Together with a Collection of New Airs, Marches, Trumpet Tunes, and other Lessons*.[55]

By the end of the seventeenth century or shortly after, each regiment took pride in its "hautboys" or military band. Even though few in number, they were able to play in four-part harmony, and their effect was so desired by the military that the fife was completely overshadowed for half a century in England. In an effort to reinforce the inner voices and achieve a new tonal color, the french horn was added during the first quarter of the eighteenth century. At the same time one or more trumpets appeared occasionally, normally for use in flourishes or signals, and not yet as an integral part of the band. Originally, the hautboys marched to the rhythm of the drums they accompanied, but as the group enlarged and as its musical literature grew, it tended to draw away from the regimental drummers, who remained as part of the field music. Throughout the eighteenth century the order of march of a regiment was for the pioneers to march first, next the band of music, and then the colonel, followed by the regiment in line of companies, with the drums marching either behind or to the flank of the companies. Musical considerations entered into the band of music, and as the century progressed, the drums were less and less included in the band, until their return with the Janissary instruments at the end of the century. An example of the band around 1725 may be seen in figure 5, in which there are four hautboys, consisting of three oboes and one bassoon, to which are added two horns played hunting style and one trumpet. The trumpet had normally been associated with the kettledrums, and logically both were introduced into the band and orchestra at the same time. Adam Carse stressed that where trumpets are included in a score (other than as soloist) there were always kettledrums, whether or not a part was written. This might pose some problems on the march, but no such limitation applied during outdoor stationary performances such as concerts and serenades.[56]

A grandiose example of the use of the military hautboys can be seen in George F. Handel's *Fireworks Music*. To celebrate the Treaty of Aix-la-Chapelle in 1749, Handel was commissioned to write a concert for "warlike instruments." Even though preferring to write for orchestra, Handel was persuaded to follow the king's wishes, and he produced a score calling for 24 oboes, 12 bassoons, contrabassoon, 9 horns, 9 trumpets, and 3 pairs of kettledrums. Observers to the festivities were more interested in the fact that the fireworks intended for the celebration caught fire prior to cue than in telling who the performers were, but it must be assumed on the basis of the king's desire for martial instruments and the number of such instruments required for the performance that the bands of the regiments stationed in London at the time were called upon to provide the musicians. Considering the variety of uniforms worn by the military musicians, it must have been a very colorful spectacle, as would befit the celebration of a peace treaty.[57]

In dealing with the records of the period, one must not be confused by the constant reference to hautboys. The term came to mean any military musician, regardless of the instrument he played. As late as 1834–35 in England the term was still being used officially in the Army Estimates to indicate the members of the band. Kandler noted that "hautboy" denoted the infantry musician in Germany as late as 1918. Therefore when one reads that a regiment of dragoons stationed in Ireland had six hautboys in 1739, it does not mean that only oboes were present. Most likely the band was balanced by the addition of two bassoons and maybe two horns. The same might be said for the directive of 1743 which prescribed four oboes for German dragoon regiments. Fortescue referred to another use of the word as it frequently was placed on the muster rolls to signify a noneffective whose pay went to the band fund.[58]

The term *Harmoniemusik* in German (*harmonie* in French) is still used today to refer to a band of wind instruments, which indicates its great impact upon the European scene. In English today it refers to a specific instrumentation, however, and in that sense it is used here. With the addition of two horns to the hautboys, and the reduction from three to two oboes, the basic *Harmoniemusik* developed. The rise in popularity of the clarinet after the middle of the century resulted either in the addition of that instrument to the other combination or its substitution for the oboe. The term *Harmoniemusik*, therefore, can signify any of the following combinations: pairs of oboes, horns, and bassoons; pairs of clarinets, horns, and bassoons; or pairs of oboes, clarinets, horns, and bassoons. Since it was standard practice in that century to double the bass line, at times only one bassoon part was included, with the understanding that it be doubled by the two players. Because of this small number of parts, from five to eight, it has been assumed that the music written for these combinations was chamber music, and their military significance has been ignored. These compositions, played by the military bands of the period, were not necessarily performed by one player per part, although this was the common practice dictated by financial considerations. Regiments that could afford additional players would double the parts, and quite frequently the octet would play music written for sextet or quintet, the oboes and clarinets playing the same part for greater volume. With this understanding in mind, a whole new world of band literature opens to the researcher and military historian. As an example of how much music was written for this combination, Bobillier mentioned an oboist who was principal of a school that instructed French Guards, who had spent considerable time in composing and arranging seven hundred pieces for outdoor performances. None of his music remains, and that was the fate of almost all of the other wind music of the period as technical improvements and Janissary music brought about a change in taste.[59]

The exact date of the transition from hautboys to *Harmoniemusik* cannot be determined, but it probably occurred sometime between 1743 and 1762. A *Treatise of Military Discipline* published in the former year referred to "Hautboys," whereas the 1762 edition changed the word to "Musick." In the latter year the band of the Regiment des gardes françaises was authorized sixteen men, doubling the basic octet. This was also the year of the "Articles of Agreement" of the Royal Artillery Band. In Prussia, Frederick the Great fixed the strength of the army bands at the basic octet in 1763. The next year, 1764, saw the appearance of the first theoretical work for the clarinet by Valentin Roeser. Its primary use can be gained from the title *Essai d' instruction à l'usage de ceux qui composent pour la clarinette et le cor avec des remarques sur l'harmonie et des examples à deux clarinettes, deux cors et deux bassons.* In 1766 the British light cavalry had their authorized hautboys replaced by trumpets, but instead of losing the musicians, simply required them to play trumpet when mounted, reforming the *Harmoniemusik* sextet when dismounted. During the next decade many British infantry regiments formed bands of eight to ten men. By 1788, French infantry regiments had followed the lead of the Gardes and had bands of sixteen musicians, but in that same year the Gardes increased their band to 24 men, and in 1789 to 32, or each of the basic eight parts played by four performers.[60]

A great number of important composers wrote for *Harmoniemusik*, and Wiggins commented on the predominance of this combination even into the nineteenth century. Throughout Europe every nobleman, whether of high or low means, attempted to have his own private little band of music for the entertainment of his court or simply for his own pleasure. The second act of Mozart's *Don Giovanni* comes to mind as an example of one such situation, where a personal *Harmoniemusik* octet performs contemporary operatic excerpts for the Don's supper entertainment. The musicians who performed in the private bands normally were engaged as servants, a common practice in the eighteenth century. As such, they would be required to wear the livery of their employer. In the smaller German states, it would be logical to assume that the nobleman required the regimental band to perform both for his court and for his regiment. The musicians were uniformed either in livery or regimentals, and sometimes the two were identical. The line between military music and outdoor civilian music, as the serenades, cassations, and divertimenti have been called, is therefore obscured. The *Harmoniemusik* was used at the *Concert Spirituel* of the Prince de Conti in 1766 and also in the next year by the Duc d'Orleans in public concerts. Sadie stated that the only full wind bands in England in the latter half of the century were the military bands. The Guard bands gave concerts in St. James's Park by 1770 at the latest, and Burney commented on their excellence compared to the outdoor concerts by military bands he heard on his journey through Europe in 1772. Kastner noted the practice of military bands playing selections for the spectators during parades or before retreat. By 1780 public concerts by military bands were being given in all the European capitals. These bands provided the general populace with their entertainment, and their repertoire ranged from marches to transcriptions of operatic and orchestral works. On a smaller scale the pleasure gardens of London tried to provide the same type of entertainment, but were limited by funds to combinations of two horns and two clarinets or other smaller groups.[61]

Orchestral works in the eighteenth century could be played in many different combinations ranging from a string quartet to an orchestra of forty to fifty players. It would be logical to assume that the wind players forming bands had had some orchestral experience prior to joining the military and would most likely continue to perform in the local orchestras, if not in fact forming a military orchestra of their own, such as in the Royal Artillery and others. Parke wrote that the musicians of the three British Guard regiments up to 1783 consisted of excellent players taken from the king's and commercial theaters, whose only military responsibility was to play the changing of the guard daily. Gottlieb Graupner, the noted composer and music publisher of early nineteenth-century America, was an oboist in a Hanoverian regiment prior to going to London where he performed under Haydn. Both Carse and Dart point out that the absence of a part in a symphonic composition does not necessarily mean that the instrument was not included. Bassoons normally doubled the bass line, particularly if other winds were present, and the kettledrums always accompanied the trumpets, even when no part was included. Oboes were used to double the violin parts, and clarinets, flutes, and oboes were used interchangeably. Because of the nature of the instruments, the performance techniques, and the quality of the players, and because the music was technically easy, Carse pointed out that the general standard of orchestral performance was not very high.[62]

Using Mozart's wind music as the epitome of the *Harmoniemusik* style, a description of his divertimenti of 1775–77 will give some idea of the type of music that was being performed at these outdoor concerts:

They are true garden-music; the sonata-like movements are as simple as possible, and to the minuet are added other dances—a *contredanse en rondeau*, a polonaise. Pastorales mix with fanfare-like phrases in the horns, and, despite the fact that the voices usually proceed in pairs, in thirds or sixths, there is the most sensitive feeling for the sound of the whole and of the individual instruments. The form is toyed with, without contrivance and without strain; it is songlike and yet never vulgar. If any works characterize Mozart as an eighteenth-century composer, it is these; they are "innocent" in every sense . . . written for summer nights under the light of torches and lamps, to be heard close by and from afar; and it is from afar that they sound most beautiful.[63]

Haydn also wrote many compositions for *Harmoniemusik*. The prejudice many musicologists have against military music and its musicians shows itself in Geiringer's description of Haydn's *Feldpartiten*: "The simple construction of each *partita*, the use of the same key for all movements of the short suites, the insertion of marches and little character pieces all show that Haydn had no intention of discouraging the members of Prince Esterházy's military band by setting complicated music before them.'' Considering that musicians of the military band probably performed the wind parts in the orchestral concerts, it is unlikely that Haydn would have insulted them in the manner Geiringer assumes. The biographer seems to have forgotten that the musicians performed these pieces on the parade ground, probably before and during military exercises. Music racks or lyres were unknown for use in marching, so the music would have to be memorized, and quickly. The horn players probably would not have had time to change crooks while on the field, and even if they did, would certainly not carry a whole bag full of them on the parade, and so the choice of keys became dependent upon the nature of the instruments used. Pictorial evidence indicates that the hunting horn was usually used on these occasions instead of the horn fitted with crooks. Compositions created for musicians to play while marching are normally less difficult than those for concert performances by the very nature of their use, and it is a general rule of thumb in playing for marching troops and outdoor performances that the simpler the better. In spite of his criticisms, however, Geiringer did find Haydn's marches to be ''strongly rhythmical pieces of a vigorous and virile character.'' It would be quite unfair and illogical to demand anything more from any composition intended for what the title specifies, the accompaniment of marching troops.[64]

A lithograph representing the ceremony of guard mounting at St. James's Park in 1753 illustrates the *Harmoniemusik* of the period. This print, shown in figure 6, depicts the basic octet marching before the grenadier company. The musicians are not gaudily dressed and have a discreet nobility about their appearance. The horns are still performed hunting style, the best manner for outdoor performances, and it is probable that the four woodwinds in the rear row are playing oboes and clarinets. If Grose is correct in his figures for the Establishment of 1753, the Regiment of Foot Guards had three hautboys at one shilling sixpence per day, one drum major at the same wage, and two drummers per company at sixpence less. The private soldier was paid tenpence per day.[65] That the band consists of eight men shows that five were being carried unofficially, either as privates or wholly paid from the band fund. Since the grenadiers were the elite corps of the regiment, no undersize persons were admitted. The only exceptions were the drummers, so the two small grenadiers in the third row, partly obscured by the officers in the foreground, must have held that position. Another drummer is depicted on the flank of the penultimate rank of the foot company, but the second drummer is nowhere in evidence, nor is the drum major, who certainly would not have been portrayed as a boy. The drummers, by their placement, would not have been able to coordinate with the master of the band as to selections played, and so it can be assumed that they acted independently from the band and possibly even from each other.

In writing about this type of *Harmoniemusik*, Farmer stated that "modern authorities on drills, evolutions, and exercises must have often wondered how troops on the march or at exercises ever kept precise step and time respectively to music supplied by so meagre and pulseless an assemblage as the above, since drummers were not utilized in the bands of those days. These, with their congeners the fifers, were kept separate and distinct as a unit in themselves."[66] Farmer advanced two reasons for the lack of drums in the bands of the period: the conservatism of the bandmasters and the taste of the officers in preferring *Harmoniemusik*. Certainly the officers, who were paying for the pleasure of the band, could determine its instrumentation, and what pleased them at the time was what they had become accustomed to in their own homes and those of their acquaintances among the nobility. The bandmasters, or music masters, having been professionally trained as musicians, not as soldiers, could be depended upon to provide compositions based upon musical considerations rather than the requirements of the steady cadence of the march as provided by the percussion section. An example of this conservatism can be seen from the description Burney gave of the music of German troops garrisoned at Ghent in 1772:

I found two Walloon regiments here; and though no general officer was on the spot, yet there were two bands attending every morning and evening, on the *Place d'Armes*, or parade. The one was an extra-band of professed musicians, consisting of two hautbois, two clarinets, two bassoons, and two French horns; the other were enlisted men and boys, belonging to the regiment; the number of these amounted to twenty. There were four trumpets, three fifes, two hautbois, two clarinets, two *tambours de basque* [tambourines], two French horns, one *crotolo* or cymbal, three side-drums, and one great kettledrum. All these sonorous instruments, in the open air, have a very animating and pleasing effect.

The professionals marched without drums and were evenly balanced according to the taste of the time. The amateurs, the boys and men of the regiment (implying they were enlisted), played whatever they had available and had succumbed to the Janissary craze.[67]

The writers and performers who advocate adding drums to the

Harmoniemusik compositions should remember that the cultivated taste, as with Burney's "professed musicians," did not favor the use of drums. How shocked one would be to hear drums accompanying the band playing for Don Giovanni's entertainment referred to above, and yet this same type of music was performed outdoors for precisely the same purpose. Even more shocking would be the use of drum accompaniment to the serenade of Ferrando and Guglielmo in *Cosí Fan Tutte*, and yet it is a military band that provides the music. Mozart was well aware of Janissary or "Turkish music," with its bass drum, triangle, cymbals, and tambourine, having used it in the *Abduction from the Seraglio* (1781) and other works. Had he wanted that effect, or had that been the prevailing style for bands in general, he certainly would have used Janissary instruments in *Don Giovanni* (1787) or *Cosí Fan Tutte* (1790). Even when he did use Janissary instruments, it was without the snare drum. This reinforces the belief that the Janissary instruments entered into the *Harmoniemusik* first, and not until considerably later did the snare drum become an integral part of the band. Standing orders of the 29th Foot as late as 1812 still designated that "cymbals, big drum, and tambourines when employed are considered as belonging to the Band," and not the field music. The use of the bass drum in "Revolutionary" fife and drum corps is therefore historically incorrect.[68]

Another example of the separation of the band of music from the field music can be seen in figure 7. When the news of General Howe's capture of New York spread through Europe, the "newsreel" makers of the time provided illustrations to accompany their information. These were lithographs put into shadow boxes carried by itinerants and would be made as soon after the event as possible, while the news was of interest. It can, therefore, be assumed that this illustration was made shortly after 15 September 1776. While the illustration cannot be relied upon as an accurate depiction of the event, since the German maker probably had no notion of the New York skyline or the line of march, it can be taken as an accurate reflection of the normal practice of the time. At the head of the grenadier company can be seen a band of six men, playing horns, bassoons, and either oboes or clarinets. The drummers of the grenadier company have been portrayed in the front rank of the company, contrary to British practice at the time, but are still too far removed from the band to be able to coordinate their activities. Presumably each drummer accepted the cadence and rhythm of the master of music at the head of the line, but one should not be too idealistic with regard to musical requirements. The mounted trumpeters and kettledrummer seem to be in the act of performing, adding to the general sound level of the scene. This was most likely a general practice or the lithographer would not have depicted the scene in that manner. As a sidelight on this situation of military tradition or ceremony taking precedence over musical considerations, as late as 1946 the manual for United States army bands requried that ''as the colors 'dip' in salute he [the sergeant bugler] will give the proper signal to the field music to COMMENCE PLAYING and render the prescribed ruffles and flourishes. The band continues to play without regard to the field music.'' Since the flourish consisted of a dominant-tonic figuration in the key of G on the bugles, it would never be in tune with the band which normally played in flat keys. In addition, it mattered not where in the particular march the flourish was sounded, so that there was most likely a conflict of rhythm and melody as well. The manual of 1957 changed this procedure, but contained the admonition, ''at no time will the field music render the honors while the band is playing,'' so that some bandmasters must have continued the practice up to that time.[69]

Such a cacophony must have made it difficult for the men to keep a steady cadence while marching. The British *Rules and Regulations* of 1794 tried to correct the situation:

The use of MUSIC or DRUMS to regulate the march is absolutely forbid, as incompatible with the just and combined movements of any considerable body, and giving a false aid to the very smallest.—They never persevere in the ordered time or in any other, are constantly changing measure, create noise, derange the equality of step, and counteract the very end they are supposed to promote. The ordered and cadenced MARCH can be acquired and preserved from the eye and habit alone, and troops must by great practice be so steadied as to be able to maintain it, even though drums, musick, or other circumstances, should be offering a different marked time.[70]

By the time the above regulations were written, a new element had been added to the *Harmoniemusik*. While the Crusaders had come into contact with and had emulated the concept of the military bands of the Turkish Janissaries (*Yenicheri*), it was not until 1720 when the Sultan gave a complete band to Augustus II of Poland that this new style became noticed in Europe. The craze spread quickly and is reflected in the literature, costume, art, and music of the time. Stories and illustrations of the Turkish harem, or seraglio, came into vogue. Particular percussion instruments were added to any musical composition to give a ''Turkish'' effect, and bands, always the exemplification of the popular culture of the time, followed suit. The appearance of this Janissary music constitutes the third phase in the development of band music in the eighteenth century.

At first the term "Turkish music" meant any or all of the various instruments borrowed from the Janissary bands, but by the end of the century it had standardized into a reference to the use of the bass drum, cymbals, tambourine, and triangle.

The idea of a bass drum was not new to Europe, since the Turkish drums were not much larger than the drums used in the sixteenth century, and drums without snares were not unknown. Europeans were impressed by the manner of playing as well as by the bizarre costumes of the performers. Instead of using two sticks on one head, the player suspended the drum across his abdomen and used a stick on one head and one or more birch twigs or switches on the other. The sound of the switch on the head compares very favorably with the sound of the snare drum, and the bass drummer was thus able to achieve both effects on one instrument. The various strokes were distinguished in the music by having sticked notes written with tails down on the staff, while the birch strokes were written with tails up. The Janissary drum was not the bass drum of today with its large heads and relatively thin, cylindrical body; rather, it had a shell depth and head diameter roughly equal in size, generally around 28 inches. Curt Sachs noted that until the nineteenth century this instrument was known as the Turkish drum.[71]

The cymbals have not changed considerably from that time to the present, except that the Janissary instruments were generally a little smaller, allowing for greater freedom in performing movements with the pair.

While the tambourine, under the name timbrel, was familiar to Europeans, particularly in Biblical references, its actual use had declined during the Renaissance. With the other Janissary instruments, it was reintroduced into Europe with great effect. As at present, the tambourine was a drum with a single head stretched over a hoop of wood, with metal jingles inserted around the edge in one or two rows. The Turkish tambourine was at least twice the size of that used today, as shown by contemporary illustrations. An instrument dating from 1750, measuring 20 inches in diameter, may be cited as typical.[72]

The triangle had been known in Europe prior to the interest in Janissary music, but not always in triangular form. The Janissary instrument was slightly heavier and larger than that previously used and frequently retained the loose metal rings strung over the horizontal section.[73]

While kettledrums had been copied from the Turks during the time of the Crusades, the concept of a single timpanum carried and played by one performer was reintroduced along with the other Janissary instruments. The drum was slightly smaller in size, for greater portability, and was not used extensively. It was replaced in the nineteenth century by the tenor drum and is not generally included in the term "Turkish music."[74]

Another instrument borrowed from the Janissaries became popular after 1800 in the military bands of Europe. This was the Turkish crescent, or "jingling johnny" taken from the Turkish name *chaghana*. The concept of a staff with tinkling jingles is common among many primitive cultures, particularly as used in religious ceremonies. The Turkish form was surmounted by the crescent, which gave it its English name. Some crescents had been brought back from the Crusades, but the instrument was not generally common until the nineteenth century. Since it is known to the French as *pavillon chinois*, Sachs believed that it may have been introduced more because of the French taste for *chinoiserie* than for Turkish considerations. The instrument is still used by some German bands, but has been generally replaced by the glockenspiel.[75]

At first the performers were Turkish, but as the supply became insufficient for the demand, Negroes were used. These players became extremely popular by reason of the antics they displayed in performing on the percussion instruments. Farmer described them thus: "The modern cross-handed drumming on the bass drum, the leopard or tiger skin apron, and a few other oddities, are survivals of their *régime* as percussionists. Dressed in high turbans, bearskins, or cocked hats, with towering hackle feather plumes, and gaudy coats of many colours, braided and slashed gorgeously and gapingly, they capered rather than marched, and flung their drumsticks and tambourines into the air, adroitly catching them in discreetly measured cadences. Their agility with fingers, arms and legs was only equalled by their perfect time in the music."[76]

With such crowd pleasers, every regiment tried to outdo the others in unconventionality. Burney had seen cymbals used in military bands at Florence, Lille, and Maastricht while on his journey in 1772, but they were so new to him and presumably to his English readers that he described them at great length. The 22d Foot obtained a pair of cymbals in 1767 and a second pair in 1769. The 24th Foot had a pair in 1777, and the 25th Foot had its drum major playing a pair in the same year. By 1787 the Royal Artillery Band had obtained cymbals, a bass drum, and a tambourine. There is no mention of other bands obtaining Janissary instruments in England prior to this time, and since the Household bands stationed in London received theirs after the

American Revolution, it would be logical to assume that the regiments of the line were still using *Harmoniemusik*. The 25th Foot did not serve in America, so the colonists would only have had the opportunity of seeing Janissary instruments in the form of cymbals in the 22d and 24th Regiments of Foot. [77]

After the American Revolution, the Janissary instruments became common throughout Europe and England. A print of the guard mounting at St. James's around 1790, as illustrated in figure 8, depicts the band in England just before the turn of the century. Comparing this print to the same guard mounting in 1753, figure 6, one can see that the original *Harmoniemusik* has been altered. A serpent has been substituted for one of the bassoons in order to strengthen the bass line; a trumpet has replaced one of the clarinets or oboes; and the horn is the type with tuning crooks instead of the earlier natural horn. The bassoon, on the other hand, appears to be a double curtall, a remnant from the sixteenth and seventeenth centuries. In front of the combined band and field music marches the drum major. His baton is more like a gentleman's walking stick, more French in form than the British mace. As part of the field music, he wears drummer's lace, as do the rest of the fifers and drummers. Following the band is the Janissary section, consisting of three turbanned and costumed Negroes and two young boys. The Janissaries march separately from the band, and following them is the field music, including small figures representing boys. The illustrator has portrayed all the musicians in the act of performing, but with such a balance it would be unlikely that the band would be heard over the percussion and the high pitch of the fifes. This is probably artistic license, and the band and the field music alternated on the march, as in fact they do to the present. In 1778, Hinde instructed that the slow march should be accompanied by the full band of music, but that the quick march was to be accompanied by the fifes and drums. Since the guards would march past the reviewing officer at both cadences in the guard mounting, both band and field music would display their abilities, there could be no mistaking the rhythmic vitality of the band. [78]

By 1820, as represented in figure 9 illustrating *La Musique Royale* in France, the Negroes had disappeared, and so too had their costumes, all of the men now being similarly uniformed. The bass drummer is clearly seen using a switch on one head and a stick on the other. On his right there is a drummer, but since this drum is considerably longer than any of the snare drums depicted in French illustrations of the period, it is most likely a tenor drum, the later replacement for the timpanum. The other Janissary instruments, including the Turkish crescent, complete the section. By this time the percussion section had become so large that additional winds had to be included in the band in order to provide some musical balance. New instruments, such as the trombone and piccolo, were added, and mechanical improvements were made to the older instruments. These events all took place, however, after 1783. The *Harmoniemusik*, therefore, is of most importance in considering the military bands of the American Revolution.

2. THE FOUNDATIONS OF AMERICAN MILITARY MUSIC

The traditions of American military music are rooted in the very foundations of the nation. Three important influences shaped these traditions—the colonial militia, the British army, and the colonial musical environment—and a knowledge of each is necessary to understand this heritage.

THE COLONIAL MILITIA

After the Assize of Arms in 1181 the English freeman was required "to provide himself with arms, to train periodically under the local militia officer, and to be ready for the king's call to service." This concept of militia was among the many English institutions brought to the colonies by the early settlers. The militia in England atrophied after the organization of a standing army by Charles II, but it became ever more important in the American colonies. Weigley noted:

[These colonies] were much too poor to permit a class of able-bodied men to devote themselves solely to war and preparation for war. Every colonist had to contribute all the energy he could to the economic survival of his colony, and no colony could afford to maintain professional soldiers. Yet through most of the [seventeenth] century every part of the colonies remained subject to military danger, potentially from Spain and France and actually from the Indians. Therefore every colony needed military protection, and every colony save the Quaker settlements sought to obtain it by invoking the historic English principle of a universal obligation to military service, in order to create a military force of armed civilians.[1]

The militia was patterned after the military organizations of Europe at the time, and, as seen in chapter 1, music was an important part of every military unit. Even before the founding of the American colonies, music performed an important role in the New World. When Jacques Cartier visited the village of Hochelaga in New France in 1535, his trumpets and other musical instruments cheered the inhabitants. John Utie, a professional musician in England, brought his viol with him to Virginia in 1624, where he served as an ensign in the militia. In 1633, Virginia colony's drummers received one thousand pounds of tobacco and six barrels of corn per year for their services. New Hampshire in

1635 had at least two drums to use on training days and no less than fifteen "hautboys and soft recorders" to cheer the immigrants in their solitude. Some of the oboes undoubtedly were used on festive occasions, and Pichierri observed that they must have been held in high esteem to have been granted shipping space otherwise given only to the transport of basic essentials. The directors of Amsterdam supplied their new colony with drums for the militia in 1659, and Montreal was never without at least one drummer, even when the garrison consisted of as few as ten privates. Trumpets were used to give commands during Bacon's Rebellion of 1676, and Colonel William Farrar of Virginia bequeathed a drum emblazoned with the family arms in the same year. In 1687 the Virginia counties voted to purchase such drums, trumpets, and colors as were necessary for the use of the militia, using tax money to pay for them, thus establishing an important precedent regarding the purchase of musical instruments. While every free white male was required to serve in the militia and furnish arms and accoutrements at his own expense, the musician was furnished his instrument at the public expense. (In some colonies it was at the expense of the officers or from fines for nonattendance at musters and for minor infractions of regulations.) Since the musician did not carry arms other than perhaps a small sword, the instrument might have been his financial responsibility in place of the cost of his weapon, but that such was not the case indicates the high esteem in which military musicians were held. Some military instruments were privately owned, for Thomas Hill had his own trumpet and sword in 1710, and "4 howboys" were listed in the estate of Captain William Tyson in 1719.[2]

The English identified drums with foot troops and trumpets with horse troops. When Colonel John Barnwell led an expedition against the Indians in 1712, he had two trumpeters and two drummers to sound and beat his commands. At a county fair in 1737 it was reported that "a Flag was displayed, Drums were beating, Trumpets sounding, and other Musick playing, for the Entertainment of the Company, and the whole was manag'd with as good Order, and gave as great Satisfaction, in general, as cou'd possibly be expected." The militia had yearly training days when all the members of the company assembled on the public grounds, practiced the manual of arms and drill, and passed in review and inspection before the militia officers and public officials. Refreshments, games, and socializing usually followed the military activities. The presence of the trumpets and drums at the above-described fair may have indicated that it was held in conjunction with one of the training days or that the militia company musicians had been engaged to help in the festivities. The trumpet was used commonly throughout the colonies to sound public assembly and martial calls and most likely for secular amusements. One sounded the starting signal at a horse race held at Williamsburg, Virginia, in 1739, certainly an appropriate use for a military instrument.[3]

The trumpeter may have been a Negro, for the previous year the Virginia legislature had enacted a statute that required all "free mulattos, negros, or Indians" to serve in the militia. They could be employed as drummers, trumpeters, or pioneers, but were forbidden to carry arms. This practice spread to the other colonies, and Negro musicians were seen often in the militia units.[4]

As the population of the colonies increased, the whole militia was seldom needed at any one time. A division arose among the able-bodied men into a "common" and a "volunteer" militia, with the former serving as a training ground for the latter. When troops were needed, the legislatures would assign quotas to the local militia districts, and units would be formed. If there were insufficient volunteers, the men would be drafted by lot. The men would be required to serve for a stipulated emergency situation and normally only within the limits of their colony.

The volunteer militia began to take on the status of an elite organization, whose members were chosen with the proviso that they would be the first to serve in case of emergency. The eliteness "often became social as well as military, with the volunteer militia sometimes choosing their recruits on some basis of exclusiveness." Predominant in this exclusiveness was membership in the Society of Freemasons, and even into the early nineteenth century the great majority of army officers were members. The Ancient and Honorable Artillery Company of Boston, organized in 1636, is an example of an early militia volunteer unit that was quite exclusive in its membership. As early as 1643 volunteer militia units had been organized into small groups to be ready at thirty minutes' warning, the forerunners of the Revolutionary minutemen.[5]

Over 160 members of the Freemasons of Philadelphia paraded on St. John Baptist's Day in 1755, "attended by a Band of Music." As the Freemasons included the prominent men of the city, the band marching before them must have been representative of their station. Since many of the members of the Society were also officers in the volunteer militia, their band may have paraded. Two points should be considered: first, a band of music at that time, as seen in chapter 1, consisted of but four to eight players. Second, this could not have been the first appearance of the band, for if it were a novelty, greater attention would have been given it by the press than the mere statement that a band was present.[6]

In 1747, during King George's War, the Pennsylvania colonists formed regiments for their own protection. One of the leading citizens who had encouraged the formation of the militia units was Benjamin Franklin, who, in 1756, commanded the Regiment and Artillery Company of Philadelphia. The regiment paraded in that year with over one thousand men, and the newspaper report of the event specified that the "Hautboys and Fifes in Ranks" preceded Colonel Franklin, who rode alone. The drums were placed behind the companies, considerably distant from the hautboys. A new element had been introduced into the American scene, in which Franklin, as a publisher as well as a militia officer, took great interest. This new element was the appearance of regiments of the British army, who brought with them their bands. Following the European practice, it is likely that the term "hautboys" did not refer solely to oboes, but to the military musicians in general, and that Franklin had a well-balanced band. While very modest by modern standards, this band was the standard size for its time. Until further research is accomplished, and assuming the Freemasons' parade of 1755 was not attended by a military band, this occasion marks the first appearance of an American military band in the colonies.[7]

THE BRITISH ARMY

The American colonials were required to provide for their own defense, relying upon whatever men were available who had had some military experience in Europe. In many cases officers were sent to help organize the militia units in the very early period of colonization, but later the militia posts were filled by elected officers of American stock, usually with only militia experience and training to guide them. The colonists had no opportunity to see the well-disciplined regular troops of the British army and no way to become familiar with European tactics except through printed drill manuals.

As the struggles between England and France grew in intensity and became global conflicts, the combat was fought increasingly on American soil. The British government found that in order to carry the fight to the French in the New World they must rely primarily on the regular army, using colonial militia only in a sustaining role. In 1755, England appointed Major General Edward Braddock to be commander in chief of all military forces on the American continent; he was accompanied by the 44th and 48th regiments of foot.[8] The plan was to recruit Americans to bring each of these regiments up to strength and to raise two additional regiments. Lieutenant Colonel George Washington served as aide-de-camp to Braddock on his ill-fated expedition to conquer the French at Fort Duquesne, in which the general and over one-third of his men were killed by a combined French and Indian ambush, the remainder fleeing in a total rout. Many Americans, later prominent in the Revolution, gained their experience from serving with these British regulars during the hostilities. While Europeans refer to this as the Seven Years' War, it is better known in America as the French and Indian War.

Recruiting in the colonies for the two regiments Braddock had brought with him at first went so well that the British ministry decided to raise a completely American regiment, officered by British regulars. This unit was called the Royal American Regiment, later taken into the line as the 60th Foot, and organized at Governor's Island, New York, in 1756. Pargellis wrote of "eager subalterns marching their small detachments into town, there wheeling into line, beating the drums, and setting out to accost all likely men between the ages of eighteen and forty." Americans soon became disenchanted with the cause of European power struggles, and that, with the elimination of some of the abuses in recruiting such as proscribing forced impressment and the employment of drunkenness as a technique in finding "volunteers," prevented the recruiting officers from filling their quotas. As a result, the British ministry decided in 1757 to send only full-strength regiments to serve in the colonies. New regiments arrived each year during the conflict and brought with them the latest military fashions from Europe. One such fashion, as described in the previous chapter, was the military band of music.[9]

The American colonists were very much interested in European news and fashions, and events were reported as quickly as possible. The Horse Guards order of 23 July 1766, substituting trumpets for the drums of the mounted regiments, was reported in the *Virginia Gazette* of 13 November 1766. The reporting of such an order, which had no relation to the colonists, nor to any British regiment serving in America, illustrates the colonists' awareness of changing military concepts and fashions. A movement as popular as the introduction and development of bands of music in the line regiments logically would gain quick attention in the colonies and be emulated by the colonial militia wherever possible. The appearance of British bands in the colonies did much to stimulate the already blooming musical environment and served as an important tradition contributing to the development of indigenous bands of music.

For many years it was the fashion for writers to deprecate the musical environment of the American colonies. Recent researchers have completely disproved these earlier writers, and it has been determined that the musical culture of eighteenth-century America mirrored that of the great European cities, particularly London. The subject need not, therefore, be considered at this point, except to extend its scope to include the military musical aspects.

The greatest cultural centers were the important seaports of Boston, New York, and Philadelphia. Williamsburg, capital of the Virginia colony, and many other settlements, also had flourishing musical environments. Because the military life of the community permeated all civilian activities through the militia requirements, it would be detrimental to any overview of the period to try to isolate any particular aspect. It is best, therefore, to consider each of the above geographical locations and its environment.

Edward Enstone might be considered a typical European musician who immigrated to the American colonies and tried to continue his profession in spite of the frontier conditions of the early period. Brought to Boston from England in 1714 as organist for King's Chapel, he shortly opened a school as "Master of Music and Dancing." Within two years he had established a music store that was able to supply a "choice collection of Musical Instruments, consisting of Flageolets, Flutes, Haut-Boys, Bass-Viols, Violins, Bows, Strings, Reads for Haut-Boys, Books of Instructions for all these instruments, Books of Ruled Paper." He offered to teach all of the above instruments and would repair any instrument, tune virginals and spinets "at a Reasonable Rate," and teach the latest dances.[10]

Concerts were advertised in Boston newspapers as early as 1729. In 1742, Peter Faneuil donated a multipurpose building to the city. Faneuil Hall, as it was called, housed town offices and a large assembly hall over a marketplace, a practice common in England at the time. The assembly hall was frequently the scene of musical performances. The musical climate of Boston must have been encouraging, for in 1754 the musician Stephen Deblois felt sufficiently confident of success that he built Concert Hall for the purposes of concerts, dancing, and other entertainments. With his brother Gilbert, organist at King's Chapel, Deblois had a shop on the ground floor, underneath the Concert Hall. In 1764 they offered almost a full range of items available in Europe at the time, including music, accessories, musical instruments, and even some maps. Significant to the military historian is the inclusion in the listing of "the 55 New Militia Marches, . . . 40 Tattoos and Night Pieces for serenading (18 Divertimenti . . .) [and] Tutors for Singing and for all Instruments singly, . . . by Rutherford, Johnson and Thompson." The musical compositions are significant because they were the standard fare for the military band. The publishers are significant because both Rutherford and Thompson, around 1759, published fife tutors which served as the text for Revolutionary fifers.[11]

That same year, 1764, saw the appearance of *A Collection of the Best Psalm-Tunes, in Two, Three, and Four-parts* by Josiah Flagg, engraved by Paul Revere on paper manufactured in the colonies. Many psalm books had been published before, but this marked the appearance of a musician who figured prominently in the military life of the community, as we shall see.[12]

When British regiments landed in Boston on 1 October 1768, the inhabitants witnessed their entry onto the Common "with muskets charged, bayonets fixed, colours flying, drums beating, fifes &c. playing." "Yanky Dudle" had already become popular, and the British fifers quickly learned the tune. There were bands of music along with the regiments in addition to the fifers and drummers, for John Rowe noted in his diary that the procession installing him as Grand Master of Masons for North America in 1768 was accompanied by "two Brass Bands of Musick, the 59th & 64th Regiments." Later advertisements tell that the 64th Regiment band had oboes, bassoons, and french horns, or the standard *Harmoniemusik*. Rowe's diary mention of brass bands must be attributed to his familiarity with the hautboy combination (oboes and bassoons), resulting in his commenting on the appearance of the horns. These brass instruments would have made quite an impression when added to the band, both visually and aurally.[13]

Even though the presence of the soldiers made the situation tense, life went on as usual, and Deblois continued to give performances. Concerts frequently ended with a ball, but apparently Deblois did not provide this as part of his entertainments. The newspaper account of his concert on 25 January 1769 describes some interesting problems in being an eighteenth-century impresario:

Some officers of the army were for a little *dancing* after the music, and being told that G——r B——d [Governor Bernard] did not approve of their proposal, they were for sending him home to eat his *bread* and *cheese*, and otherwise treated him as if he had been a mimick G——r; they then called out to the band to play the *Yankee Doodle* tune, or the *Wild Irishman*, and not being gratified they grew noisy and clamorous; the candles were then extinguished, which, instead of checking, completed the confusion; to the no small terror of those of the *weaker sex*, who made part of the company.—The old honest music master, Mr. D——bl——s, was roughly handled by one of these sons of Mars; he was actually in danger of being *throatled*, but *timorously* rescued by one who soon threw the officer on lower ground than he at first stood upon; . . . Mr. D——s has acted in character, having delivered up the room, which he held from the Commissioners, returned the subscription money, and wisely determined not to give another concert, until he should again have it in his power to preserve order and decency in such an assembly.[14]

The *Boston Evening Post* of 6 February 1769 carried an announcement of the resumption of the weekly concerts at Concert Hall. A later article explained: ''A concert Hall is again opened to all who have, or may commence subscribers to such musical entertainments. We are told proper concessions have been made Mr. D——bl——s, and that G—— P——y [General Pomeroy, commanding officer of the troops in Boston], has engaged that the o——ff——rs of his core, shall for the future behave with decency, and agreeable to the regulations of such assemblies.''[15]

Interesting in the above account is the apposition of the *Wild Irishman* with *Yankee Doodle*. Apparently the British officers at the time regarded both melodies as marks of derision. The tune must have been fairly common, or they would not have assumed that the band would know it on call. The words of the song were still being printed in popular collections as late as the middle of the nineteenth century, and yet the melody does not appear in any of the standard printed fife books. A manuscript collection of old psalm tunes and popular songs, appended to a music theory book in the possession of the Boston Public Library, is the only instance located to date of this tune. Because of the pejorative insinuation linking it with *Yankee Doodle*, and because it is one of the few melodies specifically mentioned by title, the *Wild Irishman* is included as example 1.

EXAMPLE 1: *Wild Irishman*

In March of 1769 a performance was given at Concert Hall for the benefit of the "Fifer-Major of the 29th Regiment." Tickets were available at the printer's and at "Mr. McLean's, Watch Maker." Rowe attended the concert and noted that "there was a large genteel Company & the best Musick I have heard performed there." The name of the fife major is not given, nor is the instrumentation or nature of the performers. The regiment is not identified further than the number, so it might have been an American militia regiment, although the British 29th Foot was in Boston at the time. Sonneck raised the question of the militia unit because of the inclusion of "Mr. McLean, Watch Maker" and suggested that the fife major and watchmaker were the same man. In June of the same year Josiah Flagg advertised a concert which he called "Last Concert this season." The fife major's concert may have been one of a series, and performers may have been the same in both. The instrumentation is unknown, but the concert ended with the apparently popular *British Grenadiers*. The musicians may have been from the 29th Foot or from the band of the 64th Regiment, as Flagg later gave many concerts with their assistance. The men in one or both cases may even have been local musicians who were attempting to form a musical organization, for Flagg in an advertisement of 1773 claimed that he was the "First Founder, [and had] at great Expense of Time, Trouble, etc., instructed a Band of Music to perform before the Regiment of Militia in this Town." Information about this first militia band has not yet surfaced, other than Flagg's statement, but the concert of 1769 may have been performed by this band. Flagg had seen the example of the British regimental bands and wished to organize the same for his own militia regiment. The band may not have been very large at first, or may not have had a permanent organization, but could still have been called a band. Rowe witnessed a parade in 1770 where there were "Three Flags Flying, Drums Beating & a french Horn—." Colonial standards may not have been as high as European, nor the officers' purses as full, for one-man bands were not restricted to the above parade. Roberts commented on the commander of the Central Militia Company who employed a one-eyed clarinetist "to march about eight paces in front" of the company.[16]

The band of the 64th Regiment was quite active in Boston's musical life. Flagg and W. S. Morgan both gave concerts at Concert Hall in 1771, assisted by this group. The band had french horns and "hautboys, etc.," so it must have been the standard *Harmoniemusik* popular at the time. The 64th band continued to participate in concerts throughout 1772, 1773, and 1774, sometimes at the Concert Hall and on at least one occasion at the Coffee House. Since they were a military unit, supported by the officers of their regiment, it must be assumed that the majority of their performances were for these officers and in the normal military ceremonial routines. Rowe attended the funeral for one of his military friends, for example, at which the band of the 64th Regiment led the procession.[17]

To support the rising musical interest in the colony, John Boyles published in 1769 *An Abstract of Geminiani's Art of Playing on the Violin, and of Another Book of Instructions for Playing in a True Taste on the Violin, German Flute, Violoncello, and the Thorough Bass on the Harpsichord, with Some Additions*. Warner described this work as the "first known instrumental tutor printed in America." This beginning was certainly very modest and a bit naive in attempting to fulfill its title's promise in a brief fourteen pages. The military were not forgotten by the publishers either, and in 1773, T. and J. Fleet brought out a Boston edition of *The Manual Exercise as Ordered by His Majesty in 1764*, the standard British military regulations of the period. That same year Gilbert Deblois was selling "French horns, Bassoons, Hautboys, fifes, drums, English and German flutes," with tutors for each instrument, plus "a great assortment of gold and silver Regimental and Train of Artillery Laces, Bindings, Shoulder Knots, Apaulets, Hat Loops, etc.," swords, hangers, belts, and powder flasks. The obvious appeal to military purchasers adds significance to the order of the instruments named in the advertisement, aimed at officers seeking to form regimental bands.[18]

The militia bands must have been quite resplendent in these accoutrements. John Andrews described in detail his impression of the new volunteer militia units:

Am almost every minute taken off with agreeable sight of our militia companies marching into the Common, as it is a grand field day with us; and I assure, were you to see 'em, you'd scarcely believe your eyes, they are so strangely metamorphos'd. From making the most despicable appearance they now vie with the best troops in his majesties service, being dress'd all in blue uniforms, with drums and fifes to each company dress'd in white uniforms trim'd in ye most elegant manner; with a company of Grenadiers in red with every other apparatus, that equal any regular Company I ever saw both in regard to appearance and discipline, having a grand band of musick consisting of eight that play nearly equal to that of the 64th. What crowns all is the Cadet company, being perfectly compleat and under the best order you can conceive of, with a band of musick likewise, that perform admirably well. What with these and Paddock's company of artillery make ye compleatest militia in America.

The occasion was the celebration of the birthday of the king. The troops participating were the Company of Cadets commanded by John Hancock with a band of music, the Company of Grenadiers with their band of music, the Massachusetts Artillery Company, a cavalry troop, and the "militia of the town," or common militia. Following the review, "the band of music belonging to the regiment of Cadets and Major Paddock's fifes and drums, after dinner, were in the balconies in King-Street, and alternately played a great variety of tunes before a vast number of spectators." The Company of Grenadiers had been formed the previous year according to accounts published in the *Boston News-Letter* of 11 June 1772. Some indication of the interest taken in these volunteer militia units can be observed from the great achievement of organizing, clothing, and equipping this company in such a brief space of time. In September of that same year the Independent Cadets and the Company of Grenadiers, each with its own band of music, participated in the celebration of the king's coronation, and "in the evening [there] was a grand concert of Music at Concert Hall, and a number of fireworks were played off on King Street."[19]

Colonel John Hancock, who later became the president of the Continental Congress, was the commanding officer of the Independent Cadets. At this time the Cadets had a band, presumably of eight musicians like that of the Grenadier company, who played "admirably well." A year later when the Independent Cadets dissolved because of the rising frictions leading to the Revolution, the musical instruments and equipage were turned over to Hancock for safekeeping until the Cadets could be reactivated.[20]

British musical units were active in Boston at this time in addition to the famous band of the 64th Regiment. Rowe attended a funeral procession in December 1774 that was led by the 4th Regiment and its band of music. They had just recently arrived in Boston and must have entered immediately into the musical activities of the city. A "Grand Concert of Vocal and Instrumental Music" given at Concert Hall in September of that year, by the same Morgan who had featured concerts with the 64th Regiment band in previous years, featured "clarinets, Hautboys, Bassoons, French horns, Trumpets, Kettle Drums, &c., &c." The advertisement noted that "the Gentlemen Performers of the Army, Navy, and of the Town, have promis'd Mr. Morgan their assistance in Concert; likewise some of the best Performers from the several Bands of Music of the Line."[21] This combination of the best military and civilian musical forces speaks well for the cultural integration of the city a brief seven months prior to the "shot heard round the world."

Music also played a role on less pleasant occasions. *Yankee*

Doodle had become popular with the British fifers and drummers as a form of musical taunt toward the local populace, and John Andrews complained of the field music of the 4th Regiment playing that melody near a church during religious services to annoy the congregation in March of 1775. That same month a visiting farmer was seized on a false charge, tarred and feathered, and paraded through the streets accompanied by twenty fifers and drummers of the 47th Regiment playing that same melody. The battles of Lexington and Concord were but one month distant, and the treatment of this poor colonial, surrounded by the British military, carrying a sign about his neck declaring him to be "AMERICAN LIBERTY, OR A SPECIMEN OF DEMOCRACY," did much to incite popular opinion against the perpetrators of such a deed.[22]

New Yorkers also participated in a thriving musical environment. At stores such as Rivington's one could purchase any musical instrument and its tutor, plus all the necessary accessories. By 1773, Rivington was advertising such important military musical items as "French horns, . . . hautboys, English or common flutes, fifes, tabors and pipes, . . . bassoon, hautboy and bagpipe reeds." French horns and trumpets were advertised for sale in 1761, and horns were being made locally by John Dash as early as 1765. In 1775, David Woolhaupter advertised that he "makes and sells all sorts of DRUMS and FIFES— Drums made of Mahogany, cured Maple, and Beech wood, in the best and neatest manner, and has now a quantity ready made for sale—He also makes Clarinets, Hautboys, German and common Flutes, and all sorts of Instruments, &c." Those that preferred private instruction to a self-tutor could avail themselves of the services of music teachers such as Charles Love, who announced in 1753 that he "teaches gentlemen the violin, hautboy, German and common flute, bassoon, French horn, tenor and bass viol."[23]

The social life of the city was enhanced by the opening of the Ranelagh Gardens in 1766, patterned after the London pleasure gardens. A complete band of music played weekday evenings throughout the summer, and dancing was taught in a special dance hall. Concerts were advertised in Mr. Burns's assembly room, with balls frequently being held after the performance. The program of a concert given by a horn player, Mr. Stotherd, advertised in the *New York Journal* of 1 February 1770, gives an indication of the versatility and popularity of the natural horn. At this concert Stotherd performed two of his own horn concertos, two hunting songs presumably featuring the horn, many other works including "select pieces for four French horns," as well as two Handel overtures. After the concert there was a ball, with

Mr. Stotherd presumably providing the music, since the whole concert was for his benefit.[24]

Military musicians were active in the city. The Feast of St. Patrick was celebrated with fifes and drums in 1766, and the following year saw what has been reputed to be the earliest known band concert in the United States. This was performed by, and for the benefit of, the band of the Royal American Regiment (60th Foot) and consisted of vocal and instrumental music. The officers were foreign mercenaries appointed by the British, but the recruits were American, and the regiment had not left the colonies. The officers may have been emulating European fashion in forming a band, but the musicians, their instruments, and their music were all indigenously American. This regiment could be considered the only standing army of the American colonies up to 1775, and one can take rightful pride in its concert being one of the earliest, if not the first, provided by an American military band.[25]

The anniversary of the repeal of the Stamp Act was celebrated in 1768 by "a numerous company of the principal merchants and other respectable inhabitants of this city, friends to constitutional liberty and trade, [who] met at Mr. Jones's and Mr. Bardin's taverns, which are nearly adjoining, where Union flags were displayed, and elegant entertainments provided." There were twenty-one toasts after dinner, and "a band of musick was provided, and in the evening some curious fireworks played off, for the entertainment of the company."[26]

John McLane, the fife major of the 29th Regiment, gave a concert for his own benefit in January of 1771, at which he performed a solo on the flute. The other performers are not mentioned in the advertisement, but since it is stated that "after the concert several pieces of Music [will be] performed by the Fifers and Drummers of the said Regiment," the instrumentalists for the concert itself were probably the members of the regimental band. Another military band became prominent in the musical life of the city in 1773. Intermissions of dramatic plays were filled with musical interludes, and the band of the Royal Welch Fusiliers (23d Foot) performed at a presentation of Milton's *Comus* and later accompanied a soprano soloist in *The Soldier Tired of War's Alarms* during one of the intermissions of *Romeo and Juliet*.[27]

Philadelphia also had a well-organized concert life. Michael Hillegas and others had stores where one could purchase practically all the standard musical instruments, accessories, and music books. Private instruction was available from such teachers as John Beals, "Musick Master from London," who advertised in 1749 that he taught "violin, Hautboy, German Flute, Common Flute and Dulcimer by note" and provided "musick for balls or other entertainments." Concerts were given at least after 1757, and bands of music were accompanying opera performances and theatrical plays.[28]

British army bands also were in evidence. The commencement exercises of the College of Philadelphia in 1767 were enhanced by the performance of the band of the Royal Irish Regiment (18th Foot). They are reported to have performed at the exercises of 1773, so they may have been frequent visitors to the college. This may have been the band that a young Philadelphian wrote about to his sister, Mrs. Philip Francis, in 1768, describing a popular pastime: "We—with four or five young officers of the regiment in barracks—drink as hard as we can to keep out the cold, and about midnight sally forth, attended by the Band which consists of ten musicians, horns, clarionets, hautboys, and bassoons, march through the streets and play under the window of any lady you choose to distinguish, which they esteem a high Compliment. . . . I have been out twice and only once got a violent cold by it."[29] One can feel sympathy for the performers if the situation resembled that described by William Congreve in a letter to a friend: "The Hautboys who played to us last night had their breath froze in their instruments till it dripped of[f] the end of 'em in icicles, by god this is true."[30]

The military bands also gave formal concerts. John McLean, "Instructor of the German Flute," advertised a concert in Philadelphia for December 1771, in which a "full Band of Music, with Trumpets, Kettle Drums, and every instrument that can be introduced with Propriety" was promised. A John McLane, fife major of the 29th Regiment, gave a concert in New York in January of that same year, at which he performed a solo on the german flute. Two years earlier, the fife major of the 29th Regiment gave a concert in Boston, at which tickets were available from a Mr. McLean, watchmaker. It is possible that all three are the same person, and that McLean, or McLane, had left the British service and was attempting to succeed musically in America. The Philadelphia concert concluded with "an Overture composed (for the Occasion) by Philip Roth, Master of the Band belonging to his Majesty's Royal Regiment of North British Fusileers" (21st Foot). The musicians were most likely from either the 21st or the 29th Regiment bands, or both combined, judging from the military instruments included in the advertisement. Particularly significant at this point, however, is the fact that this same Philip Roth became the music master of Lee's Legion of the Continental army.[31]

During the period 1699 to 1780 when Williamsburg served as the capital of Virginia, it was the cultural center of the colony. Its influence stretched throughout the southern colonies. Like the great seaports just described, Williamsburg had its musicians, concerts, and music stores. William Atwood advertised in 1771 that he would teach the gentlemen of Williamsburg the french horn, hautboy, and german flute, and Peter Pelham, the organist of Bruton Parish Church, was active in performing and teaching. Concerts were presented, and some idea of the size of the performing groups may be gained from the instrumentation of the concert advertised for 30 December 1766. The orchestra consisted of three violins, one tenor, one bass, two flutes, one oboe, one horn, and one harpsichord. The string family was in a state of transition at that time, and the word "tenor" could have meant a viola, violoncello, or an instrument somewhere between the two. The "bass" similarly could have meant a violoncello, a *viola da gamba* the size and range of the violoncello, or an actual contrabass. The most balanced sound from such a small combination of instruments would have been if the two terms represented the ranges of the modern viola and violoncello respectively. Small instrumental combinations were common in the social life of the plantation owners, and Fithian wrote of a ball in 1774 where the music was provided by two violins and a french horn. Horns and trumpets provided entertainment during the intermissions of dramatic works at The Theatre.[32]

The environment must have been very encouraging, for musical instruments were available from two different stores. John Greenhow was selling bugle horns, hunting horns, german flutes, fifes, and other accessories, while one could purchase flutes, violins, and music books at the nearby office of Purdie and Dixon, which served also as post office and publishing house for the newspaper. German flutes and guitars seem to have been especially popular, for in 1777, Ann Neill offered to sell them "for ready Money only" at her general merchandise store right opposite that of John Greenhow.[33]

The social life of the southern colonies was quite different from the active city life of the northern seaports. Large plantations tried to emulate the customs of the fashionable cities on a smaller scale. An additional consideration was the presence of slaves, both as field workers and as domestics. A slave who was capable of playing a musical instrument was particularly valuable. Those capable of playing the horn were in great demand, presumably for their ability to sound the calls of the hunt. Typical of the many advertisements featuring such performers is the following: "To be SOLD, a Young healthy NEGRO fellow, who has been used to wait on a Gentleman, and plays extremely well on the *French* horn. For further particulars apply to the printer."[34]

The ideal of the southern plantation owner may be summed up in a letter written by Thomas Jefferson during the Revolution to a friend in Italy requesting help in securing domestics for his plantation:

I retain for instance among my domestic servants a gardener . . ., weaver . . . a cabinet maker . . . and a stone-cutter . . . to which I would add a vigneron. In a country where, like yours, music is cultivated and practised by every class of men, I suppose there might be found persons of those trades who could perform on the French horn, clarinet or hautboy and bassoon, so that one might have a band of two French horns, two clarinets and hautboys and a bassoon, without enlarging their domest[ic] expences . . . . Without meaning to give you trouble, perhaps it mig[ht] be practicable for you in your ordinary intercourse with your pe[ople] to find out such men disposed to come to America. Sobriety and good nature would be desirable parts of their characters.[35]

In addition to the large seaports, many other settlements could boast of musical activities, though not on as grand a scale. The Moravian settlements at Bethlehem, Bethabara, Wachau, and Salem all had highly developed musical environments. In addition to the famous trombone choirs of the Moravians, flutes, strings, horns, and trumpets were being used in community services as early as 1743, somewhat prior to the concerts in the larger cities. Charleston, South Carolina, had a Saint Cecilia Society in 1771, whose concerts were highly regarded in the colonies. Charleston also had its music stores and complement of music teachers. Concerts were advertised in addition to those of the Society, showing that the musical activities were not restricted to one organization. Norfolk, but a short distance from the capital of Williamsburg and its shops, had a store where one could purchase german flutes, tabors with pipes, and some printed music. Annapolis, Maryland, formed a traveling group of players in 1752, who gave performances of *The Beggar's Opera* accompanied by "a set of Private Gentlemen" and featuring "a Solo on the French horn."[36]

When a modern writer ventured that "the Continental Army had neither band instruments nor men to play them," he was certainly doing a great injustice to the colonies that produced the Continental soldier. It would have been a very primitive frontiersman who would not have come into contact with the flourishing and musically varied environment in the years before the outbreak of open hostilities.[37]

3. FROM LEXINGTON
TO VALLEY FORGE

Conditions between the mother country and her colonies deteriorated steadily after the close of the French and Indian War, when the British ministry decided to maintain regular troops in America. While not actually anticipating an outbreak of war, military preparations were being made in all the colonies. As a result of the incidents at Lexington and Concord on 19 April 1775, Boston was besieged by militia units called to duty for the emergency. Some attempt was made by the Provincial Congress to provide a Continental army, but it was left to George Washington to try to mold such an army from the miscellaneous militia units serving around Boston.

To gain an understanding of the first years of the Revolution, it is necessary to view several separate aspects: the preparations for war, the siege of Boston, the Continental army of 1776, the enemy it faced, and the army of 1777. This phase of the war drew to a close as Washington led his troops into winter encampment at Valley Forge in December 1777.

PREPARATIONS FOR WAR

By the time the first shot was fired at Lexington in 1775, the colonists had already done a considerable amount of preparation for any possible outbreak of hostilities. The famous Boston Tea Party had occurred a year and a half previously, and steps were taken then to form revolutionary governments in each colony. Committees of Safety were established, and the First Continental Congress had gathered at Philadelphia in September 1774. The Massachusetts Provincial Congress, like similar groups throughout the colonies, had reorganized the militia units, forcing out Tory officers and replacing them with sympathetic leaders. Companies of minutemen were established, to be ready to respond at a moment's warning. Military stores and ammunition were accumulated, such as at Concord, the aim of General Thomas Gage's sortie precipitating actual warfare.

The militia units were patterned after British models, as they had been since the founding of the colonies. *The Manual Exercise as Ordered by His Majesty in 1764* was the basic textbook, supplemented by the drill manuals of Humphrey Bland and William Windham. As early as 1766 the *Manual* had been reprinted in the colonies, but it had not been adopted officially for use by the militia. In October 1774 the Massachusetts Provincial Congress recommended that the colony's inhabitants learn the *Manual*, "it being in the Opinion of this Congress the best calculated for appearance and Defence." Virginia followed in March 1775 and ordered the work reprinted locally. In 1772, Thomas Simes, an English officer, had written his *Military Guide for Young Officers*. This work became very popular in the colonies and was reprinted at Philadelphia in 1776. The New York Provincial Congress directed that each Continental colonel in the state was to receive eleven sets of this work and two copies of Bland's treatise.[1]

The militia units were reorganized, each colony taking steps to prepare for the possibility of war. In 1775, Virginia organized units of seventy-six men, four officers, one drummer, and one fifer per company, the soldiers to "be clothed in a hunting shirt, by way of uniform." The "drums, fifes, colours, and halberds" were to be provided at the public expense. In December, when six additional militia regiments were raised, Virginia allowed one drum major to be appointed by the colonel. Connecticut, in its reorganization, authorized two drummers and two fifers per company. If there were more than one hundred men in the company, three drummers and three fifers were authorized. Distinction in the dress of the musicians had already been established. The drummers were to have white lace and black feathers on their hats, and the fifers black feathers and red cockades over the hat buttons. The third drummer, when authorized, was to be assigned to and dressed as a grenadier in a blue coat with scarlet jacket and cap, white breeches and stockings. Pennsylvania, in 1777, allowed but one drummer and one fifer per company, the drums, fifes, and colors being purchased from the state treasury. A drum major and a fife major were also allowed, who "shall be persons experienced in the duties of their respective offices."[2]

One measure of the state of preparedness is the number of men involved in the running fight engaged with the British in their return from Lexington and Concord. In spite of the short warning allowed them by Paul Revere and William Dawes, by the end of that day, 19 April 1775, 3,763 Americans had become involved at one point or another, though not all at the same time. The poor results obtained from such a large force fighting for a full day amply demonstrates the great lack of organization, discipline, and training of the militia. What cannot be denied is the fact that they were there, however, and that they did respond to the call. Significantly, that call was first sounded by a military musician, William Diamond, a teenager serving as drummer in Captain John Parker's militia company from Lexington.[3]

THE SIEGE OF BOSTON

From all over New England men responded to the news from Lexington, and within a few days a large, undisciplined, unorganized mass of men were besieging Boston. The Massachusetts Provincial Congress resolved that eight thousand men immediately be enlisted and formed into companies of seventy-nine men each, including one drummer and one fifer, nine companies forming a regiment. New Hampshire sent regiments of ten and twelve companies, Maryland of eight companies, and a Canadian regiment reported with twenty. There was no standardization of size among units, but all depended upon the drum for commands.[4]

In order to continue the siege, the Massachusetts Provincial Congress decided to ask for support from the Second Continental Congress. When the delegates arrived at Philadelphia in May, they were met by "the company of riflemen, and a company of infantry, with a band of music, who conducted them through the most public streets of the city to their lodgings amidst the acclamations of near 15,000 spectators." Their mission was successful, and the Congress in effect adopted the New England army on 14 June 1775, the date since celebrated as the birthday of the United States army. On the same date Congress called for the raising of a regiment of riflemen consisting of ten companies from Pennsylvania, Maryland, and Virginia. Each rifle company was to have eighty-one men, including a drummer or trumpeter.[5]

On the next day, 15 June 1775, Congress appointed Colonel George Washington of Virginia as the commander in chief of all Continental forces. Washington did not accept until the following day. He set out for Boston and formally assumed command on 3 July.

In the meantime, the New England army was engaged in a battle on Breed's Hill, better known to history as the Battle of Bunker Hill. A drum alleged to have been beat by John Robbins at that battle is now in the possession of the Bostonian Society. It was given by Robbins to Daniel Simpson, who used it in the War of 1812 and for many years in the New England Guards and various militia bands in Boston. Simpson's portrait, with the Robbins drum, is included as figure 10. A comparison with figures 1 and 2 clearly shows the differences between the snare drums of the sixteenth and the eighteenth centuries.

All over the colonies men were preparing for war. Connecticut emblazoned its standards and drums with the colony arms and the motto *"qui transtulit sustinet!"* which they interpreted as "God, who transplanted us hither, will support us." Fifes and drums were on sale in Virginia, Pennsylvania, and probably elsewhere in the colonies. Thomas Sterling and Thomas Hookins advertised that they would "willingly learn any number of Boys the MILITARY MUSICK of the FIFE and DRUM" for a fee. Sometime later advertisements appeared for drummers and fifers "who can teach the others the DUTY, to act as Drum and Fife Majors." A concert was given in New York "for the benefit of a Band of Music" on 27 April, but the band is not identified. When the newly formed Marines went recruiting, their drums were emblazoned with a rattlesnake and the motto "Don't Tread on Me," perhaps similar to the famous flag of that design. Philip Fithian was speaking only of Virginia, but the scene he described most likely was duplicated all over the colonies: "The Drum beats & the Inhabitants of this Village muster each Morning at five o Clock . . . Mars, the great God of Battle, is now honoured in every part of this spacious Colony, but here every Presence is warlike, every Sound is martial! Drums beating, Fifes & Bag-Pipes playing, & only sonorous & heroic Tunes —Every Man has a hunting-Shirt, which is the Uniform of each Company."[6]

Washington gallantly attacked the many problems besetting the new army. Some recognition of rank was needed so that rudimental discipline and organization could be achieved. Since the army was not uniformed, rank was indicated by means of different colored cockades for officers and epaulettes for noncommissioned officers. The generals were distinguished by colored sashes worn across the breast over the waistcoat. Attention also was paid to music for the army. Washington ordered that "the Drummers and Fifers of the Regiment in and about Cambridge, are to be order'd constantly to attend the Drum and Fife Major, at the usual hours for instruction." Military courtesy and honors between the combatants were not neglected either, and Washington instructed the manner in which flags of truce were to be received. Following the European practice, drummers and trumpeters often were used for this purpose.[7]

Washington's senior officers were not completely ignorant of military matters. Spaulding noted that of thirteen general officers appointed to the Continental service in 1775, all but two had had war service, eight of them in the grades of lieutenant colonel, colonel, or general officer. These men had become familiar with British military music and knew its importance to the service. Brigadier General William Heath, for example, commented in orders of 7 November 1775:

As good musick is not only ornamental to an army but so absolutely so essential that the maneover cannot be performed in a regular manner without it Bridgen Heath Orders that the fifers and drums of the 10th 26th 30th 31st 36th Regt Except those who are orderly for the Day in their prospective Regt attend at his Quarters at Nine O'Clock in the Morning & at Sun Set to perform their Several Beatings to its Troop and Retreat for Mounting Guard & Roll Callings —and to perf. at them in thar duty—the Commanding officer of Each Regt will see that this order Be strictly Complyd with unless the Weather is foul. Thomas Guy of Colo Greatons Regt is appointed Drum Major of the whole. Therefore due obedience is to be paid to his Command.[8]

General Heath must have been very much interested in their performance, for even if the musicians were not at full strength, five regiments at an average of two per company would easily have involved over fifty fifers and drummers. To have that many men, particularly if the majority were beginners, practicing "at his quarters," would be quite an ordeal.

Since he assumed command of the Continental forces in July, Washington had been striving to mold the loose aggregations of men around Boston into an army patterned on European models. With the help of a committee of Congress, a plan was developed in October to form a Continental army of one artillery and twenty-seven infantry regiments, all enlisted for the year 1776. Each regiment was to consist of a headquarters staff and eight companies of ninety officers and men, including one fifer and one drummer. It was hoped that the enlistments would come from the militia units already in service, and Washington was faced with the problem of trying to form a new army from the one that was already disintegrating beneath him in December 1775. Reducing the thirty-eight regiments on duty to the proposed twenty-eight meant that a number of officers would become excess. Because men would not serve under any but officers of their own choice from their own state, the recruiting officers found it difficult to bring the new regiments up to strength. The emphasis on music was continued, and Washington encouraged the new colonels to provide their regiments with good drummers and fifers while forming their commands.[9]

THE CONTINENTAL ARMY, 1776

By March 1776 the new army that Washington had struggled so hard to create still had a strength of only slightly over nine thousand men, not the twenty thousand authorized. The general supply situation had improved somewhat, and with the aid of short-term militia units and artillery pieces brought from Fort Ticonderoga by Henry Knox, it was decided to force the British from Boston. On 17 March, a day easily remembered by the Irish patriots of the city, Major General William Howe evacuated his troops to Halifax, Nova Scotia.

The new Continental army had not changed considerably from the New England army it replaced. The regiments were not fully recruited, and differences in size persisted. Each was primarily associated with one colony and was part of a quota assigned by the Congress. Soldiers of one colony were rarely to be found in the regiments of another. The militia units upon which Washington continually had to rely came to him in various forms of organization, since their organization was controlled by the individual colonies and not by the Continental authorities.

The year 1776 can be divided militarily into several separate operations. Some troops merely waited for action, protecting an important area, such as General Artemas Ward's command in Boston. Among the troops engaged in offensive activities were the commands of General Richard Montgomery and Colonel Benedict Arnold, which had moved against Quebec in 1775. Despite Montgomery's death in action, they continued the attempt to make Canada the fourteenth colony. Washington himself directed the actions centered in New York and New Jersey, while General Charles Lee and Colonel William Moultrie successfully thwarted British advances toward Charleston and the southern colonies.

Faced with many obstacles from the very start, the Canadian campaign had little time for music except for the standard drum signals and need not be considered at this point. To illustrate the variety of military concepts and practices utilized by the army, the three remaining areas of military activity will be discussed with regard to musical procedures: Boston, the central colonies, and the South. A comparison of the three highlights the need for standardization which was not to be accomplished until the winter of 1777 at Valley Forge.

When Howe evacuated Boston in 1776, Washington was not sure which direction the British forces would take. Fearing that New York might be the next objective, he ordered four brigades and the artillery regiment to that city, leaving General Artemas Ward in command of six regiments in and around Boston for the protection of the entire area.

Ward was apparently not too pleased with the music of his little army, for less than two weeks after assuming command he ordered that his chief executive officer, the brigade major, set up his office in the general's own quarters and that the ''drums-and-fifes majors of the whole brigade'' meet in that office on the following day. The meeting must have been amicable, for Ward publicly encouraged his musicians that same evening. General orders normally were read to the troops at Retreat parade, and that day's orders contained the statement that "the General observes with pleasure the improvement the drums and fifes have made in martial music, and their attention to duty. He hopes that the drum-and-fife majors will continue to exert themselves in instructing those under their care in every branch of their duty." To ensure that the fife and drum majors would continue "to exert themselves," a chief drum major and chief fife major were appointed in orders the very next day. So that there would be no question in anyone's mind as to the importance placed on the music, explicit details were given:

All the drums and fifes in town are to attend the stated exercises at the time and place appointed. All the drums-and-fifers majors of this division of the army are to meet twice a week, on Tuesday and Friday, on the bottom of the Common, for practice. The drums and fifes of each regiment off duty are to practice separately, under the direction of their respective majors, till the chief drum-and-fife majors shall think them sufficiently instructed to join in one body. It is recommended the musicianers of each regiment that they emulate each other in striving to excel in this pleasant part of military discipline.

To reinforce the total effect of this drive, Ward decreed that the next day's parole, or sentry's challenge, would be "MARTIAL," to be answered by the countersign, "MUSIC." This concentrated emphasis in a brief four days seems to have had its effect, for no further mention of music is contained in the orderly book.[10]

Meanwhile, Washington was in the central states, faced with tremendous problems of organization, the logistics of feeding and equipping his army, and the enlistment of men to fill the authorized Continental regiments. Washington had to rely upon his various brigade commanders for the regulation of the interior details of camp management. For example, within a month of Major General John Sullivan's arrival in the New York area, he ordered "Mr. Gerry Brigade Drum Major to appoint a place to meet the Drummers and fifers of the Brigade to instruct them in beating the drum and playing the fife, a spell each morning and afternoon. The Drummers and fifes to assemble as he shall direct for beating the Troop Tatoo &c. and follow such directions as he shall give them."[11] Sullivan's brigade apparently had no appointed drum or fife majors in the various regiments, for the brigade drum major was ordered to train all the musicians of the brigade personally. Usually, the brigade drum major would work with the regimental drum majors, who would then be depended upon to train the men in their care.

The lack of sufficient musical instruments plagued Washington.

The militia units brought their instruments with them, as they did their weapons, but the Continental units were to be supplied from congressional funds. Always mindful of public expense, Washington issued a decree which set the precedent for such actions up to the present day: "The Colonels of every Regiment are to see that their Drums are put in good Order, at the public Expence, after which they are to be kept so at the charge of the Drummers, who have extra-pay on that account; from which deductions will be made if necessary: But in case of unavoidable accidents, the charge of repair will be borne as heretofore." At that time the private was paid six and two-thirds dollars per month, with the drummer receiving seven and one-third per month, another indication of the important position of the military musicians.[12]

No provision had been made in the regimental organization authorized by Congress for the inclusion of drum and fife majors. Regimental or brigade commanders officially appointed one of the company drummers to act as drum major. His position and pay remained that of a company musician, and he was normally expected to continue to function as a company drummer. Drum and fife majors were authorized in some of the militia units, and the Continental army was rarely without some militia support. Delaware, for example, authorized drum and fife majors to be employed in teaching the drummers and fifers of the battalion, who were to be paid "any sum not exceeding Seven Shillings and Six-pence" per day from funds collected by petty fines for nonattendance at musters and the like. Maryland established the pay of its drum major in the regular service to be eight dollars per month. In order to help raise, equip, and support the army, Congress had established on 12 June a Board of War and Ordinance composed of its own members and an appointed secretary. This board raised the question of the status of sergeant majors, drum majors, and fife majors in the army and asked Washington what pay and allowances he thought should be given them. While he served with the British in 1755, Washington had become familiar with their method of deducting a small sum from each drummer to pay the drum major for instructing them and had ordered sixpence per month deducted from his drummers for that purpose. Twenty years later, however, he believed that this method "cannot be well done in ours, all stoppages being attended with difficulty and giving uneasiness. I would therefore propose, that an additional allowance of a Dollar per month should be made to their several pays as now established, as a sufficient compensation and satisfaction, for any extraordinary trouble attending their offices." Congress accepted Washington's recommendation, and on 25 July he announced in orders that the pay raise was granted retroactive to the

16th. The order stipulated the pay of these positions, but neglected to indicate their organizational status. Some units considered the majors as the musicians of one of the companies, while in others they were carried as part of the staff in addition to the musicians. Over a year later, General William Heath wrote for clarification: "I also beg to be informed whether Serjeant Fife & Drum Majors and the Quarter Master Serjeant in the respective Regiments are to be considered as included in the ordinary number of those Officers and consequently as belonging to particular Companies; or as distinct from & not connected with any Company." No reply has been found in Washington's correspondence, but the reorganization of the army of 27 May 1778 resolved the problem by including these majors as part of the regimental staff.[13]

In an attempt to adapt to the irregular fighting techniques of the American Indians, and to prevent another disaster such as befell Braddock, the British introduced light infantry companies in their regiments. These troops were an elite corps of men chosen for their swiftness, agility, and physical strength. Their uniform was somewhat abbreviated, and they were trained to move at a quicker pace than the regular infantry. They often were used to protect the flanks of the regiments while on the march. When the light infantry company of the 3d Foot was organized in 1770, it was authorized two drummers as in all other infantry companies. The drum was considered too cumbersome for rapid movement, and in 1773 the light infantry of the 43d Foot had a trumpet. The following year, inspection reports commented on a new instrument in use in the 4th and 20th Regiments. This was a "German post-horn," used to give signals to the light infantry companies. The bugle signals were not taught to the regular infantry companies. It was necessary, therefore, when mixed units were operating together, to sound the signals on each instrument. Simcoe, for example, described on one occasion when "the enemy's sentinels fired, and in succession the bugle-horns, drums, and bagpipe of the Queen's Rangers sounded."[14]

The Americans had not yet adopted the bugle horn for their light infantry. Just one week after the Declaration of Independence, a Philadelphia newspaper described the occasion of its proclamation in Easton: "The Colonel and all the other field officers of the first battalion repaired to the court-house, the light infantry company marching there with their drums beating, fifes playing, and the standard (the device for which is the Thirteen United Colonies,) which was ordered to be displayed." Obviously, the light infantry company was still using drums in 1776. At the Battle of Harlem Heights, the Americans met some of the British light infantry and Hessian *jäger*. These latter were special companies of hunters, uniformed in green, and serving as light infantry. At the beginning of the battle, as Washington's adjutant Joseph Reed described it, "The enemy appeared in open view, and sounded their bugles in a most insulting manner, as is usual after a fox chase. I never felt such a sensation before—it seemed to crown our disgrace." Being familiar with the customs and signals of the fox hunt, both Washington and Reed would have understood the implication of "a fox gone to earth" and justifiably could have been incensed at the insult. Another participant later wrote to his wife regarding the same incident that "the Enemy Halted Back of an Hill, blode a french Horn which whas for a Reinforcement, and as soon as they got itt, they formed in to two coloms." The bugle horn of the period came in various shapes and sizes and sometimes was referred to as a hunting horn. It is easy to understand the witnesses mentioning the sound as coming from two different instruments, when even writers in the present century regarded the two as interchangeable.[15]

Boston had a strong heritage of bands of music in the elite militia units, as shown in the previous chapter. No documentation for bands in the Continental army in 1776 has been found, but some may have existed. John Hancock, in Philadelphia, wrote to General Philip Schuyler requesting a favor:

On the Departure of our Troops from Boston to New York, Colo Greaton & I believe some other of the Cols from my Colony, Without my Knowledge or Consent took into their Possession & out of the hands of the proper officer with whom I had left them, some French horns, Bassoons & other Instruments of Musick which I purpose imported for the Use of a Military Corps under my Command. I have to request the Favor of you to Give Orders to Colo Greaton, or any officer who may have them, to deliver them to you. I shall esteem it a Favor, if you have any good opportunity, You would please to order them to be sent to me. I believe you will find my name on them.

It will be remembered that when Hancock's Independent Cadets dissolved in 1774, the musical instruments of the band were left with him for safekeeping. These may have been the instruments that were taken, and it is known that Hancock did seek his own command during the Revolution, at one point even competing with Washington for the position of commander in chief. General Schuyler was away from the main part of the army, so he requested his second in command, General Horatio Gates, to collect the instruments and forward them to his house at Albany. Schuyler then wrote to Philadelphia of his instructions to Gates, hoping that he would soon be able to forward the instruments to Hancock. Apparently, he was not successful, for six months later Hancock reminded Schuyler: "I never heard anything of my band of musick since I wrote you." Schuyler's correspondence does not indicate a reply, nor does Gates's correspondence to the request. Nothing more has been located regarding these instruments. Colonel John Greaton commanded the 24th Continental Infantry, later the 3d Massachusetts, and the instruments may have remained with the regiment and been used by a band.[16]

During the campaign of 1776, Washington met reverses in the battles of Long Island and Kips Bay. Despite the victory at Harlem Heights, the entire New York campaign was practically a disaster for the Continental army. Washington was forced to retreat through New Jersey until he crossed the Delaware into Pennsylvania where he received some respite from Howe's pursuit. To give the army some small confidence in itself and to act before the periods of enlistment of the whole Continental army expired at the end of 1776, Washington decided on a surprise attack on Trenton in the morning of 26 December. Among the prisoners gained by this success were two Hessian bands of music. The army, after another success at Princeton just after the new year, went into winter quarters at Morristown.

General Andrew Lewis, commanding the troops stationed at Williamsburg, Virginia, also attempted to organize his musicians. Shortly after he took command in 1776, he appointed a drum major and a fife major and ordered them "to practice the young Fifers & Drummers between the hours of 11 & 1 o'clock every day." To provide them with extra money, Lewis employed the standard British method of stoppages from the pay of the musicians:

As the Drum Majors pay is not more than the common Drummers, and he being oblijt to teach the young Drummers and keep their Drums in Repair, General Lewis has thought proper to order and it is what is custommerry in the army that each young Drummer shall pay the Drum Major 5s. pr month untill the Drummers are capable of doing duty, and keeping their Drums in order.

The fife Major, for his trouble of teaching, the young fifers are to pay him 5s. pr month untill they are capable of doing duty, and should any young Fifer break or render his fife unfit for service, he is to pay for it.[17]

Lewis ordered this practice as customary, yet just one month later Washington wrote that this practice would not work in the Continental army. The drum major's was clearly a teaching position, since the stoppages were made only until the musicians were "capable of doing duty."

Virginia had required its militia to be clothed in hunting shirts since at least 1775, and Lewis made some distinction for the various ranks. Officers were to have fringed shirts, while those of the men were to be plain. Sergeants and drummers were to have small white and dark cuffs respectively.

At this same time, General Charles Lee was advertising for young men to form companies of light dragoons. These troops included "a trumpet, or horn sounder." There was no mention of a drum, even though this instrument was still being authorized for the cavalry in Virginia one month later.[18]

THE ENEMY

Although hampered by the logistical problems involved in supporting a war on a distant continent, Britain met each colonial military act with a corresponding escalation of troops and equipment. Shortly after the news of Lexington reached London, Parliament voted an army of fifty-five thousand men and sent out recruiting parties. One member of Commons, serving as an infantry major, arrived in Cork with a large purse of gold to reward volunteers and "an elegant Band of Music, consisting of French Hautboys, Clarionets and Bassoons" playing *God Save the King*. Preparations were made all over the kingdom, and the news of a shipment of upwards of 1200 drums being put on board transports bound for America even reached the Virginia newspapers. This seems like a bit of propaganda spread for psychological effects, however. By the end of 1776 there were only thirty-eight regiments stationed in America, eighteen more than in 1775. Even if a complete new issue were made, which seems unlikely as Britain was pressed for funds, thirty-eight regiments at ten companies each with two drummers would require only 760 drums. If the ministry were anticipating the addition of two companies per regiment, which was authorized in November, there would still be more than 125 percent of requirement.[19]

Although some colonists were expected to come to her aid, England had to turn to the smaller German states for additional manpower. The enemy the Continental army faced was primarily regiments of the British army, but supported by German mercenaries and American loyalists.

As shown in the previous chapter, British regimental bands had performed in America prior to 1776. Bands of music had become popular throughout the British army, but except for a few special regiments, all bands were unofficial and supported totally or in part by the officers of the regiment. The officers were normally gentlemen in the eighteenth-century sense of the word and very frequently were capable of playing an instrument themselves. Several must have brought instruments with them to America, for Lieutenant John Barker mentioned a flute among the effects of a deceased officer of the 52d Regiment offered for sale in Boston in 1775. The instrument must have been highly prized by the owner to warrant its being brought to America when baggage space was relatively scarce, even for officers. The regimental band provided the officers' evening entertainment. Music was performed during and after meals and at the social occasions so delighted in by the officers.[20]

A compilation of band references from various inspection reports, account books, and announcements of musical performances may be found in Appendix A. Regiments normally were inspected just prior to leaving for overseas duty, thus the records are not complete. Of the seventy regiments of foot that were on the British establishment in 1775, forty-nine, or 70 percent, had bands of music. In only a few cases did the inspection reports state that there was no band, so very likely the percentage should be much higher. In some cases, such as the 26th Foot, a regiment was stationed in the colonies for the whole period of consideration and was not inspected. These regiments may have had bands, since the Royal American Regiment was able to raise a completely indigenous band. Additional evidence may someday be found to show that the figure should be much higher.

At the beginning of 1775 nine British regiments were stationed in Boston: the 4th, 5th, 10th, 23d, 38th, 43d, 47th, 52d, and 59th. The 52d Regiment, the only one without any indication of a band from the inspection reports, had been stationed in the colonies since 1766, so may easily have had an American band.[21] In addition to the units in Boston, ten regiments were stationed throughout the colonies, at least five of which had bands of music. It may have been two of these that participated in the festivities of the British soldiers on the occasion of the capture of General Charles Lee, whom they considered one of the ablest American generals. The newspaper report stated that the British "showed an ungenerous, nay, boyish triumph, after they had got him [Lee] secure at Brunswick, by making his horse drunk, while they toasted their king till they were in the same condition. A band or two of music played all night to proclaim their joy for this important acquisition."[22]

Ward wrote of the British bands playing the *British Grenadiers* on the Brandywine battlefield in September 1777: "There was no irregularity, no hurry. They came on with the arrogant assurance that marked the disciplined troops of that period of formal, dress-parade warfare." Two weeks later the British and Hessians marched into Philadelphia "with a band of music playing *God save the King*."[23]

While Washington and his army suffered through the ordeal of Valley Forge, Howe and his command were comfortably settled in Philadelphia. A gay and busy social season was climaxed in May by a

Mischianza given as a farewell to Howe who was returning to England. The participants in this grand festival were dressed in medieval costume, and the elaborate affair included a tournament complete with jousting and tilting. The procession commenced by water, three flatboats with a band of music in each at its head. *God Save the King* and other pieces of martial music were played during the festivities. Philadelphians must have seen at least one of these bands of music, and the affair was publicized extensively throughout the newspapers.[24]

The British recruiters were finding it difficult to enlist men to serve in the colonies against those whom they considered to be brother Englishmen. Turning elsewhere, Britain obtained soldiers from some of the princes of Germany. While they came from Brunswick, Ansbach, Hesse-Cassel, Hanau, and Waldeck, they became known and hated by the single name Hessian. In 1775, England contracted for complete German regiments, fully equipped and trained, with their own officers, amounting to 17,775 men.[25]

The treaties that the British minister, William Faucitt, arranged were explicit with regard to the organization of the regiments to be supplied. That signed with the Landgrave of Hesse-Cassell on 15 January 1776 called for four battalions of grenadiers, fifteen regiments of infantry, and two companies of *jäger*. Each company, four in the battalions and five in the regiments, was to include 105 privates and three drummers. The grenadiers had two fifers per company, but the line regiments had a band of six hautboys and a drum major included in the staff of headquarters section. Neither drums nor hautboys were permitted the *jäger*, their place being taken by three french horns. A certificate dated 12 April 1776 indicates that the three brigades of Leopold von Heister's division did indeed have the full complement of fifers, drummers, and hautboys when they were mustered into the British service. The treaties with the Duke of Brunswick and the Prince of Waldeck were similar in most respects, except that only four hautboys were permitted, while the treaty with the Margrave of Ansbach-Bayreuth included only field musicians. The hautboys, probably in *Harmoniemusik* combination, were brought with their regiments to America. Trevelyan wrote of the Hessian grenadiers at the Battle of Long Island in 1776 advancing "two deep with colours flying, and to the music of drums and hautboys, as if they were marching across Friedrich's Platz at Cassel on the Landgrave's birthday." When they landed in New York in October, a loyalist newspaper described the scene in glowing terms, including the poetic statement that the Hessians made "the Hills resound with Trumpets, French Horns, Drums and Fifes, accompanied by the Harmony of their Voices."[26]

Colonel Johann Gottlieb Rall commanded three regiments of Hessians stationed at Trenton in December 1776. As described by one of his officers, Rall was a pleasure-loving man who enjoyed drinking and gambling late into the night. He also took great pride in his band and never failed to watch the morning guard mount. "Since the guardhouse was only six or eight houses distant from his quarters and thus the trumpeters could not play long enough to satisfy him—he had the officer and picket march first around a church. . . . He would always follow the parade as far as the guardhouse, only to hear the music during the relief." This band of four musicians was among the 948 prisoners taken when Washington surprised them on 26 December. The band of the Lossberg regiment, consisting of five musicians, also was captured. The news of the victory spread throughout the colonies, and the impressive list of captives, including the nine musicians, was repeated time and again. Washington lost no opportunity to gain psychological advantage from the victory, and on the first day of 1777 paraded the prisoners through Philadelphia. The two bands were combined into one and remained in Philadelphia, parading on several occasions. The band attended and heightened the festivity of the first anniversary of the Declaration of Independence with some fine performances suited to the joyous occasion. This scene caused one member of Congress to write back home that the band "performed very delightfully, the pleasure being not a little heightened by the reflection that they were hired by the British Court for purposes very different from those to which they were applied." The same letter mentioned that the band had been used in celebrations on 28 June and that their appearances most likely would have been quite popular in Philadelphia.[27]

Among the spoils taken at Trenton were a number of brass drums used by the Hessians. These drums were used by the Americans in their own army, for in the early years of the war equipment always was short.

There were other German regiments still in British service after Trenton and, with them, their bands. When General John Burgoyne needed supplies of horses and cattle, he organized a raiding expedition into the countryside. To keep the true mission of this expedition secret, he ordered a German band of music along with the troops as if it were a ceremonial parade. In November of that same year, the Hessians "marched into the great city of Philadelphia with band playing and colors flying."[28]

In addition to the German mercenaries, the British crown enlisted regiments of loyalists to serve in their cause. These troops were supplied by the British, and so were much better dressed and equipped than the Continental soldiers. The loyalist orderly books read practically the same as those of the British or the Continentals. The drummers, as traditional in the British army, were clothed in the reverse colors of their regiment. The regimental organization emulated the British models in every detail. It was probably a Tory colonel who advertised in New York's loyalist newspaper in 1778: "Musicians wanted for a regiment, two good horns, a Clarinet, a Bassoon, and a person capable of directing a band, to all of whom good encouragement will be given." It may even have been the Volunteers of Ireland, a loyalist regiment, for on St. Patrick's Day 1779, they marched into New York "preceded by their band of Music."[29]

Throughout 1775 and 1776, while the colonials were struggling to form their army, they saw ample numbers of the European type of bands of music to use as models.

THE CONTINENTAL ARMY, 1777

The army of 1776 had been discharged. To avoid the problem of raising a new army each year, Congress had authorized eighty-eight regiments to be enlisted for the duration of the war. These were to be raised and equipped by the colonies according to assigned quotas. All officers and men would be appointed by the colonies, Congress reserving the right to appoint general officers. Recruiting was slow, and when Washington left his first winter encampment at Morristown he had but eight thousand of the legislated seventy-six thousand men. The supply picture had brightened somewhat, for France had agreed to send muskets, powder, and other badly needed military stores. In addition, a number of foreign volunteers arrived to help build and mold the army. Most important among these were the Marquis de Lafayette and Baron Friedrich von Steuben.

The military music of 1777 is best described by its two aspects, the company musicians and the bands of music.

The procedures begun in 1776 regarding the company musicians were continued in the new year. Regimental and brigade commanders applied their own interpretations of the various drum signals and attempted to improve the music of their command through the teachings of their appointed drum majors. Some improvement was needed, particularly with the newly formed Continental troops that had not served in the campaigns of 1776, for a mere week after he had left the winter encampment Washington commented that "the music of the Army being in general very bad; it is expected, that the drum and fife Majors exert themselves to improve it, or they will be reduced, and their extraordinary pay taken from them. Stated hours to be assigned, for all the drums and fifes, of each regiment, to attend them and practice—Nothing is more agreeable, and ornamental, than good music; every officer, for the credit of his corps, should take care to provide it.''[30] Washington then ordered the exact times and procedures for the daily camp duties, standardizing them at least for that portion of the army that was serving with him. Throughout the Revolution the hours for daily practice by the drummers and fifers were listed in orders, and musicians practicing at any other time were subject to severe punishment.

Normally, the drum major was responsible for the training of the company musicians. In some cases, there was no such major assigned, and a fife major acted as instructor. The musicians were not quartered together, but rather with their company, and the drum major had control over them mainly when they performed in a musical capacity. While the spelling may not be perfect, the intent of the following order cannot be misconstrued: ''Enos Fountain is appointed Dr. Majr. to Doe Drum Majrs Duty till further orders & is to be obayd accordingly & is to take Perticuler Care that the Several Beets beet in Camp are beet in their Proper Season.'' Usually one hour in the morning and one in the afternoon were devoted to practice, but commanders could increase this amount as they wished. One colonel, for example, ordered that the musicians practice at least four hours each day. General Sullivan ordered his drum and fife majors to report to him for orders on the very day following his assumption of command of the division at Princeton. It is hoped that not all commanders went as far as the colonel who one evening ''Confined 9 Drumers and fifers for not attending their Duty Better & Released them again in the morn after that they Promisd to Doe Beter for the futur.''[31]

The fifers and drummers were truly company musicians. Since August 1777, all able-bodied fifers and drummers were furnished with arms and were required to do duty as soldiers. The men of the unit regarded these musicians as part of themselves and grew very attached to their music, even in social situations. Dr. James Thacher, in writing of the retreat from Ticonderoga in July, commented, ''The drum and fife afforded us a favorite music''; several bottles of wine were found among the hospital stores, which undoubtedly enlivened their spirits. Chaplain Robbins described one evening when he prayed with his brigade: ''Sometime Tibbals, who strikes the drum admirably, gives it a touch at the right time when we are singing—it is beautiful harmony. A soft fife is also an addition.'' The degree to which the men associated with their musicians can be seen in the predicament of General William Smallwood of the Maryland Line. When the Independent Company of

Baltimore was discharged, he wished to keep the drummer and fifer as an aid to recruiting. In spite of an officer and a file of men who were sent to escort the musicians, the company refused to give them up and insisted upon taking them back to Baltimore with them. The company commander expressed his regrets to the general for the incident, but was powerless to do anything.[32]

Since the Middle Ages, trumpets had been associated with troops of horse. British dragoons were still using the drum in 1761 when Dalrymple made his suggestions for the improvement of these mounted infantry units: "It will be observed that trumpets are proposed preferable to drums; it is because they are infinitely more animating than the hoarse unaccompanied sound of the latter; they pour an acid into the blood, which rouses the spirits and elevates the soul above the fear of danger." The plea must have convinced the administration, for in 1764 brass trumpets were substituted for the drums of the light cavalry. Seeing the success of the light infantry with the bugle horn, the dragoons adopted this instrument for use with detached parties. The same musician was expected to sound the trumpet when signaling the whole troop and the bugle horn when signaling small detachments. When the Continental army began recruiting for its 1st Regiment of Light Dragoons in April 1777, it was modeled after the British regiments. An advertisement appeared in the Pennsylvania papers seeking a trumpet major. The uniform of the dragoons was to be brown faced with green, and the trumpeters, following the British tradition of reversed colors, were to have green coats faced with brown. The trumpet was to have a banner, or tabard, "the Colour of the Ridgmantal Facings," or the same color as the trumpeter's coat. "Next, to make up for the lack of trumpeters, the regimental quartermaster was to procure seven trumpets and seven fifes, and one man from each troop was to be selected to learn the two instruments." While the dragoons were mounted, the trumpet would remain the standard instrument. While they were dismounted, since they served as infantry, the fife and drum would provide the signals. Since they did not have drums, the colonel probably wished the trumpeters to learn fife to provide cadence for the march. It was not uncommon to find troops marching to the fife alone, and later in the war it was even mandated for all formations after retreat. Other units seem to have followed a similar practice, for an account book of Pulaski's Independent Legion contained a debit for teaching the fife and trumpet. There was also an entry for three french horns, which may have been used in place of the bugle horns.[33]

On 27 May 1778 the Congress voted a reorganization of the army. The changes were put into effect by general orders of 7 June. The infantry regiment was raised from eight to nine companies by the addition of light infantry. This company was to be composed of picked men and was to be kept complete by drafts from the other companies. The field-grade officers, or colonel, lieutenant colonel, and major, were each in command of a company in addition to their regimental duties, following the British custom (an important point for band researchers, for frequently the members of the band were carried as privates in the colonel's company). The infantry drum and fife majors received a raise in pay to nine dollars per month and were included in the regiment as part of the staff, that is, in addition to the regular complement of company musicians. The drummers and fifers remained at the same rate of pay as the corporal, or seven and one-third dollars per month. This was sixty cents more than the private, who received six and two-thirds dollars per month, as the dollar at that time contained only ninety cents. The artillerymen fared much better than the infantry. The drummers and fifers received eight and two-thirds dollars per month, while their majors received ten and thirty-eight ninetieths. The artillery matross, equivalent to the infantry private in rank, was paid the sum of eight and one-third dollars, or more than an infantry corporal.

As already shown, British and German regiments usually had bands of music in addition to their fifes and drums. The Americans had seen these bands in concerts and in the normal performance of their duty as the show element of ceremonial parades. Reference has been made to the hautboys of Benjamin Franklin and the bands of colonial militia units. The Continental army also had its bands. Except in one instance, the men were not mustered separately as a band, nor often even as musicians, but as privates in the individual companies. Their existence has long been denied simply because they did not appear as a separate unit. It is necessary to turn to the various journals, diaries, newspaper accounts, and sometimes orderly books to find traces of these units. While there may have been others in existence, so far only three actual Continental army bands have come to light for the year 1777. These were the bands of the 3d and 4th regiments of Artillery and Webb's Regiment of Infantry.

After having been appointed commander of the Regiment of Artillery stationed at the siege of Boston, Henry Knox recommended to Washington that three regiments be formed in order to strengthen the Continental forces. Congress approved this plan on 24 July 1776, but it was some time before the regiments were raised and actually in the field. Colonel John Crane's regiment from Massachusetts, later numbered the 3d Regiment, did not join the army until the late spring of

1777. Prior to that time it was stationed in Boston under the command of General William Heath. Boston had been peaceful since Howe left in March of 1776, and the distance from the actual site of warfare seems to have given the inhabitants some sense of assurance that military preparations were no longer an emergency. On 29 May 1777, Heath gave the following order to the troops in Boston:

The Honble House of Representatives having represented that the frequent Drumming around and near the Court House greatly interrupts the Debates of the Assembly, and desire that a stop may be put thereto, the General therefore forbids any Beating of Drums during the sitting of the Council or House of Representatives (except on some special occasions) either for practicing or on Duty, above the Coffee House in Congress Street, or between the Old Brick Meeting House, and the Town Pump in the Main Street. Fife Major Hywill will fix a parade for the Musick of Colo Crane's Battalion, somewhere without the before mentioned limits.[34]

The fife major referred to in the order was John Hiwell, who had been appointed to that position in Knox's Regiment of Artillery on 1 February 1776. Prior to that time he had been a sergeant, but little else is known about his early life. On 1 January 1777, according to Heitman, Hiwell had been promoted to the rank of second lieutenant, yet the above order refers to him as fife major. It is very possible, in the light of subsequent events, that Hiwell carried on the duties of fife major, with the rank, pay, and allowances of a second lieutenant because he was responsible for the regimental band of music. If only the fifes and drums were meant, there would be no need to single out Hiwell and "the Musick of Colo Crane's Battalion" in the order. Nothing else has been found about this band during the year 1777, but since Crane did have a band in 1778, the same one probably existed a year earlier.

In June of 1777, less than a month after the above order was given, Hiwell received 180 dollars from Colonel Crane "to recruit men for his Reg. of Arty." At that time a Continental bounty of twenty dollars and one hundred acres of land was offered to anyone who enlisted for the duration of the war and ten dollars to anyone enlisting for three years. Since Hiwell was fife major and a skilled musician, he may have been sent to recruit additional men for the regimental band.[35]

In October 1775, Captain Thomas Proctor commanded the 1st Company of Pennsylvania Artillery, a militia unit. By July 1776 his company included one fifer, two drummers, and six musicians. Proof of the existence of bands of music in the colonial militia can be found in a letter which Proctor, by then major of the Pennsylvania Artillery Battalion, addressed to the Council of Safety in Philadelphia. Dated 24 October 1776, the letter complained:

As the times of sundry of the Artillery men for which they enlisted, will expire the 27th of next month, in which matter beg to have your advice especially as my band of musicians are in the number, who from private encouragement offered to them are intending to join some other corps, at said expiration; I cannot find out who the persons are, as they keep it secret, but I am convinced the persons thus acting use me very ungenerously, as I have been at a considerable expense having bought all their musick and instruments, and paid each person who played on the viol, 5s. per month for their strings. I hope you will take premises in consideration and order it as in your wisdom you may think meet.[36]

Whoever the "ungenerous" people were, they must have been successful, for only one of the musicians of 1776, Thomas Menckle, appears on the muster roll of Proctor's band in 1777. Another, Christian Coon, went on to become the trumpet major of the Pennsylvania Regiment of Cavalry. The significance of Proctor's appeal is that he had a band of six men, in addition to his company fifers and drummers, and that at least some of these six were double-handed, or capable of performing on both string and wind instruments.

When the enlistments of Knox's Regiment of Artillery expired at the end of 1776, Proctor's battalion was the only artillery unit still in existence. Because of the great need for this arm, Pennsylvania offered the battalion to the Continental army. Congress approved on 19 July 1777, and the unit was incorporated into the Continental army as the 4th Regiment of Artillery. It entered service unchanged from its militia form, the officers' commissions dating from the time of their entrance into state service. That organization, as resolved by the Pennsylvania Council of Safety on 6 February 1777, consisted of a complete regiment of eight companies, each with a fifer and a drummer, and a staff including a drum major, and twelve musicians. Throughout the war this regiment was manned by Pennsylvanians, and it is possible that Moravian influences contributed to the high regard for music and the continued existence of its band.[37]

The question of which of these two bands of music can claim seniority cannot be answered until further information is gained. Crane's was the senior regiment, ranking from 1 January 1777. Proctor's regiment was not taken into Continental service until July, but with date of rank of 6 February. The earliest mention of Crane's band is in the order of 29 May 1777, quoted above, but additional research may provide earlier documentation. On the other hand, Proctor's militia company had a band of six in July 1776, and at least one of the musicians remained with the unit when it entered Continental service. Because the Continental army was completely disbanded in 1784, a definite break was made in the lineage of all units with one exception, a battery of artillery. The United States army, however, dates its lineage to 14 June 1775, completely ignoring this break in service. It should therefore be quite proper, unless some documentation for the existence of Crane's band can be found in Continental service in January 1777, to recognize the band of music of the 4th Regiment of Artillery, commanded by Colonel Thomas Proctor, as the senior band in the United States army.[38]

On 27 December 1776, Congress authorized the forming of sixteen additional Continental regiments to be raised at large and known by the names of their colonels rather than by number. Colonel Samuel B. Webb of Connecticut was appointed to command one of them. Webb had been an aide to General Israel Putnam and later to General Washington and had been wounded at both Bunker Hill and Trenton. In his service as aide he must have become familiar with regimental bands, British or Continental.

Timothy Olmstead had served in the Connecticut militia as a fife major from January to April 1776. On 1 May 1777 he enlisted in Webb's regiment for three years. A request for clothing for the band of music of Webb's regiment dated 30 December 1778 lists eight names, including Olmstead's. Three of the others were already in the regiment when Olmstead enlisted in 1777, the remaining four enlisting shortly after. When he returned from the war, Olmstead settled in Hartford and became a psalmodist of some renown. He also wrote *Martial Music*, or *a Collection of Marches, Harmonized for Field Bands in Various Keys, such as are the Most Familiar and Easy to Perform on the clarinet, oboe, bassoon, &c,* which contained seven easy lessons "for young practitioners," and thirty-five marches scored for primo, secundo, and bass. This volume was most likely an outgrowth of his experiences and repertoire in the Revolution. He was probably in charge of Webb's band in 1777, as indicated by his name being placed first upon the clothing request mentioned above. The men later included as members of the band were all enlisted by June 1777. Webb must have been proud of them, for his journals mention several occasions near the end of the year when the band was present as he entertained young ladies and officers.[39]

With Howe comfortably settled in Philadelphia, Washington moved his diminished army into Valley Forge for the second winter encampment of the war. He was buoyed somewhat by the success of Gates in capturing Burgoyne at Saratoga, but knew that he would have to resolve many serious problems before attempting another campaign. The difficult times and the shortages of food, clothing, and shelter have all been recounted many times. The devotion of this small group of men may perhaps be summarized by von Steuben's comment that no European army would ever have remained in existence under such desperate conditions.

Baron Friedrich von Steuben arrived at Valley Forge in February 1778 and offered his services as a volunteer. Washington instituted a new staff position and asked von Steuben to serve as acting inspector general of the army, in charge of training the troops. The conditions that he saw and described—the lack of clothing, the confusing jumble of understrength and irregular units, the lack of standardized drill techniques, the poor equipment and ignorance of its proper use, and the general lack of any systematized organization—have been cited many times. Von Steuben immediately set to work developing a drill manual that adapted the Prussian techniques to American individualism. He then organized a model company and began to drill it himself in these new techniques. Using the model company as cadre, he then extended the new drill to the remainder of the army in the encampment. Greatly pleased by the results, Washington had von Steuben confirmed as inspector general with the rank of major general and recommended to Congress that the drill regulations he had developed be adopted for the entire army. On 29 March 1779 the *Regulations for the Order and Discipline of the Troops of the United States* were officially adopted. The date is misleading, however, for several reasons. First, von Steuben applied these regulations to the troops that he personally drilled at Valley Forge in 1778. Second, the regulations usually were published in the general orders as they were written and so became adopted by decree of the commander in chief. Third, von Steuben, as inspector general, was responsible for the supervision of all training by the army and, with his subordinate brigade inspectors general, ensured that the regulations would be followed as directed. These regulations were therefore in force in the Continental army from the period of Valley Forge until the end of the war and remained basically in force until superceded by the *General Regulations for the Army* of 1821.

One of the shortages that plagued the army was musical instruments. Washington called for a return of missing fifes, drums, and accessories, in February and again in March. It was not just a musical consideration that pressed the need for these items: the drum was the signaling instrument of the army and regulated the march of the troops in the techniques being taught on the drill field. The lack of drums must have hampered training, for when they finally were available, orders were very explicit: "The Drums and fifes having now arrived from Lancaster, it is the Genl's positive Orders, that each officer exert himself in perfecting the men in their march and wheelings, for which purpose they will have them out twice a day at the hours directed in Genl Orders.'' Specific hours were determined for drill and for the practice of the musicians. Drummers practicing at other times would be severely punished for ''the use of Drums are as signals to the Army and if every Drummer is allowed to beat at his pleasure, the Intention is entirely destroy'd, as it will be impossible to distinguish whether they are beating for their own pleasure or for signal to the Troops.''[40]

As the skill of the army grew, so did its esprit de corps and morale. Parades and formations took on ceremonial significance, and the men became proud of their regiment and their army. As conditions improved, some relaxation was possible. Anderson has described some of the social activities participated in at Valley Forge, such as theater productions and dancing assemblies. May Day was ''spent in mirth and jollity the soldiers parading marching with fife & Drum'' around maypoles that had been erected. General Charles Lee had been a prisoner of the British, and Washington arranged to have him exchanged and returned to service. When Lee arrived at Valley Forge in April, he was greeted by all the principal officers of the army, and the troops formed a line almost two miles long leading back to camp. ''All the Music of the Army attended,'' and he was brought to ''Head Quarters, where Mrs. Washington was, and there he was entertained with an Elegant Dinner, and the Music Playing the whole time.'' Another participant, Elijah Fisher, was more explicit regarding ''all the music of the army'': ''Gen. Washington with all his attendance went to the Lines to Meet Gen. Lee and to Accompany him to Head Quarters where they arrived at two of the Clock in the Afternoon where they was received with a kind of salute of arms Drums fifes and Band of Musick.'' A short time later Fisher noted in his journal that the French and Spanish ambassadors were received at headquarters with ''the salute of arms and Drums and fifes and band of Music.'' Fisher did not include any further details regarding this band of music, but did specify in both cases that the band was in addition to and separate from the fifes and drums. Fisher mainly noted the two reception ceremonies in his journal, and the music was merely a sidelight. Diaries normally contain only those events which the writer considers important or unusual, and the common occurrences were not noted. Music was so naturally accepted as a part of everyday life that it was frequently considered unworthy of comment. When news of the alliance with France reached Washington, he decided to stage a formal review and celebration. While the procedures for the day were detailed in orders, there was no mention of any music. Ewing described the festivities in detail, but again made no mention of music. The newspapers carried Washington's orders and described the thirteen rounds of cannon and the *feu de joi*, but not music. Only from the letter of an unnamed soldier published in the newspapers does one learn that "an excellent band of music attended during the entertainment."[41]

As seen in the previous section, there were at least three bands of music in existence in the army at this time: Crane's 3d Artillery, Proctor's 4th Artillery, and Webb's Infantry. Crane's regiment was at Valley Forge, but no documentation has been found for the presence of the band. Webb had been taken prisoner in December, and no information has been located regarding his band at this period. Proctor's regiment was also at Valley Forge, and the assumption must be made that Proctor's band performed on each of the occasions mentioned above. The band's existence is proved by an entry in Washington's own account of expenses, under the month of February 1778, for "Cash paid the 22d Inst. to Proctr band—15s." John C. Fitzpatrick, the editor of the published edition of the account book, went to great length to comment on this "first public recognition of Washington's birthday," but stubbornly insisted that it was the fifers and drummers who serenaded the commander in chief. Fitzpatrick then listed from "the returns of Colonel Proctor's regiment" the names of one fife major, one drum major, one music master, five musicians, seven drummers, and six fifers.[42]

Fitzpatrick never seems to have considered the second indication of the existence of Proctor's band. The regimental returns, from which he gained the names of the musicians, were submitted to headquarters and then consolidated into a general return of the whole army. The returns were consistent throughout the encampment and that taken for 19 January can be considered as representative. That portion of the return which applied to the three artillery regiments is reproduced as figure 11. A column between those of the "Drums and Fifes" and "Mattrosses," is headed "Band." It shows that five men were present fit for duty in Proctor's Regiment on 19 January 1778. This was just one month prior to the date of Washington's birthday, when five musicians, rather than drummers and fifers, serenaded the general. Below the report, an additional three musicians in the band are listed as "Sick Absent." The regiment was authorized one drummer and one fifer for each of its twelve companies, or twenty-four men. The return indicates twenty-seven drums and fifes, so that Proctor had his full complement, plus the drum major, fife major, and music master. The five musicians in the band were in addition to the field music and were unquestionably a band in the eighteenth-century definition of that word as described in chapter 1.[43]

The encampment at Valley Forge is important to the military historian. Standardization was achieved by means of von Steuben's *Regulations*, and the new drill techniques developed a strong nucleus that served as a cadre for the remainder of the army. Valley Forge is also extremely important to the military musician, for everyone who participated in the encampment would, at some time or other, have come into contact with Proctor's band. This band of music, which many observers noted as excellent, suffering through the hardships of Valley Forge along with the small Continental army, served as a model for other commanders to emulate in their own regiments.

4. OF THE DIFFERENT
BEATS OF THE DRUM

As seen in chapter. 1, the drum was used primarily as a means of communicating military signals and commands and only secondarily as a musical instrument. This important primary function cannot be overstressed. While mentioning the nature of the calls and their names, the early military writers, with few exceptions, neglected to give the actual notation of the signals. These writers wrote as individuals, not in any official capacity, and merely gave their suggestions or described actual usage in particular armies. The official manuals of the time determined the placement of the drummers, fifers, and musicians in the ranks, but did not in any way attempt to regulate what these performers executed on their instruments. William Windham's *A Plan of Discipline Composed for the Use of the Militia of the County of Norfolk* is an exception which can be explained by its title. Printed for the militia, it was official only for the county of Norfolk and was not ordered into use by the king. A corps of experienced men was not available to train the militiamen, so detailed instructions were necessary. Unfortunately for historians, these instructions did not include the actual notation of the beats and melodies. One can gain very little, for example, from the following complete entry (p. 93): "The Serjeants and drummers calls are almost needless to mention, as well as the DEAD-MARCH, and some other trifling beats." The armies apparently depended upon the traditional instructions of their drum majors for the training of musicians, just as the noncommissioned officers were depended upon to train and drill the private soldiers. It is significant that the fife books published at the time always included the statement, "as performed in the Guards & other Regiments," implying that the tunes had been adopted by the fashionable regiments, rather than having been prescribed by regulations.

The army that Washington found camped by Boston was a composite of various training methods and levels of experience. What fifers and drummers there were had been trained by rote in British military traditions. Whatever fife books were available had been imported from England and usually consisted of three parts: the melodies of the English duty, those of the Scots duty, and miscellaneous popular marches. These tutors were published for the fife alone and were aimed also at commercial sales by including the statement that they were playable on the german flute or other instruments.

As the Continental army grew larger, the need for standardization became more pressing. Washington could not depend upon a trained corps of noncommissioned officers or drum majors. The whole army had to be developed, as described in the previous chapter, from raw materials utilizing experienced men as cadre. As part of his work in codifying regulations for the army, Baron von Steuben considered the importance of standardized musical signals. Chapter 21 of his *Regulations for the Order and Discipline of the Troops of the United States*, entitled "Of the different Beats of the Drum," listed the various beats and signals ordered into use for the Continental army and described their functions. Unfortunately, von Steuben did not include any musical notation. Starting with the Valley Forge encampment of the winter of 1777–78, these beats and signals were standardized for the whole Continental army, and von Steuben, as inspector general, was able to enforce their acceptance. For these reasons, von Steuben's *Regulations* are used as a basis for this chapter.

The soldier's day was regulated by the various *beats* of the drum which indicated to him the passage of time as well as the action that was expected from him. In addition, occasions that were not regulated by the clock, or that did not apply to the whole army, were included in the *Regulations* as *signals*. All these beats or calls were referred to as the camp duties. The private soldier was expected to "acquaint himself with the usual beats and signals of the drum, and instantly obey them." All signals were to be given by the drum, and no orders were to be given on the march by "calling out." The drummer had to be capable of the proper execution of the signals and would most likely be expected to help the privates in his company become familiar with them.[1]

THE BEATS

Nine *beats* are listed in von Steuben's *Regulations: The General, The Assembly, The March, The Reveille, The Troop, The Retreat, The Tattoo, To Arms,* and *The Parley.* The colonials were able to hear two different sets of signals in the British army, the English duty from those regiments and the Scots duty as performed by the Scottish regiments. The Scots duty was discontinued in the British army by order of the War Office in 1816 when Samuel Potter's two manuals were officially adopted. Some portions of the Scots duty are to be found in the early American fife books, and the "Slow Scotch" and "Quick Scotch" were incorporated into the nineteenth-century sequence of melodies for the reveille formation. When the French arrived in 1780, a third set of beats, or calls, was introduced to

America. Von Steuben's instructions were similar to those of the Windham plan used by the Americans prior to 1778. Considering the British heritage, it is natural to assume that the calls would be predominantly those found in the English duty. No Revolutionary American fife tutor has been located, telling exactly which melodies were used by the Continental musicians. A comparison of the fife tutors published in England prior to and during the Revolution with tutors printed in America after that period yields an idea of which actual tunes were used by these musicians. The problem is compounded by the unavailability of any drum manuals published prior to the Revolution, so that all beats presented are based upon nineteenth-century works. The fife tutors contained only fife music, while the drum manuals sometimes contained fife and drum parts, but never in score form. Drum beats were not written in musical notation, but rather in symbols or words for drum rudiments. These notations were unmeasured, and the specific melody referred to is often omitted. As an illustration, Daniel Hazeltine explained the *Rogues March* in the following manner in 1810:

1st Part. A five and a half drag, and two and a half drags, three times over; then a five, a rough and two and a half drags.
2nd Part. Eight fives; then a five and a half drag, and two and a half drags three times over; then a five, a rough and two and a half drags.

Hazeltine also included the fife tune for the march, thus indicating that the beat was meant to accompany a specific melody. The interpretation found below in example 15 is that of the writer, based on the above rudiments. If a drum manual of the period were to become available, greater certainty would be possible in stating that beats and signals were performed in a specific manner during the period. This is not possible today, and the interpretations included here are only suggested as being close to Revolutionary beatings in consideration of the following assumptions:

1. The general level of ability of the drummers of the period was not of a high standard, and there were few rudiments required of the average company musician. If the standard of drumming were as high as that of the nineteenth century with its many additional rudiments, it would have been impossible for Congress in 1782 to order that "in future no recruit shall be inlisted to serve as a drummer or fifer. When such are wanted, they shall be taken from the soldiers of the Corps in such numbers and of such description as the Commander in Chief or commanding officer of a separate army shall direct, and be returned back and others drawn out as often as the good of the service shall

make necessary."[2] Because only one drummer was authorized per company and he was vital to provide signals for that unit, such a man could not be dispensed with for a period of many months in order to train a new man "as often as the good of the service shall make necessary." The implication must certainly be that the drummer could be trained to perform adequately within a short period of time.

2. As shown in chapter 1, there is no verification for the use of bass drums in the Continental army. The bass drum was introduced into the band of music as a part of the Janissary section near the end of the century and should not be considered as a part of the field music during this period. The first drum manual to make any mention of this instrument was published in 1817, and then only as an additional page to the main body of the manual. As late as 1829, Ezekiel Goodale's *Instrumental Director* still combined the bass drum with the cymbals, tambourine, and triangle, as the rhythm section of the band.

3. It is logical to assume that during times of peace greater emphasis was placed on music and ceremony. The technique of drumming normally would improve, though retaining the basic format of the beats. This progression can be seen by a comparison of the manuals of 1810 through 1820 with those of the Civil War, where rolls of seven and nine strokes have been enlarged to nine, eleven, and even fifteen strokes. In plotting this progression backward, one might venture that the seven- and nine-stroke rolls of the early nineteenth century may have been five- and seven-stroke rolls during the Revolution.

With the above problems and considerations in mind, each of the directions in von Steuben's *Regulations* is considered in turn, and an interpretation of the music is presented.[3]

"*The General* is to be beat only when the whole are to march, and is the signal to strike the tents, and prepare for the march."

The eighteenth-century army moved primarily on foot. So as not to be surprised while on the march or while in the process of establishing a new position, the army moved and camped in battle order. The *General* was beat to warn the army that they were to move that day, and a chain of events was instituted upon its sounding. The *General* would be substituted for the *Reveille* as a signal for the men to rise, dress, and prepare themselves for the march. The baggage would be packed and loaded on the wagons. The advance party, consisting of the regimental quartermaster, the pioneers, artificers, and guides, would assemble and begin their march to the new location. There was no limitation with regard to time, and in summer the *General* was frequently beat as early

EXAMPLE 2: *The General*

as two or three o'clock. This beat was a signal for all the troops to march, and if only a portion of the army was involved, the *General* and the *Reveille* both would be omitted, and the *Assembly* substituted. The first four bars of the *General* were also used as the signal to cease fire.[4]

"*The Assembly* is the signal to repair to the colours."

Within a reasonable time after the beating of the *General* indicating that the troops were to march that day, the *Assembly* would be sounded. This was the signal for the men to form their companies and then form on the regimental line, ready to march. At this time the quarter and rear guards would be recalled.[5]

    Drum beats frequently had more than one interpretation, depending upon circumstances. Windham stated that the beat for the *Assembly* was the same as that for the *Troop*. Washington's "Standing Regulations" of August 1777 used the word "troop" to indicate this call, and von Steuben's later adaptation changed the word to "assembly." The various fife tutors included a call marked *Troop, or Assembling*, so one may assume that the same music was used for both functions. The soldier would understand which interpretation was meant by the call that preceded this beat, the *General* for days when the troops were to march or the *Reveille* on other days.[6]

"The March for the whole to move."

During the sixteenth century each nation had its own particular drum beat or pattern. While these patterns, or marches, were quite simple, they became increasingly more complex as the skill of the performers developed and as more interest was taken in the performance. The *March*, as a signal to advance, was identical with the march pattern used in tactics for maintaining the cadence of the troops. Humphrey Bland (1743) directed that the *March* was to be used when a battalion was to march forward, with the beat for *Retreat* used when marching to the rear. Windham (1759) broadened this interpretation to include any portion of a battalion marching, but never played unless the men were carrying shouldered arms. He also referred to it as "The Batallion, or Foot March," as if there were a specific beat or melody associated with that particular battalion and no other. This was probably the case, at least concerning melodies. The fife books abound in tunes titled in honor of a particular unit or regimental commander, most likely included for greater commercial attraction to the general public. The tradition for each unit having its own regimental slow march and quickstep had its foundation in this period.[7]

Von Steuben did not give the actual rhythm of the *March* signal. An inspection of several of the drum manuals printed in the early nineteenth century shows striking similarities, so a Revolutionary pattern probably was the common ancestor of the beats for the ordinary step given in example 3.

The cadences of the marches in the British army at the time were 60 for the ordinary step and 120 for the quickstep. Following British manuals and techniques, the early Continental army maintained the same cadences. Von Steuben, schooled in the Prussian tradition, raised the cadence of the ordinary march to 75 twenty-four-inch steps per minute, without changing the rate of the quickstep. When this new cadence was introduced at Valley Forge, one participant commented, "This forenoon the Brigade went thro the Manouvers under the direction of Baron Stuben the step is about half way betwixt Slow and Quick time an easy and natural step and I think much better than the former."[8] Melodies for both cadences can be found in the fife tutors. The ordinary step is usually indicated by an *alla breve* (¢) time signature, though sometimes C or $\frac{4}{4}$ are indicated. In each case, according to the

EXAMPLE 3: *The March*

regulation, a cadence of 75 was required. The quickstep was usually indicated by time signatures of $\frac{2}{4}$ or $\frac{6}{8}$, which would have been played at the cadence of 120 steps per minute.

Von Steuben ordered that "*The March* [is the signal] for the whole to move." It was not implied that the drum beat was to continue for the whole period of the march, as in modern parades, for the men would be on the road for the greater portion of the day. The pattern was beat once, "and upon the last flam . . . being struck the whole are to move." The men marched at an uncadenced pace (the modern route step), and the drummer would unsling his drum and carry it over his shoulder by means of the drag rope. Drummers who tried to take it easy by putting their drums into the baggage wagons instead of carrying them on the march were to be "immediately flogg'd by any officer comm[andin]g the Baggage of such waggon."[9]

On at least one occasion, Washington ordered the cadence of the marching troops modified. In August 1777, moving to engage with Howe whom he believed to be advancing toward Philadelphia, Washington determined to impress the populace with his command. He ordered the army to halt just outside the city, and every man was given the opportunity of refreshing himself to look his very best. The men in tattered uniforms, the women followers, the baggage—all that would have spoiled the effect—were ordered to travel circuitously around the city under the control of the wagon master general, who was strictly ordered that no one from his train be allowed to slip into the city. Choosing a route directly through the center of Philadelphia, Washington paraded his men in ranks of eight across, regiment by regiment. For greater effect, the company musicians were collected in the center of each brigade. Since there were normally four to six regiments per brigade, this would mean that approximately eighty to one hundred and twenty fifers and drummers would have been massed in the center of each marching unit. The musicians were instructed to play a tune for the quickstep, "but with such moderation, that the men may step to it with ease; and without dancing along, or totally disregarding the music, as too often has been the case."[10] This order very frequently has been quoted by modern writers, often with incorrect applications. It has been applied to all foot marches, for example, rather than merely to this one parade. It also has been used to indicate that the quickstep cadence was normally ignored or modified, even by Washington. The elite units of the time, the grenadiers and light infantry, normally marched at the quickstep. Apparently Washington felt that he would have to modify the cadence somewhat so that the whole infantry would maintain such a quick pace. In modern concepts, it would have been as if he had ordered his troops to parade through the city at double time, or on the run. This analogy is not as strange as it may seem. The cadence of all human activities has increased considerably since the colonial period. When the regular infantry marched at the ordinary step, the elite marched at the quickstep. Today, when almost all troops march at the quickstep, the elite march at the double step. The light infantry units in the British army maintain a quickstep cadence of 140 steps per minute, approximately the same as that of the Italian Bersaglieri and the French Chasseurs Alpins. The United States army specifies 180 steps for double time, the cadence of all normal activities for such elite units as the Rangers, airborne troopers, and Military Academy cadets. By having his troops pass through Philadelphia at the quickstep, Washington was able to give the psychological impression that his whole army was composed of elite troops.

"*The Reveille* is beat at day-break, and is the signal for the soldiers to rise, and the centries to leave off challenging."

It is important to remember the two-fold meaning of this beat: the signal for every soldier in camp to "rise and comb his hair and clean his hands and face and be ready for the duties of the day" and the cessation of challenging by the guard. Windham stated that it was to be sounded by the drummers of the guard in front of the guardroom as soon as it was light enough to read writing. Some of the Continental drummers during the siege of Boston must have forgotten this meaning, for Washington chided them in orders: "Certain Drums in and near Cambridge, very improperly beat the Reveille this morning before day; Although the Troops are ordered to be under Arms half an hour before day light, it does not follow the drums are to beat at that time. The Reveille is to beat when a Centry can see clearly one thousand Yards around him, and not before."[11]

EXAMPLE 4: *The Reveille*

The *Reveille* was omitted on days when the troops were to march, the *General* being beat in its place. Some commanders seem to have omitted the *Reveille* on Sunday, as one soldier noted his surprise at being awakened by the drums and fifes of his regiment. Orders have been located exempting the *Troop* and *Retreat* on Sundays, but no exemption has been located for the *Reveille*. Washington encouraged church parades, with the whole regiment attending services. Since the call was also important to the guards, and this duty was never omitted, this incidence of being awakened indicates the lack of standardization and organization of the early part of the war and certainly is not representative of the whole army.[12]

A morning gun was fired by the artillery at least as early as May 1777; the practice was extended to the whole army by the general order of 6 June 1777, making this one of the oldest general orders still in force. By this time *Reveille* had become ceremonial, in that all the fifers and drummers were required to perform while marching along the regimental color line, rather than just the orderly drummer performing in place before the adjutant's tent.

When the eighteenth-century army encamped, it did so in battle formation. Each battalion set up camp according to the plan outlined in von Steuben's *Regulations*; his plate VIII is included as figure 13. The front of the camp was not allowed to occupy more space than the battalion in formation. One tent was assigned to the noncommissioned officers of each company, and one tent for each six men, including the drummers and fifers. The adjutant's tent was in the center, at the head of the widest or "grand" street, with the drums piled six paces in front. The colors were planted before the drums, and this formed the "color line" or parade ground of the battalion. The drummers would pick up their drums from in front of the adjutant's tent and perform the beats in unison. Starting in front of the adjutant's tent, they paraded along the front of the battalion to the right, then to the left, and then back to the center. It is doubtful that the beat was performed more than once through, with repeats, for the elaborate *Reveille* formations with the *Three Camps* and as many as seven different fife melodies and accompanying drum rhythms did not appear until the beginning of the nineteenth century.[13]

"*The Troop* assembles the soldiers together, for the purpose of calling the roll and inspecting the men for duty."

Windham stated that this beat was the same as that for the *Assembly*, and the various fife tutors have a melody entitled "The Troop, or

Assembling,'' as given in example 5. When the companies were ready to come up to their position for the regimental formation, "the drummers [were to] march forward, beating the troop, ten paces beyond where the front rank is to draw up; opposite to the centre of the company: then face to the right about, continuing to beat till the officers are at their posts, when they are to cease."[14] It was also used by the grenadiers in going for or returning the colors, but since a "Troop for the Colours" is included in some of the fife tutors, this latter melody would most probably have been used.

EXAMPLE 5: *The Troop or Assembling*

The *Troop* was used in several contexts. When sounded after the beating of the *General*, it signaled that the men were to strike their tents and put them in the wagons, ready to wait for the beating of the *March* as a signal to form and parade to the regimental color line. When sounded in garrison, after the *Reveille*, it normally signaled the formation of the regiment, but in some commands it was used as the signal for the formal guard mount. In either case, the *Troop* normally was sounded in the morning, between 8:00 and 9:00 A.M., though on marching days it would often be earlier. Washington seemed to prefer the *Troop* at eight o'clock, as can be seen from his orders of 4 June 1777 and 8 February 1778, while General Heath ordered nine o'clock.[15]

"*The Retreat* is beat at sun-set, for calling the roll, warning the men for duty, and reading the orders of the day."

As mentioned under the section on the *March*, Bland indicated that this signal was used for the troops to march to the rear, or retreat. Windham enlarged the meaning to include the ceremony held at sunset, at which time the rolls were called and orders given. The ceremony is an ancient one and has vestiges of the period of the medieval walled towns. At the completion of the beating of *Retreat* by the drummers around the city walls or in the open fields just before them, the gates were shut, the drawbridge raised, and the city sealed until the following morning at the beating of the *Reveille*. The Prussian *Regulations* of 1759 still contained instructions for the "Ceremony of Opening and Shutting the Gates." A drummer beat *Retreat* upon the ramparts one-half hour prior to the gates being shut, to give notice to the townspeople. The French *Ordonnance* of 1753 called for the beating of *Retreat* at sunset, with the drums marching the full length of the regimental encampment and back to their original position.

The working day in the Continental army ran from *Reveille* to *Retreat*, or from sunrise to sunset. During the summer months when

EXAMPLE 6: *The Retreat*

campaigns were most vigorous, this meant a very long day. An artillery round was also fired as the signal for *Retreat*, similar to the morning gun. Sometimes even then the day was not over for the soldiers, but the drums were forbidden to beat after *Retreat*. If there were any fatigue parties or guard details still marching after that time, they were to be accompanied by the fife alone.[16]

"*The Tattoo* is for the soldiers to repair to their tents, where they must remain till reveille beating next morning."

The earlier form of this word gives additional meaning to the function of the beat: tap-too. Reputedly taken from the Dutch expression "doe den tap to" meaning to turn off the taps, it was the signal for the innkeepers or sutlers to shut the taps of their casks and close business for the day. Windham stated that the call was generally beaten at eight in winter and ten in summer, and it required that the sergeants check the men in their quarters. In January 1776 the officers of the Massachusetts Brigade were requested to "visit their Troops in Quarters at Tattoo Beating [8:00 P.M] & see that they retire to Bed & that the fires are secured." Washington seemed to have preferred a later hour, for the general orders of 8 February 1778 and 9 September 1779 stipulated 9:00 P.M. This may have been due to the influence of Simes's *Military Guide*, which states that "the Taptoo beats at ten o'clock every night in summer, and nine in winter."[17]

All the drummers and fifers of the regiment that furnished the guard for the day were to march through the line up to the general's quarters and back again, escorted by a sergeant and a file of men. The sutlers were required to "shut their Doors & sell no more Liquors that Night upon Penalty of severe punishment." Other vestiges of medieval traditions can be seen in instructions contained in orders that at the beating of the *Tattoo* "the gates of the fort [were to be] drawn up, which must not be let down till the reveille beats," or "upon the return of the Drums to the Barrack [after beating the signal] the gates to be immediately locked." The *Retreat* had become more a military ceremonial, and so the old signal to shut the gates had been absorbed by the *Tattoo*. Unless they had leave in writing from the commanding officer of their regiment, soldiers who were found away from camp after *Tattoo* would be suspected of desertion and would be punished.[18]

At the beginning of the nineteenth century this signal began with the *Three Cheers*, followed by the "Singlings of the Tattoo." Ashworth's manual (1812) instructed that "some favorite Air is then played by the Drums and Fifes: at the end of each part of the Tune the

EXAMPLE 7: *The Tattoo*

Drums Beat the Singlings. When through the tune the Signal is given from the Right to begin the Doublings, which are beat but once through, after which the Singlings as at first, and so on alternately 'till the Signal is given for Rolling off; End with the three Rolls [*Three Cheers*] and the Doublings once through.''[19]

    Since any ''favorite Air'' could be played, none of the nineteenth-century fife tutors contains a melody for this signal. The eighteenth-century fife books do contain a *Tattoo* as part of the English duty, which may well have been used during the Revolution. It is therefore included as example 7. The $\frac{3}{4}$ time signature is misleading, for it would have been quite difficult to play the melody at one beat per bar in a cadence of 75 or even the British 60 steps per minute. It would be much more plausible if the meter were $\frac{6}{8}$, at two beats per bar, cadence of 120. The melody could then fit the Singlings at one pattern per bar. The Doublings could fit the second strain, with the repeat, and the coda one restatement of the Singlings.

    ''*To Arms* is the signal for getting under arms in case of alarm.''

It is indeed unfortunate that von Steuben did not include musical notations in his *Regulations*. Since the melody in example 8 appears in most of the eighteenth- and nineteenth-century sources, it may be accepted as authentic. No such verification is available for the drum beat. Many references of the period indicate that the long roll was the signal *To Arms*, and not the beat included in the example. The long roll consisted simply of a continuous series of paired strokes rapidly executed on the drum, which could easily accompany any fife tune. Orders are somewhat confusing, and it seems there was no standard practice, particularly in the early years of the war. General Charles Lee, for example, used the roll as a signal for "collecting under arms," but did not specify whether this was the same as *To Arms*, which he cited as the signal for the alarm. Shortly after, the roll was beat every morning at seven o'clock for the men to turn out for roll call. The *Troop* was used to summon the new guard to the parade. The opposite was true in the garrison of Fort Ticonderoga, where the *Troop* was sounded at 8:30 A.M. for the men to form, and the long roll beat one hour later "for the Guards to parade fresh shav'd and well powder'd, Arms & Accoutrements in good order." One may wonder at how "fresh shav'd" the guards were at 9:00 A.M., for on a similar occasion the troops were ordered to "shave this evening, and to see that they are well powder'd, with the Arms in good Order ready to be turned out at 8 o'clock tomorrow Morning on the Parade, or at such time as they may be order'd."[20]

* *Alternate drum part : long roll*

British version, c. 1903 *, Drum only*

EXAMPLE 8: *To Arms*

The long roll was also the signal at Princeton for the guards and fatigue parties "to parade ready to march to the grand parade as Soon as the Troops begin to beat" one-half hour later. General Andrew Lewis, in Virginia, ordered the long roll to be beat every morning and evening as a signal for the men to turn out for exercise. Three months later he ordered that the officer turn out the guard at all times when he heard the long roll, and "if he finds it is not occasioned by an alarm, he is then to dismiss them." The orders did not mention whether the guard was required also to turn out for the morning and evening beatings of this call or whether that practice had been discontinued.[21]

Washington was just as vague. While conducting the siege of Boston, he ordered "that the main guard on no Account whatever, be without a Drum, which is to beat To Arms on any Alarm and be followed by all the drums in the Camp; On which every Officer and Soldier is immediately to repair to the Alarm post." Apparently the men were not to fall into their company formations, but rather to an assigned post. Washington therefore ordered, "Upon any Alarm, the Drums are to beat through the whole lines, *To Arms*, as quick as possible, and continue beating till the whole line is formed."[22] In neither case does he specify whether the drums were to beat the long roll or some other recognizable pattern such as that included in example 8. The regulations did specify that the long roll was the signal to reform units after a halt while on the march, but this does not preclude its use for *To Arms*, for in either case the troops were required to form their units.

Some of the confusion may have existed among the colonials, for Deacon Tudor described an event in May 1775 while the British army was stationed in Boston: "This evening between 8 & 9 o'clock a fire broke oute in the Barracks of the 65th Regiment . . . upon the discovery the Troops beat to arms, which being unusual on such occasions, caused great consternation among the inhabitants." The Germans had been using the roll as a fire-alarm signal, and since European signals were fairly ubiquitous, the British may have adopted the same meaning. Presumably the Bostonians were not familiar with this use of the beat, but must have been familiar with the signal in other contexts in order to have become concerned by its beating. Heath recognized the call and remembered that both the British and American drums had beat *To Arms* at the Battle of Bunker Hill. Regardless of which drum rhythm was used, its meaning was universally understood: "The Drums beat to Arms. And instantly this vast Body of Men were at their Respective Posts! . . . Drums & Fifes on all Quarters making the very Air echo *To Arms! To Arms!*"[23]

"*The Parley* is to desire a conference with the enemy."

Considering its normal use in battle, the *Parley* probably was a beat for the drum alone, which explains why no melody of that name appears in any of the eighteenth-century fife tutors. Since no British drum manuals of the time have as yet been located, it is difficult to state with certainty what that drum beat was.

It is certain that there was such a beat and that it was used by the Americans. Writing about the Battle of Bennington in 1777, Ward related that the Hessian commander "beat a parley, a call to a conference for a surrender. But the untutored Americans did not know its meaning. To them it was just drums beating. They kept on shooting."[24] On another occasion this unfamiliarity with the beat resulted in serious confusion: "The drum beating a parley to summon a surrender was mistaken for a retreat; a panic seized our bewildered troops; and while one band believed itself in the full tide of victory, another would be hastily retreating thinking all was lost."[25] The Americans may have been using a different beat at this time from that of the British. According to all the eighteenth-century rules by which the war was fought, one always respected a flag of truce, particularly with a drummer to beat the *Parley*, yet Chastellux related that "an American officer was sent [to parley] who being preceded by a drum, and displaying a white handkerchief, it was imagined, would not incur the smallest risque; but the English answered this officer only by a musquet shot, and killed him on the spot." Chastellux must have been relating an incident early in the war, for by 1781 it was recognized fully on both sides. Ebenezer Denny wrote of the thrill of seeing and hearing a lone British drummer beat the *Parley* to arrange for the surrender of Lord Cornwallis. Denny recognized the beat, understood its meaning under the circumstances, and noted in his journal his great joy in anticipation of the victorious close of the Yorktown campaign.[26]

Three nineteenth-century manuals include a melody for this signal, two of them with accompanying drum beats. There is a surprising similarity between these beatings and the British version published in 1815. This latter has remained virtually unchanged to the present; the Revolutionary *Parley* could be the common ancestor. Without the corroboration of eighteenth-century tutors or manuals, example 9 is included only as a suggestion of what may have been played. The drum beating is the British version of 1815. The modern British version has a *da capo*, and since the melody ends on the dominant, it would seem logical that a return to the beginning was made. If the melody were to be played three times through, with repeats and *da capo* each time, the

EXAMPLE 9: *The Parley, or Church Call*

sequence of drum beatings to accompany it could then be (1) First Part, Doublings of the first Part, each repeated; (2) Second Part, Doublings of the second Part, Doublings of the first Part; and (3) Third Part, Doublings of the third part.

THE SIGNALS

In addition to the various beats of the army, a number of signals were used. These were directions to portions of the army or were simple facing or marching commands used to direct the troops when voice commands were not possible or desirable. Windham included the following signals, which he claimed were taken from the French:

Turn, or face to the right!	Single stroke, and flam.
[Turn or face] to the left!	Two single strokes, and flam.
[Turn] to the right about!	Three single strokes, and flam.
Halt!	Flam.
Wheel to the right!	Roll, single stroke, & flam.
[Wheel] To the left!	Roll, two single strokes, & flam.
[Wheel] To the right about!	Roll, three single strokes, and flam.
[Wheel] To the left about!	Roll, four single strokes, & flam.
Make ready!	Preparative.
Cease firing!	The General.
March!	March, and a flam.
Retreat!	Retreat, and a flam.
Advance by the double [quick] step.	Grenadiers March.
Charge!	Point of War.
Divisions to close up.	Troop.
Form Battalion!	To Arms.
Club, marching!	Drummers Call, and a flam.
Shoulder, marching!	March, and a flam.
Fix bayonets, marching	Roll, and flam.
Return bayonets, marching	Two ruffles, and flam.

The flams indicated when the movement was to begin, so that no confusion would result from men anticipating the command at the first strokes of the drum. The author was very wary of too many signals, however, and felt that most of the above, other than the march, retreat, troop, to arms, preparative, ruffles, and flams, were "of no use but to cover the deficiencies of the officers and men, and their want of knowledge in the real grounds and principles of exercise."[27] Regardless of Windham's feelings, these same signals were included by Simes in two of his military guide books. Simes added the following signals:

To ease your arms	Tow-row-dow
To secure your arms	First part of tat-too
To shoulder your arms	Last part of ditto
To call the Adjutant	First part of the troop
To call a Serjeant and Corporal of each company	Three rolls, six flams
To call all the Serjeants and Corporals	Three rolls, nine flams
To assemble the pioneers	Pioneer's March
To assemble the drummers and fifers	Drummer's Call

These works served as a basis for Colonel Samuel Elbert when he ordered them into effect for his 2d Georgia Regiment. Some of these signals were also used by the Pennsylvania line, and Henry Knox adopted some of them for the Brigade of Artillery just two weeks before von Steuben's *Regulations* were ordered into force.[28]

Von Steuben chose to include only twelve signals for the drum: *Adjutant's call, First Serjeant's call, All non-commissioned officers call, To go for Wood, To go for Water, To go for Provisions, Front to halt, For the front to advance quicker, For the front to march slower, For the drummers, For a fatigue party,* and *For the Church call.* All but three are brief drum beats without fife melodies, and even the three exceptions often were performed by the orderly drummer alone.

''Adjutant's call—*first part of the troop*.''

The association of the *Troop* with the adjutant is very logical. As the chief executive officer of the regiment, the adjutant was responsible for forming the regiment for parades and guard mounts. The adjutant's call was a signal to mark the beginning of the ceremony, a function it has maintained to the present.

''First Serjeant's call—*one roll and three flams*.''

The sergeants of a company were numbered one through four. The first sergeant's pay and allowances were those of every other sergeant, but he was the ranking noncommissioned officer in the unit. It was his responsibility to be the chief executive and administrator of the company, similar in function to the adjutant of the regiment. At a certain time of the day the adjutant would assemble all the first sergeants of the regiment, give them the orders for the day, and assign the details for the following day. These orders were copied by the sergeants into orderly books, which were then taken back to the company and the orders disseminated to the command. This signal, sometimes referred to as ''orderly call,'' would be used for assembling the first sergeants on such occasions.

"All non-commissioned officers call—*two rolls and five flams.*"

This beat is similar in intent and in execution to the First Sergeants call, but orders all the sergeants and corporals to report to the adjutant's quarters.

"To go for Wood—*poing stroke and ten-stroke roll*"

"To go for Water—*two strokes and a flam*"

Proper security was always a problem, and guards formed a chain around the camp. In order to pass through the chain, a soldier had to have the written permission of his regimental commander. The rigors of military discipline made desertions an ever-present consideration. For these reasons, men were not allowed to wander about at will, and all details were closely regulated. The *Regulations* stated (p. 85):

When any of the men want water, they must apply to the officer of the police, who will order the drum to beat the necessary signal; on which all who want water must immediately parade with their canteens before the colours, where the officer of the police will form and send them off under the care of two non-commissioned officers of the police, who are to be answerable that they bring back the whole detachment, and that no excesses are committed whilst they are out. Wood and all other necessaries must be fetched in the same manner. Except in case of necessity, not more than one detachment is to be out at a time.

Just what the "poing" stroke was has been the subject of some controversy. Hazeltine (1810, p. 5) stated that the stroke "is beat by giving a light flam and strike each stick nigh the hoop of the drum, lightly touching the hoop at the same time." Ashworth, less than two years later, described it simply as a hard stroke and used the symbol in many different beats in that context. Lovering (1819, p. 9) instructed that the player "strike the head about three inches from the lower side with a smart sliding stroke." Robinson, in the 1818 edition, paraphrased

Hazeltine. Some have interpreted this as a rim shot, which is unlikely for it appears in many of the beats in Ashworth where such a modern technique would be impractical and out of context. The stroke probably was a single heavy glancing blow on the drum, utilizing the full extent of the stick to make the head vibrate. The drum heads of the period were considerably thicker than those used at present, and a heavy stroke would be required to achieve a full sound. Drum Major and Music Master John Moon of the modern Colonial Williamsburg restoration instructs his drummers to place the left stick on the drum head and depress, then striking the left stick smartly with the right stick.

"To go for provisions—*roast beef*."

EXAMPLE 10: *Roast Beef*

There were no mess halls in the the Continental army, nor any men whose duty was specifically to cook. The rations were issued raw to the men, and they were responsible for the cooking. Usually the six members of a tent would choose one to perform that task or rotate the duty. When the provisions were ready for issue, the *Roast Beef* was the signal for the men to come and draw their rations.

In the early part of the eighteenth century a celebrated bass singer, Richard Leveridge, wrote "A Song in Praise of Old English Roast Beef." The words and music became very popular as the *Roast Beef of Old England* and were reprinted many times. It must have been so well known to the colonial soldiers that von Steuben felt the brief notation "roast beef" would tell everyone which melody was meant. This signal is still used as one of the "dinner" calls in the British army and has two alternate beatings. The second is identical with that of the American drum manuals of the nineteenth century and is given in example 10 as line C. The first beating is considerably simpler in execution than the second, so may very possibly date from the Revolution. This beating is included in example 10 as line D. Line A is an eighteenth-century form of the melody, while line B is from the nineteenth-century manuals. The two forms of the melody and two separate beatings are presented in score form so that comparison may be made easily. It is suggested that the earlier form of the melody, line A, and the simpler beating, line D, are closest to the actual signal used during the Revolution.[29]

"Front to halt—*two flams from right to left, and a full drag with the right, a left hand flam and a right hand full drag.*"

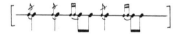

While on the march, the soldiers were permitted to proceed at their ease, at open intervals. Except when in the presence of the enemy, the weapons were carried at will, but with the muzzles elevated for safety. The line of march would stretch over several miles, and some form of control obviously was necessary. The *Regulations* stated (p. 71) that "on the march no orders are to be communicated by calling out, but must be sent by the adjutant from regiment to regiment. The signals for halting, marching slower and quicker, must be given by beat of drum." When the commanding officer thought proper to halt while on the march for refreshment, water calls, or because of a defile, he would command the orderly drummer to beat the signal for the front to halt. The drummer in each regiment assigned as orderly for the day would be required to carry his drum slung for the transmission of signals. The beat would be repeated by each orderly drummer until it reached the front, whereupon the command would be executed.

"For the front to advance quicker—*the long march.*"

If the commanding officer at the rear of the line of march saw that the troops were marching too slowly, or became too clustered in formation, he would command the orderly drummer to beat the signal for the front to advance quicker. This would be repeated up the line by each regimental orderly drummer until the command was executed. The *Regulations* stated simply that the signal was to be "the long march." Presumably this meant the same signal as the *March*, discussed previously. It was possibly performed in a faster tempo, to imply the acceleration desired. This may account for the inclusion by Ashworth, in 1812, of a beat for the "Quick Step, or Long March." This beat is included above as example 3, C.

"For the front to march slower—*the taps.*"

Similarly, if the commanding officer in the rear felt that the leading elements were marching too quickly, he would order that the signal for the front to march slower be beaten. The *Regulations* stated only that this was "the taps." The actual number of rhythmical notation of these taps is unknown, but Ashworth included the pattern

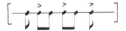

Again, like the previous signal, the drummer may have beaten the taps in the cadence desired, in which case a steady, even stroke may have been used.

"For the drummers—*the drummers call.*"

Except for the drum used by the orderly drummer on duty at the adjutant's tent or guardhouse, all drums were piled in front of the adjutant's tent on the color line. In order to gather the musicians prior to the beating of any call, the *drummers call* would be beaten.

EXAMPLE 11: *The Drummers Call*

EXAMPLE 12: *The Pioneers March*

In the nineteenth century the odd nine-bar call was reduced to the more familiar eight bars by eliminating the rest and one flam-tap and treating the sixteenth notes as an anacrusis. In this latter form it is still used in the British army, though the fife tune has been somewhat rhythmically changed.

"For a fatigue party—*the pioneers march*."

The word *fatigue* refers to any manual or menial chores of the soldier. Included in this would be general camp cleaning, construction of kitchen, sink, and "necessary" trenches, public works, and any other labor details. The following order is a typical example of the use of this march: "The Pioneers March to beat at 9 o'clock this Morning, at which time all the Brigade not on other Duty is to parade, and under the Direction of the officers to remove ev'ry Species of Filth from or about the Encampment."[30]

"For the church call—*the parley*."

As discussed in the section above on the *Parley*, the exact call has not been sufficiently established. Church parades were a common practice even as late as World War II, and all men, regardless of personal religion, were marched to the services. It is known that Washington greatly encouraged and at times required attendance at religious services. The following order is typical of the many reminders that Washington published throughout the war: "All Chaplains are to perform Divine Services tomorrow, and on every succeeding Sunday, with their respective brigades and regiments, where the situation will possibly admit of it. And the commanding officers of corps are to see that they attend; themselves, with officers of all ranks, setting the example. The Commander in Chief expects an exact compliance with this order, and that it be observed in future as an invariable rule of practice. And every neglect will be considered not only a breach of orders, but a disregard to decency, virtue and religion." This was not a new order to the troops, for Daniel McCurtin wrote his impression of a church parade during the siege of Boston in 1775: "This being the Sabbath day our Rifle Company were marched to Dorchester Meeting House, where we had a fine sermon, but the appearance of us as well as many other Companys seemed something strange to me, when I could see nothing else but men loaded with the ministers of death going to hear God's word; every company had their whifers and drums, and marched into the House of God under arms."[31]

TRADITIONS AND CEREMONIES

Besides the beats and signals outlined in von Steuben's *Regulations*, there is evidence that the Continental army had developed certain traditions and ceremonies. Since they are the basis for many present-day customs and practices, they are included. Standard operating procedures were developed with regard to the use of the *Three Cheers* and the *Grenadiers March*. Ceremonies for drumming undesirables from camp, for escorting the colors, for reviewing the troops, and for military funerals were formalized.

"The Three Cheers."

As the army grew in size, coordinating the activities of the regiments became increasingly difficult. Since the military units were encamped along one straight line and the various daily beats were sounded along that line, it became necessary to coordinate the musicians so that each group would begin the signal at the same time. The Continental drummers were even heard at times in the British encampment, so the sound of the drums must have carried quite far in the open countryside.

The first instructions appeared in 1777, when Washington ordered the following procedure:

For the sake of regularity, the drum of the regiment on the right of the line, to give three taps, allowing a sufficient equal space between each, as a warning to the drum of the one next on the left; which is to do the same, and so on, through the whole—the second line taking it by the right from the regiment in front, and the advanced Brigades, by the right from the regiment in the rear—these taps over, and a proper interval allowed for the warning to become general, the *drummers call* must be given as the signal for what is to follow; and then the whole music of the line begin in concert—the *reveille*, troop or retreat, as it may happen.[32]

Less than one year later, Washington reversed the order of the signals and changed the taps to three rolls. As soon as the *drummers call* was beat throughout the line, "three rolls to begin and run through in like manner as the call; then all the drums of the Army at the heads of their respective Corps should go thro' the regular beat, ceasing upon the right which will be a signal for the whole to cease."[33] The rolls were also called ruffles, which were used as warning signals in other military ceremonies. By 1779 they had become the standard commencement of the *Troop, Retreat*, and *Tattoo* beatings. There is no indication whether the fifes played with the ruffles and whether they were also performed at the conclusion of the beat, but by the early nineteenth century these three rolls had become known as the *Three Cheers* and were written as shown in example 13, A. There has as yet been no verification for the inclusion of the *Three Cheers*, in this form, prior to and after each of the ceremonial beatings during the Revolutionary period. Originating as a coordinating device, the three rolls gradually assumed musical importance. At what point the fifes were added, and the form most familiar today standardized, is not known. By the time of the Civil War, the *Three Cheers* were performed prior to and after the *Troop*, which had developed into the ceremony of the musicians "trooping the line" along the full front of the assembled regiment. This Civil War form is shown as example 13, B. With the replacement of the fife by the bugle, the melodic line was changed, but the drum ruffle remained. The present-day *Three Cheers*, officially known as the *Sound Off*, is still performed before and after the band's trooping the line. This form, for bugle and drum, is shown as example 13, C.[34]

EXAMPLE 13: *The Three Cheers*

"The Grenadiers March."

The grenadiers, the elite companies of the British infantry regiments in the eighteenth century, had their own particular march. Windham stated that it "should never be beat but with the grenadiers; or when the whole advance to charge an enemy.'' When rendering the salute during the review ceremony, the grenadiers were to beat this march, while the other drummers of the regiment were to beat ''the battalion march.'' The grenadiers, like the later light infantry, normally proceeded at a faster pace, and their march is in $\frac{2}{4}$, indicating a quickstep. The British 23d Regiment of Foot, considering itself an elite regiment, caused comment by an inspector for beating the Grenadier March on all occasions. The king observed it and ordered the colonel to see to it

EXAMPLE 14: *The Grenadiers March*

"that the same march must be beat by the Welch Fusiliers [23d Foot] as is observed by the other corps on the same establishment."[35]

Von Steuben made no reference to this march, but the colonials were also using Windham as a guide. The use of the *Grenadiers March* for the signal to advance was adopted by Henry Knox when he established "one Uniform System of Manoeuvers" for the artillery in 1779. The march appeared in the Willig fife tutor, and Ashworth (p. 20) included it with the statement that "the first part of the Grenadier March on the Roll is used when Guards Present Arms to each other—that on the Drag when a Regiment presents arms to a General." It was used in New Hampshire militia units as a march for trooping the colors along the length of the regiment, while the men were at present arms. The original meaning of the quickstep had been lost by this time, for the instructions stated that the color bearers were to march in slow time to the long *Grenadiers March*. The march is still used by the modern Grenadier Guards in both slow and quick time.[36]

"Drumming out of camp."

Discipline was very strict in the eighteenth-century armies. Persons convicted of crimes or breaches of discipline were ceremonially punished in front of their regiments or brigades. Lashings, running the gauntlet, and executions all were performed by or before the assembled troops. Where the crime was sufficiently serious to warrant dismissal from the service, but not the penalty of death, the culprit was "drummed from the army." Traditionally, the music associated with this ceremony was the *Rogues March*.

During the siege of Boston, a number of men were drummed out of the army for such various offenses as stealing, assault, desertion, and even for cursing the American army and drinking to General Gage's health. Even the women who followed the army and did the washing, tended the sick, and sometimes did the cooking for the men were subject to this punishment. James Stevens noted the important events of 8 June 1775: "This morning we preaded & went to her prars in the afternoon there was a woman dukt & drumb out of the regiment There was a funeral."[37] Frequently the culprits were lashed prior to the ceremony. Mary Johnson, for plotting to desert to the enemy, received one hundred lashes and was "drum'd out of the Army by all the Drums and Fifes in the Division." Timothy Downing was let off with an easier punishment. For the same crime, attempted desertion, he was sentenced "to receive thirty-nine Lashes upon the bare back with a Cat 'o' Nine tails, and it appearing to the Court that as the Prisoner is worthless and

incorrigible, they order him to be drum'd out of the army."[38] The
ceremony was made as impressive as possible so that it would serve
as a deterrent to others. Another soldier, found guilty of stealing a
twenty-dollar bill, was sentenced to receive thirty-nine lashes and be
drummed out of the service. A witness to the scene later wrote in his
journal that "after having his number [of lashes] he was drummed out
of the camp by fifty and two drums and as many whifers. This was the
first time that ever I heard such a number of drums beat all together,
they made such a report in my ears, when accompanied by such
screaking of whifes that I could not hear the next man to me, or
however could not hear what he said." Another spectator was impressed

EXAMPLE 15: *The Rogues March*

by the number of musicians, raising the number to fifty-five drummers and sixty fifers, certainly a most impressive showing.[39]

The actual ceremony consisted of the musicians parading the prisoner along the front of the regimental formation to the tune of the *Rogues March* and then to the gate or entrance of the camp. The prisoner's coat would be turned inside out as a sign of dishonor and his hands tied behind him. At the gate he would be sent upon his way by a kick from the youngest drummer, with instructions never to return to the vicinity. The sentence often was published in the newspapers, both near the post as well as in the prisoner's home town.[40]

This march was used unofficially in another type of ceremony. A soldier who married the widow of a comrade was "hoisted upon the shoulders of two stout fellows of his company, with a couple of bayonettes stuck in his hat by way of horns, and preceded by a drum and fife, playing 'The Rogue's March,' he is paraded in front of his regiment." The writer commented that "this has been a custom in the army for time immemorial and is still performed with the greatest punctuality and ceremony that circumstances will admit of."[41]

"The Escort of the Colors."

The colors of the unit normally were lodged in the colonel's quarters when not actually displayed before the regiment. Whenever the regiment was in formation, an escort was sent to bring the colors to the parade ground. The escort ceremony had vestiges of the earlier ceremony of "lodging the color." "In the 17th century, it was the custom before a battalion or a company was dismissed to quarters, bivouac or billets, to 'Troop' the Colour, or Colours, down the ranks, and the Ensigns then taking their Colours to their lodgings and displaying them from the window, or doorstep, or entrance to their tent, the Battalion or Company trooped past the Colour and so came to know, in case of alarm, the place of their rallying point."[42]

During the eighteenth century, the colors were brought to the men and paraded before them while in formation. When the regiment was formed, the right flank company was ordered as escort for the colors. The flank in the British regiments normally was held by the grenadier company, and this ceremony became closely associated with that unit. Arriving at the place where the colors were lodged, the bearers entered and brought them forward. Upon receiving the colors, the company presented arms, and the drums beat a "point of war." There is some confusion as to the meaning of this term. Early writers used the term to indicate any of the military signals in use at the time. Most nineteenth-century drum manuals stated that the first part of the *Reveille* served as the "point of war" in ceremonies, so this may well have been the case during the Revolution. By the early nineteenth century, the *Reveille* had become the *Three Camps*, and the first part, referred to as "mother" by the British, would be interpreted as the original *Reveille* in example 4. Duane (1814) directed the drummers to beat a roll, while the band was to play "a national air." The *Rules and Regulations* of 1815 directed the drums to beat the *Troop*, with the *Three Cheers*.

These honors completed, the company escorted the colors back to the regiment. The colors were then paraded along the length of the regiment, with the musicians marching between the line of officers and first rank of men, and the escort company marching one rank between the second and third rank of troops, the other marching behind the rear rank. These instructions appeared in Bland and Simes, both standard guides for the Continental officers, and this ceremony most likely was performed in the Continental army. By 1815, the ceremony had changed in the United States army so that the escort company no longer marched between the ranks of the regiment in formation, but the other parts of the ceremony remained basically the same.[43]

"The Review."

The end of the working day was not announced merely by the beating of drums, but was often celebrated by a full military ceremony known as the review, in which the musicians figured prominently.

Upon hearing the *Troop*, *To Arms*, or the *Assembly*, the men would fall in on the company streets and then parade to the regimental color line, there forming the regiment as in figure 12. The company musicians were divided between the right and left flanks, and the drum and fife majors were centered behind the colors. When the general officer who was to review the troops came within thirty paces of the right flank, the colonel ordered the battalion to present arms. The drums on the right flank rendered the honors, and the officers and colors saluted him as he passed along the front of the regiment. When he arrived at the left flank, the drums at that post again rendered the honors. These honors consisted of ruffles, or short rolls, according to the rank of the person conducting the review. The commander in chief, the president of Congress, all governors in their own states, and committees of Congress at the army were given a march while the officers saluted. Major generals were given two ruffles and brigadier generals one, a regulation unchanged to the present day.

The salute completed, the men were ordered to shoulder arms.

The battalion was then ordered to wheel by platoons to the right and pass before the reviewing officer. The colonel led the regiment, followed by the major. The four drummers and four fifers of the right wing then followed, preceding the companies marching in platoon formation. The four drummers and four fifers of the left wing followed after the last platoon of the regiment, and the lieutenant colonel brought up the rear. As the officers and colors passed the general, they saluted him by trailing their weapons, taking off their hats, and gracefully bringing their arms down closely to the left side until past the person saluted. The troops would march off the field, or reform, as desired.[44]

"The Military Funeral."

It has always been customary for the friends and family of a deceased person to accompany the body on the journey to its final resting place. For distinguished men, the body was accompanied by a dignified procession in proportion to the esteem in which the deceased was held by the populace. Some form of musical ensemble normally preceded the bier, providing a solemn and mournful accompaniment. These civilian marks of respect were translated into military terms for those who died in the service of their country. The body was escorted by a military unit whose size was determined in regulations by the rank of the deceased. Weapons were carried reversed, or inverted, and military symbols, such as flags or swords, were often placed upon the casket. The colors of the unit were draped in black. The drums of the period were traditionally emblazoned with the arms or designation of the unit, and as such were symbols of the regiment equal in significance to the colors. They were therefore shrouded in the same manner as the colors for funeral occasions. To achieve a more somber effect, the drums were muffled by placing a handkerchief or piece of cloth between the snares and the snare head.

The *New York Journal* for 26 October 1775 described one such funeral procession. Captain Michael Cresap commanded a company of riflemen who were returning to their homes in Maryland from the siege of Boston. Cresap died while the company was passing through New York, and he was buried with full military honors in Trinity Church yard. The newspaper account gave the order of the funeral procession: "Sergeant Major. Grenadiers of the First Battalion with their fire-locks reversed.—Two lieutenants. Drums and Fifes.—Captain of the Grenadiers, Two Sergeants. Two Adjutants conducting the funeral, Band of music. Clergymen. The CORPSE. The PALL, supported by

Eight Captains. Chief Mourner. Major with his sword drawn. Second Battalion. First Battalion. Non-Commissioned officers, Battalion officers. Ward officers. Citizens of New York.''

The drum beat that was used for such a procession, if in fact there was any one specific rhythm, has not been identified. As in so many activities in the early Continental army, there was no standardization. In describing the funeral of an army lieutenant in that same year, 1775, one writer wrote of the fifes playing ''the tune called the Funeral Thoughts. At the end of each line in the tune the Drums beat one stroke.''[45] This tune has not been located, as it does not appear in any of the standard fife tutors of the period or later.

On the other hand, Ammi Robbins commented, ''There is something more than ordinarily solemn and touching in our funerals, especially an officer's; swords and arms inverted, others with their arms folded across their breast stepping slowly to the *beat* of the muffled drum.''[46] There seems to have been one definite pattern, for Simes included in his instructions for such a procession the direction, ''the drums being muffled, beating the dead march, and fifers playing a solemn tune.'' The use of the definite article for the drum beat, while the indefinite article is used for the fife tune, is significant. The Prussians also had a specific dead march, played by the hautboys, fifes, and muffled drums.[47]

The actual melody performed is almost as elusive as the drum beat. Windham included the dead march among those beats so familiar that they were ''almost needless to mention.'' When the Duke of Cumberland was buried in 1765, the dead march in Handel's *Saul* was performed. Several post-Revolutionary writers mentioned that this composition was performed at American funeral processions, so it may very well have served this purpose during the Revolution. Carr's *Military Amusement* of 1796 included it as the *Dead March*, and Alexander Reinagle conducted it for the solemnities in Philadelphia at the death of George Washington in 1799. It was still being used as late as 1831, according to one reminiscer, who also noted that the *Merry Man Home to His Grave* was the quickstep used in returning from the funeral. A fife tune entitled *Dead March* is included in the tutors of Rutherford, Bennett, Thompson, and Willig, but its identity or source has not been determined. Hulbert, writing in 1807, included William Billings's *Chester* as the ''Death Beat.''[48]

The melody most often associated with funerals during the Revolution seems to have been *Roslin Castle*. Legend has it that this tune was played by the Scottish bagpipers stationed in New York during the Revolution, in honor of the castle at Roslyn, Scotland. Proctor's band of music used this tune in memory of massacred soldiers in June 1779 and may have used the melody for funeral services. The music and text of the song were printed in the *Boston Magazine* in November 1783, but there was no reference to its use as a funeral march. After the Revolution it seems to have become generally regarded as the standard funeral march. A soldier in Wayne's Legion in 1794 referred to it in terms synonymous with the death beat. James Hewitt, in writing *The Battle of Trenton* in 1797, included it as an expression of the "Grief of the Americans for the Loss of their Comrades killed in the Engagement." It is in the Bellamy manuscript book of 1799 and in the fife tutors of Hazeltine, Willig, Cushing, Robbins, Robinson, and Steele. Rocellus Guernsey stated that it was always used as a funeral dirge during the War of 1812. With such widespread acceptance so closely following the hostilities, it is likely that *Roslin Castle* was the most commonly performed funeral march of the Revolution.[49]

EXAMPLE 16: *Roslin Castle*

Figure 1: Drummer by Jacob de Gheyn, 1587 (courtesy of the Prints Division, The New York Public Library, Astor, Lenox and Tilden Foundations)

Der Fendrich.

¶ Zů eym Fendrich byn ich bestelt
Vom Hellen hauffen außerwelt
Weyl die das Fendleyn sehen flygen
Verhoffen sie noch ob zů sygen
Vnd sind Beherzet in der Schlacht
Vnd weren sich mit ganzer macht

Darumb laß ich meyn Fendleyn schweben
Dieweyl hie wert meyn leyb vnd leben
Setz ich hie keyn flüchtigen fůß
Drey Sóld ich wol verdienen můß
Von eynem großmechtigen Herren
Der kriegt nach preyß vnd großferrehten
¶ Zů Laitinger byn ich erkom
Zů dem Fendleyn hab ich geschworn
Wo den Fendrich leybs not an gat
Das ich verdretten wól seyn stat

Laytinger.

Vnd wól das Fendleyn helffen retten
So lt ich meyn leyb darob verzetten
Jn Sturm/scharmützel vnd streyt
Darumb man doppel sold mir geyt.

Pfeyffer vnd Drumelschlager.

¶ Pfeyffer vnd Drumelschlager gůt
Machen knechten eyn freyen můt
Weil man vmbschlecht wil geben Gelt
Auch in der Ordnung vnd zů feld

Als er wenn man den Lerman schlecht
So müssen darnach alle Knecht
Zum Fendleyn kumen auff den platz
Mit harnisch wehr gerüst zum hatz.

*Figure 2: Sixteenth-Century Musicians and Standard-Bearer by Erhard
Schoen (courtesy of the Prints Division, The New York Public Library,
Astor, Lenox and Tilden Foundations)*

Figure 3: Fifer by William Hogarth, 1750 (author's collection)

Figure 4: Highland Piper by Martin Engelbrecht (courtesy of the Austrian National Library)

Figure 5: Hautboys by Christoph Weigel, ca. 1725 (courtesy of the Austrian National Library)

Figure 6: Guard Mounting, St. James's Park, 1753 (author's collection)

*Figure 7: Triumphant Entry of the Royal Troops at New York, 1776
(courtesy, The New York Public Library, Astor, Lenox and Tilden
Foundations)*

*Figure 8: Guard Mounting, St. James's Park, ca. 1790
(author's collection)*

Figure 9: La Musique Royale, *1820 (author's collection)*

Figure 10: Daniel Simpson, with John Robbin's Drum, by Darius Cobb (courtesy of the Bostonian Society)

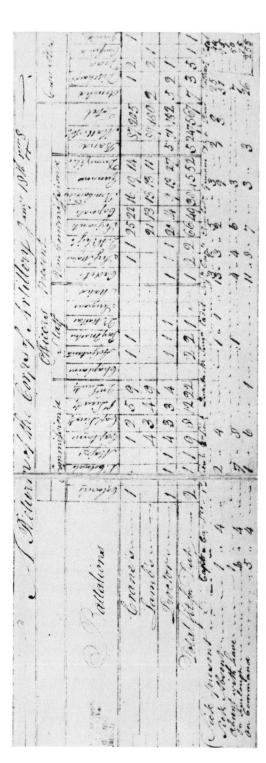

Figure 11: A Return of the Corps of Artillery, 18 January 1778 (courtesy of The National Archives)

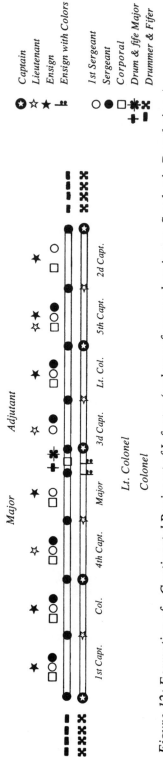

Figure 12: Formation of a Continental Regiment of Infantry (redrawn from a plate in von Steuben's Regulations)

Figure 13: The Manner of Laying out a Camp with the Order of Encampment (redrawn from a plate in von Steuben's Regulations*)*

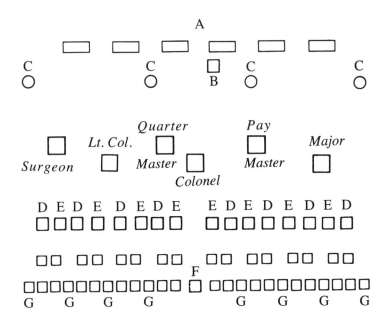

A   Waggons
B   Sutler
C   Kitchens
D   Captains Tents
E   Subalterns
F   Adjutant
G   N. C. officers

*Figure 14: Private and Drummer, Continental Line, 1781, by Donna Neary
(author's collection)*

*Figure 15: Debtors' Welcome to Their Brother
(courtesy of The British Library)*

5. THE STALEMATE IN THE NORTH

After the surrender of Burgoyne and his army at Saratoga in October 1777, France took renewed interest in the American colonies. Benjamin Franklin finally succeeded in achieving a treaty binding the two nations together in military alliance. General Sir Henry Clinton, having relieved General Howe of command in Philadelphia, received orders to leave that city and retreat to New York. This retrenchment was necessary to allow the British government to concentrate its forces in preparation for a full-scale world war. Washington, at Valley Forge, saw Clinton leave Philadelphia on 18 June 1778, and immediately entered the city.

The army that Washington now commanded had increased in size, and because of the extensive drilling by Baron von Steuben during the encampment at Valley Forge, was much better trained and disciplined. Washington followed Clinton, and determined to engage with the British forces as they were leaving Monmouth, New Jersey, on 27 June. General Charles Lee, whom the Americans had welcomed joyously upon his exchange as a prisoner of war, was given command of the attacking force. Apparently unconvinced of the new ability of the army, Lee hesitated and then began to withdraw his troops after a few brief skirmishes. Washington, moving in with the main force, relieved Lee of command and fought the British counterattack to a stalemate. During the night, while both sides held the field of battle, Clinton quietly slipped away and succeeded in reaching New York.

Washington took up a position at White Plains where he could observe Clinton and then settled down to wait. A brief expedition of French and American forces to dislodge the British at Newport almost ended in calamity, and no more major engagements with the enemy occurred in the northern sector for the remainder of the war. Washington took advantage of this period of enemy inactivity in the north to consolidate the gains made by von Steuben and to apply them to the army that was being enlarged for the coming campaign.

Congress had voted on 27 May to reorganize the army in conformity with Washington's recommendations. A light infantry company, to be kept complete by drafts from the other companies, was added as the ninth company of the infantry regiment. Each company had three officers, three sergeants, three corporals, a drummer and a fifer, and fifty-three privates. The regimental staff, in addition to the normal complement of officers, had a drum major and a fife major.

By August 1778, Washington was able to turn his attention to the condition of the army's music. On the fifth of that month he called for "a Return of drums, fifes, drum-heads, etc. wanting in the respective Brigades to be made immediately." By 16 August he was able to order the brigade quartermasters to draw the missing items from the commissary. Just three days later Washington announced the appointment of an inspector of music to supervise the musical activities of the army.

THE INSPECTOR AND SUPERINTENDENT OF MUSIC

Baron von Steuben had been confirmed in his appointment as inspector general of the Continental army. To assist him in training the army, subordinate inspectors general were appointed for each brigade. Music was considered of such importance to the army that a subordinate inspector was appointed for its standardization and supervision. On 19 August 1778 the general orders announced that "Lieutenant Hiwell of Colonel Crane's [3rd] Regiment of Artillery is appointed Inspector and Superintendent of Music in the Army and is to be respected accordingly. His Pay and Rations to be made equal to a Captain in the Train." John Hiwell formerly had been the fife major of Crane's regiment, and he was still in charge of its band of music. He held the rank of lieutenant until the end of the war, a rank that drew the salary of thirty-three and one-third dollars per month, but the orders fixed his pay to be that of a captain of artillery, which was fifty dollars per month. The order did not specify the duties entailed in the new position, but it may be assumed that they were to standardize and improve the army's music. Hiwell had been at Valley Forge and thus would have been familiar with von Steuben's work. Because the regulations did not include the actual music, as discussed in chapter 4, some supervision was necessary.

Music for the daily guard mount at 8:00 A.M. was to be provided by the combined drummers and fifers of the whole right wing, left wing, or second line, each in rotation, and Hiwell was ordered to be present. There may have been some grumbling on the part of the drum majors, who had never previously had an immediate musical supervisor and were accustomed to providing music for their own brigades or regiments without interference or restrictions. The question was resolved within a few days by a general order which left no doubt as to Hiwell's position of authority: "The Drum and Fife Majors of the Regiments on the Ground are to attend at the Inspector of Musick's tent in the rear of the [Artillery] Park tomorrow morning ten o'clock to receive his instructions.''

The adequacy of supplies was always an important consideration, and the new inspector no doubt set out to rectify the inadequacies. Entries of the issue of fifes and drums to Hiwell for delivery to various units are frequent. Damaged instruments were returned, fifes sorted according to key within the units, and the pitch standardized. In preparing for the campaign of 1779, Washington brought the army's shortages to the attention of the Board of War: ''There are upwards of one hundred Drums wanting in this part of the Army and I imagine a proportion in the remainder. I shall be obliged by having means taken to procure them if it is not already done, and forwarded as fast as finished.'' The Board of War responded within a month that they were unable to comply with all the requests for drums and regimental colors, as they did not have materials to make either of these items in sufficient numbers. They offered some hope, however, that they would be able to send a complete supply of drums in the near future. In other words, the musicians would have to use what they had for the time being. Washington was able to provide some physical comfort to the drum and fife majors in recompense, possibly at Hiwell's suggestion, for they were authorized a tent by themselves, while the noncommissioned officers and privates had to share a tent with five other men.[1]

The shortages continued. During the Morristown encampment, in January 1780, Washington again asked for a return of the ''arms, ammunition, accoutrements, drums and fifes in possession of the respective regiments.'' Shortly thereafter, he complained to the Board of War that ''there is a great deficiency of drums, fifes and standards. I presume the necessary measures are being taken to procure them with other articles of similar kind.'' Within five days the Board of War replied: ''We believe there will not be much difficulty in procuring a sufficient number of Drums & Fifes, but we wish we knew the number required. Perhaps the Adjutant General could get the Necessary Returns to enable your Excellency to inform us.'' Washington did as recommended, and the adjutant general was directed to get the requested information. The Board of War was optimistic because the commissary of military stores, Major Jonathan Gostelow, had set up a drum factory manned by three workers. In the period from 1 January to 1 September 1780, the factory had turned out 399 drums. Other instruments were made available, and on 23 August, Gostelow was able to send Hiwell 163 fifes, 54 drums, 40 pairs of drumsticks, and 20 drum carriages. After such a long wait Hiwell did not merely deliver the supplies, but insisted on careful adherence to musical standards as well. The general

orders of the 31st read: "The Brigade Conductors are to attend tomorrow morning nine o'clock at the Park of Artillery [where Hiwell's
quarters were located] for their proportion of Drums and fifes. The
drum and fife Majors are to attend at the same time with all their old
fifes for the purpose of having them properly sorted to the same keys."
To save the time, trouble, and expense of obtaining replacement drum
heads, Hiwell must have decided to prepare his own, for the commis-
saries were ordered to deliver their "sheep and Calve skins to the field
commissary of military stores with the Park of Artillery who will have
them properly dressed for Drum heads." Some time later Hiwell also
drew quantities of sash cord, presumably to make into drum cords.[2]

Washington must have been pleased with Hiwell's work, for a
voucher for "additional pay & sub: as Inspector of Music to the Army
from Dec[embe]r 19: 1779 to the 31st of July 1780," signed by
Washington, gave Hiwell 876 20/90 dollars for the seven-month period,
or 129 dollars per month. Since the voucher stated it was to be "additional pay," it must be assumed that his regular pay was not included
in that figure.

The supply picture was brighter in 1781, and the commissary
general of military stores, Samuel Hodgdon, ordered Major Gostelow
to close his drum factory. Preparations were being made for the coming
campaign, and the original estimate of 500 new drums and 1,000 fifes
was reduced to the more practical figure of 100 drums and 100 fifes,
not counting the 145 drums already on hand. The lacking drums were
ordered from local makers and were ready to be delivered by the end of
June.[3]

On 6 July 1781, Washington's army was joined by the French
forces under Rochambeau which had been quartered at Newport since
the previous summer. It has been conjectured that one reason the
armies did not meet sooner was that Washington was afraid to have his
allies see his army until it was somewhat better equipped and trained,
or it would appear in too sharp a contrast to the well-disciplined,
trained, and equipped French soldiers. With the supply picture improved, Washington was able to tend to other matters that required his
attention. General Edward Hand, the adjutant general, sent Hiwell
specific instructions on his duties as inspector of music at this important
time:

Until they are perfectly organized with their Duty, the Drum and Fife majors
of the line should be assembled at a particular time and place to practice
together. Their first attention should be to acquire a perfect knowledge of the
different beats and signals printed out in the regulations and to establish a
uniformity in the time, both which are absolutely necessary to regulate the

march of an army, and as the drum and fife majors are answerable for the conduct of the musick of their regiment it is their business to make them acquainted with every particular of their duty whether in Camp on Guard, when the Troops are under arms for exercise, or on a march. They are therefore when collected to regulate the whole so that the same principle may prevail through the line.

These instructions were given in conjunction with the general orders for the day, which directed that "untill further orders the Drum and Fife Majors of the several corps in Camp are to assemble every day at 10 o'clock A. M. in the wood in the rear of the second line to practice under the direction of the Inspector of Music who will attend for that purpose." The drum and fife majors must have been avid students, or Hiwell had been properly supervising their work previous to the order, for the majors learned quickly. Only one week after the above routine was instituted, it was ordered that "the Attendance of the Drum and Fife Majors on the superintendent of Music will for the present be dispensed with that they may attend to the instruction of the Drummers and fifers of their respective regiments who are to practice from five to six o'clock every morning and from four to five o'clock every afternoon."[4]

When Washington left on the march south that would bring him to victory at Yorktown, he went without the 3d Regiment of Artillery, which was ordered to remain stationed around New York, keeping watch over Clinton. So it was that Hiwell, still an officer in that regiment, was not able to witness the events that followed. Perhaps, had he gone, he would not have lost his silver spur on the very day that Yorktown surrendered.[5]

BANDS OF MUSIC

While Hiwell was striving industriously to improve the field music of the army, he did not neglect his responsibility to Crane's Regiment of Artillery band, of which he was still in charge. This band, Proctor's 4th Artillery Regiment band, and Webb's Continental infantry band were all in existence in 1777 and continued to perform. Several other colonels, notably Henry Jackson, Christian Febiger, and Henry Lee, attempted to form bands, with varying degrees of success. Other instances of band performances have been located, but without sufficient information to determine the specific regimental unit. These bands existed for the most part independently from the field music and were accepted so naturally that complete identification is often impossible.

Crane's Regiment of Artillery Band

The treaty that Franklin had labored so long to achieve with France was finally signed on 6 February 1778. On the occasion of its first anniversary, Congress gave a public entertainment for the French minister at Philadelphia. Similar festivities were planned for the army, but Washington was away on the actual date, so they were not held until 18 February, at Pluckemin, New Jersey. The entertainment was sponsored by General Knox and the officers of the artillery. Dr. Thacher described the event in his journal:

The anniversary of our alliance with France was celebrated in proper style a few days since near head quarters, at Pluckemin. A splendid entertainment was given by General Knox and the officers of artillery. General Washington and his lady, with the principal officers of the army and their ladies, and a considerable number of respectable ladies and gentlemen of the state of New Jersey, formed the brilliant assembly. About four o'clock sixteen cannon were discharged, and the company collected in a large public building to partake of an elegant dinner. In the evening a very beautiful set of fire-works was exhibited, and the celebration was concluded by a splendid ball, opened by his Excellency General Washington, having for his partner the Lady of General Knox.[6]

The "large public building" that Thacher mentioned was used as a training academy for the members of the artillery. A newspaper account described the great room as "fifty feet by thirty, arched in an agreeable manner, and neatly plastered within. At the lower end of the room was a small inclosure, elevated above the company, where the preceptor gave his military lessons. This was converted into an orchestra, where the music of the army entertained the company. . . . When the fireworks were finished, the company returned to the Academy; the same room that had served to dine in served to dance in." In a letter to his brother written a few days after the event, the host, General Knox, admitted that "everybody allowed it to be the first of the kind ever exhibited in this state at least. We had about seventy ladies, all of the first *ton* in the State, and between three and four hundred gentlemen. We danced all night—an elegant room."[7] For such a festive occasion, Knox surely would have wanted the best possible musical accompaniment and would have called upon the inspector of music, in charge of Crane's Regiment of Artillery band, to prepare the musical portions of the entertainment. The newspaper account specifically mentioned "the windings of a fiddle" at the dance, so that the musicians were most certainly not the regimental fifers and drummers.

As seen in chapter 3, two of the four regiments of artillery had bands of music: those of Crane and Proctor. The accounts did not specify the musicians' unit, and so it may have been either band, or perhaps a combination of both for greater effect. Crane's regiment was encamped at Pluckemin; Proctor's was not. This would not preclude the detachment of the latter band, but since Crane's band was already present, it may be assumed that this group did the performing. This is further supported by letters several months later in which Hiwell is described as having requested instruments for a band of music of the "Brigade of Artillery," implying there was only one band in the artillery at the time. Proctor's regiment, with its band, was then on an Indian expedition with a division under General Sullivan and was detached from the artillery brigade. Except for Proctor's, no band was authorized in the Continental establishment, so that references to a "Brigade of Artillery" band must indicate the existence of a band supported by the combined officers of that brigade. This may have been in addition to the band of Crane's regiment, or it may have been the adoption of that band by the whole brigade.

Samuel Hodgdon, the commissary general of military stores, wrote from Pluckemin on 14 May 1779, to Major James Pearson, commissary of quartermaster stores, regarding the receipt of stores delivered. He then discussed some of the items that had not as yet been delivered,

such as four B. Clarinets a small box of Cane suitable for reeds of bassoons and Clarinets, two French horns Concert and twelve D. Concert fifes, these are sent for by the particular desire of General Knox, the inspector of Musick having inform'd him that the band which is now a grand addition to the Brigade of Artillery, Must cease Their Martial and Animating sounds for want of instruments. Mr. Clumberg inform's me the horns may be had at the Q. M. Genl store at Philadelphia, and English Clarinets at the Musick shop, which he can inform, if this should not be the case, the Music Master says they may be had, very good of Mr. Anthony, your particular attention and speedy information of this Mater will very Much oblige the General and your friend.[8]

The music shop was probably that of Michael Hillegas, who was active in the city, and who imported musical instruments, accessories, and printed music. Mr. Anthony may have been the Jacob Anthony listed in the Philadelphia directory for 1785 as "turner and instrument maker," though that term did not necessarily mean musical instruments. A Joseph Anthony is listed in the 1791 directory as "musical instrument maker," and lived on the same street as Jacob, so one may suppose that the son specialized in one of the father's skills.

In spite of the plea for "speedy information," Hodgdon had to remind Pearson a month later that "the inspector of Musick impatiently waits the Return to the request for Musical Instruments. Please to inform me what he may expect." The delay was probably caused by the Board of War's desire to have more information on bands, particularly in view of establishing a precedent in the Continental army. Richard Peters, the secretary to the Board of War, had an estate at Belmont just outside of Philadelphia. A guest on an adjoining estate at Lansdown was James Bremner, a relative and former branch manager of Robert Bremner, the famous music publisher with offices in Edinburgh and London. Bremner had one of the most extensive and valuable catalogs of the time, and his publications were used ubiquitously by civilian and military musicians. Robert certainly would have been most familiar with the practical aspects of military bands, and James seems also to have been quite well informed on the subject. Since his reply to Peters contains a number of interesting sidelights on the practices, prejudices, and philosophies of the time, it is quoted in full:

Lansdown 22 June 1779

Dr. Sir

I received your favor from Belmount & shall with pleasure give you my opinion, partly from what I know of Millitary Bands as are used in Europe, & what I think would suit the American Army.

A Complete Band for a Regt. of Foot should consist of
A pair of Cymbals for the Master
2 Hautboys
2 Clarinetts
2 Tailles or Tenor Hautboys
2 Bassoons
2 Trumpets. a pair of Kettle Drums
2 F. Horns made in G. or F. with crooks for E♭. D. and C. and a Serpent.

—But I fear your performers in this Country are either young hands, or, too old to improve much, I therefore think that
2 Hautboys
2 Clarinetts
2 Bassoons
& 2 French horns

would be sufficient. I would recommend you to purchase 2 Ger. flutes with pieces, as the Hautboys generally play on that Instrument, which will be an addition in a private Concert.

As to the cost, Yourself can judge of the use, or pleasure, of purchasing an ordinary Violin, Ital. or any thing else. A set of good Instruments with proper care, will serve once for all, the additional cost will always give satisfaction.

—A Judge of Music will select proper pieces for such a Band. A Collection to the Amount of 4 or 5£ Ster. will be sufficient. printed music I mean, as manuscripts comes very high—If the Instruments are made in London where you may depend upon the goodness & neatness of the work the whole may amount between 50 & 60 £ Ster. perhaps a little more the Music included. —The Horns will be the dearest articles.

If you send to Hamburg, Mon. Gerard [French minister at Philadelphia] may recommend a proper person to choose the Instruments for you, but there is very little Music printed there.

I know of no French Music that will suit, the Germans are the best composers for Wind Instruments.

I have endeavoured to be as particular as possible but if I have forgot any article, I shall probably be in Town some day this Week & will then satisfy you in the mean time believe to be

Your very humble Serv.t
James Bremner

Peters's correspondence does not indicate what he did with the above information, but he must have acted favorably. In October Hodgdon wrote to Pearson thanking him for his letters, in one of which he was ''inform'd that the honble Board have order'd the Clarinets, to be made this I am glad to hear on many accounts, as the inspector of Music has been so disgusted at the delay that he has been almost ready to resign any further charge of the band—indeed the man has merited attention by indefatigable endeavors to promote the science of Musick in the Army.'' Finally, on 10 November 1779, Hiwell was able to draw two ''B Clarinetts'' and twelve reeds of various sizes, debiting them to ''Col Crane's Regt Arty.'' Nothing further has been found regarding the concert horns originally requested in Hodgdon's letter, but it may be assumed that they had been delivered long previously, since no mention of them was made in Hodgdon's correspondence after the initial request.[9]

Throughout the months that Hiwell was attempting to obtain clarinets for the ''Brigade of Artillery'' band, Crane's band continued to function. Hodgdon's original request was for four clarinets, or double the usual number in the standard *Harmoniemusik*, and for cane for bassoon reeds, even though bassoons were not requested. Obviously the bassoons were already on hand. Crane's band may have had two oboes, two bassoons, and two horns, and wished to add two clarinets in accordance with the current fashion. The additional two clarinets and two horns may have been to enlarge Crane's band or to form a new band within the artillery brigade. Only two clarinets were debited to Crane's regiment, and no mention has been located of the other two originally requested. Crane's band may have been supported in some manner by the whole brigade, for Colonel Charles Harrison, commanding the 1st Artillery Regiment, apparently ordered the band to perform at one of his functions. Dr. Samuel Adams, surgeon to Crane's regiment, noted in his diary that "Col Popkin [was] arrested by Col Harrison for disobedience of orders viz not sending the band of musick of Col Crane's Regt to play for Col Harrison at his order." Lieutenant Colonel John Popkin, the executive officer of Crane's regiment, may have refused on the grounds that the band properly belonged to his regiment and could not be commanded to perform by other officers. No further information in this regard has been located in Crane's orderly books, in correspondence of the principals involved, or in Dr. Adams's diary. It does indicate, however, that Crane's band was functioning musically, or there would have been no cause for such altercation.[10]

The winter of 1779–80 was spent at Morristown, New Jersey. The bitter cold and frequent snowfalls, the lack of adequate clothing, the shortage of provisions, and the continuing devaluation of the Continental currency all contributed to make this encampment even more difficult than that of Valley Forge. In spite of these hardships, a group of officers contracted together to provide regular dancing assemblies, in which the officers, their ladies, and many distinguished civilians of the neighborhood participated. Washington, Knox, Proctor, and many other prominent officers agreed to contribute toward the expenses of these social occasions. Chastellux remarked that the masters of ceremonies of these assemblies were "generally chosen from among the most distinguished officers of the army," and that "this important place is at present [1780] held by Colonel Wilkinson, who is also clothier General of the Army." The master of ceremonies was able to choose from among several bands, for Webb's band was present at the encampment, and the artillery must have had more than one band available. These may have been Proctor's and Crane's, or one of these two plus an additional "brigade" band. For a public hanging of two criminals of a Pennsylvania regiment, the Corps of Artillery was to send "a band of music to attend the Criminals to the place of execution," and large detachments of men from each division were to be present as escort. It is unlikely that the indefinite article would have been used if there were but one band in the artillery, so it must be assumed that General Knox, the corps commander, had a choice of which band to send. Crane's band was still known by that name, for a year later the band was mentioned in orders: "Colonel Crane's Band of Music will attend the Grand Parade every Morning," thereby relieving the fifers and drummers of that duty, so that the inspector of music could work with the fife and drum majors.[11]

Proctor's Regiment of Artillery Band

On 4 July 1778, just a few weeks after Washington had reentered Philadelphia following the British withdrawal, the members of Congress
gathered together at the City Tavern. Samuel Holton noted that there
were "several General officers & other Gentlemen of Distinction &
while we were dining there was an Agreeable band of Musick & we had
a very elegant dinner." William Ellery was more specific: "The glorious fourth of July I celebrated in the City Tavern with Brother
Delegates of Congress and a number of other gentlemen, ammounting
in the whole to about 80. . . . The entertainment was elegant and well
conducted. At the end of the Room opposite the upper Table, was
erected an Orchestra. . . . As soon as Dinner began, the Musick
consisting of Clarinets, Hautboys, French horns, Violins, and Bass
Viols, opened and continued, making proper pause, until it was
finished."[12] The musicians are not further identified, nor is any credit
given on the occasion of a dinner just one month later when "Monsieur
Gerard, Minister Plenipotentiary from his most Christian Majesty
[Louis XVI], had a public audience with Congress & dined with them;
the proceedings were conducted with great decorum. The entertainment
was grand & elegant, the band of musick was very agreeable."[13] Both
occasions were sufficiently important to the new nation that the greatest
effort would have been made to secure the most competent band of
music. Proctor and his musicians were all from Philadelphia and had
performed in that city many times. In view of their reputation and their
history of performances in the city, it seems quite likely that they
provided the music for both occasions.

There is no question that Proctor's band performed in Philadelphia
at the end of that year, for here the band is mentioned by name:

PHILADELPHIA: Monday last [28 December 1778], agreeable to the Consti-
tution of the Most Ancient and Worshipful SOCIETY of FREE and AC-
CEPTED MASONS, was celebrated as the Anniversary of St. John the
Evangelist. At nine o'clock in the morning near three hundred of the brethren
assembled at the College, and at eleven o'clock went in regular procession
from thence to Christ Church to attend divine service. The order of procession
was as follows, viz.

    1. The Sword Bearer.

    2. Two Deacons, with blue wands tipped with gold.

    3. The three orders, *Doric*, *Ionic*, and *Corinthian*, borne by
brethren. . . .

    7. His Excellency our illustrious brother GEORGE WASHINGTON,
Esquire, supported by the Grand Master and his Deputy. . . .

    15. Brother Proctor's Band of Music.

16.   Visiting Brethren.

17.   The Members of different Lodges, walking two by two, according to seniority.[14]

After services, which included a "Grand Symphony" of solos, a trio, and a chorus, "the Procession returned in the same order to the College; the musical bells belonging to the Church and the band playing proper Masonic tunes." Most Continental army officers were members of Masonic Lodges, and an extra effort certainly would have been made for the presence of their commander in chief. A general return dated 21 December 1778 stated that Proctor had nine men in the band on that date, plus twenty-seven fifers and drummers for eight companies. A return dated 19 March 1779 indicates that there were ten men in the band, so that Proctor may have had nine or ten men parading for the Freemasons. These two returns do not identify the musicians, but that of 3 April 1779 does list the names, their places of birth, and the dates of their enlistment:

Chas. Hoffman, Master Musician, Germany, 10 July 1777
Wm. Shippen, Musician, Philadelphia, 24 April 1776
Pet'r Colkhoffer [Kalckhoffer], Musician, Germany, 20 December 1777
Jacob Snell, Musician, Pennsylvania, 27 March 1777
Thos. Mingle, Musician, Pennsylvania, 12 March 1776
Geo. Weaver, Musician, Germany, 11 July 1777
Sam'l Hockuhoy, Musician, Germany, 15 May 1778
Mich'l Thurston, Musician, Ireland, 24 June 1778
Wm Moore, Musician, Scotland, 24 October 1778
Con'd Gropingeiser, Musician, Germany, 21 December 1778
Thos. Guy, Fife Major, Pennsylvania, 8 September 1776
Wm Norton, Drum Major, Ireland, 5 April 1777

Each of the men had resided in Philadelphia. Prior to the war Peter Kalckhoffer had taught the German flute, and Charles Hoffman had performed a solo on the clarinet in a public concert, some indication of the quality of musicians employed by Proctor.[15]

Encouraged by British agents, the Indians of the Six Nations had been causing great difficulty along the Pennsylvania and New York frontiers. In February 1779, Washington decided to send a military expedition to bring them under control and prevent any further marauding. On General Gates's declination to assume command, Major General John Sullivan was offered the position and accepted. He was given a division of three brigades, including Proctor's Artillery Regiment. At Tioga, he was to meet Brigadier General James Clinton's brigade and combine forces for the march into Indian country. There was no attempt at secrecy, and the reveille cannon kept the enemy informed of their advance. A number of participants kept journals of the expedition, and the band is mentioned on several occasions. William Rogers, the brigade chaplain, described one event:

Wednesday, June 23 [1779]. . . . This day we marched with regularity, and at a distance of three miles came to the place where Captain [Joseph] Davis and Lieutenant [William] Jones, with a corporal and four privates were scalped, tomahawked and speared by the savages, fifteen or twenty in number;. . . In passing this melancholy vale, an universal gloom appeared on the countenances of both officers and men without distinction, and from the eyes of many, as by a sudden impulse, dropt the sympathizing tear. Colonel Proctor, out of respect to the deceased, ordered the music to play the tune Roslin Castle, the soft and moving notes of which, together with what so forcibly struck the eye, tended greatly to fill our breasts with pity, and to renew our grief for our worthy departed friends and brethren.

Music was played one month later when the bodies of the two officers were removed from their place of interment to a more proper burying ground. "The [Masonic] brotherhood met at five o'clock, and marching by the General's marque, had the pleasure of his company. Colonels Proctor's and Hubley's regiments, with drums, fifes, and the band of music, accompanied them."[16]

A more joyous occasion took place on 22 August when General Clinton's brigade marched into Sullivan's encampment at Tioga. Portions of General Hand's brigade, to which Proctor's regiment belonged, were drawn up in smart array along the riverside to greet the new arrivals. As they came near, they were saluted by thirteen rounds of cannon "and welcomed by the band of music and drums and fifes, playing alternately." Erkuries Beatty, one of the men in the saluted column, later commented on the "Band of Musick which played Beautiful as we passed by them." Two days later, the band was again required to perform at a funeral ceremony, when "the Remains of the Unfortunate Captain Kimble [Benjamin Kimball] was Inter'd at 11 o' Clock AM with the Honours of War—Attended by General Poor and almost all the officers of the Brigade with Colonel Proctor's Band of Musick." There were again great festivities when the troops returned to Tioga on 30 September, signaling the end of the expedition. The garrison turned out to render the military honors and thirteen rounds of artillery, which were returned by the army's artillery. Following the ceremonies, Colonel Israel Shreve, the commandant of the garrison, provided an elegant dinner for the generals and field officers of the army, which they enjoyed immensely, and "great joy & good humour was visible in every Countenance. Colo'l Proctors Band & Drums & Fifes played in Concert the whole time."[17]

Returning to the main army after the Sullivan expedition, Proctor's band maintained its level of nine men. On 25 December 1779, Washington paid them the sum of fifteen pounds, but the specific reason for the payment is not given. Presumably there was some form of Christmas entertainment at which the band performed. Several months later, a general return listed the fife and drum majors, nine musicians in the band, and nineteen drummers and fifers. One year later, 5 April 1781, there were still nine men in the band, but two of them were carried as "sick in Philadelphia." The strength of the band varied but slightly throughout this period, and it would be logical to assume that the quality of performance, which had been described in very complimentary terms, remained continuously high.[18]

Jackson's and Webb's Continental Infantry Bands

Prior to his Indian Campaign of 1779, Major General John Sullivan had been in command of the American forces stationed at Providence with orders to drive the British from Newport, Rhode Island. One of his brigades was commanded by Brigadier General James Varnum and included Colonel Samuel B. Webb's regiment. Colonel Henry Jackson commanded a separate detachment assigned to Sullivan's forces. Through a series of circumstances over which Sullivan had little or no control, the Newport campaign failed, and the army returned to Providence. With the approach of winter 1778, the main army under Washington took cantonment in a semicircle around New York, with the headquarters and the major portion stationed at Middlebrook, New Jersey. Sullivan's headquarters remained at Providence, with Webb's regiment stationed at Warren, Rhode Island.

As shown in chapter 3, there had been a band of music in Webb's regiment since the middle of 1777. Colonel Webb himself had been taken prisoner at Long Island in December of that year, and the regiment was commanded by the executive officer, Major Ebenezer Huntington. Colonel Jackson was also trying to raise a band; when Washington heard of this, he had his adjutant general contact Sullivan to have the band forwarded to Middlebrook. Sullivan must have complained, and Washington himself replied:

I have your two letters of the 2d and 7th Inst. now before me. The order communicated by the Adjutant General to Col. Jackson was in consequence of my instructions. It is not however my desire to remove the band in case it has been procured at the cost of the officers, and is kept up at their private expence. This is a prerogative I could not think of assuming. But on the other hand, if it belongs to, and is supported by the public, I shall adhere to my former order, you must be of opinion with me that the necessity for such a thing is much greater here than it can be anywhere else. Under these circumstances, I could wish the matter to be considered; especially when I add that I can make no distinction in Corps. A Band is no part of our establishment; to endulge one Regiment therefore and refuse another (equal in pretensions) is setting up invidious distinctions which cannot be productive of any good but may of much evil and ought to be avoided.[19]

The major portion of the army was stationed at Middlebrook, and with the holidays approaching, Washington may have wished to provide his officers with some musical entertainment. Dr. Thacher, at Middlebrook, described the busy social activities in his journal: "30th [December 1778].—Our officers have not permitted the Christmas days to pass unnoticed, not a day without receiving invitations to dine, not a night without amusement and dancing." Whether it was to please Washington or to have a band available for the same purpose at his own headquarters at Providence, two days after Washington's letter Sullivan issued the following order:

The musicians of General Varnum's and Colonel Jackson's Bands to repair immediately to Head Quarters with their Instruments, Blankets and necessary Baggage for Tarrying one Week.

The Commanding Officers of General Varnum's Brigade and of Colonel Jackson's Detachment will send with them the best Drum and Fife from each Band. General Glover's Brigade to furnish two good Drums and Fifes.

The Barrack Master immediately to furnish a good Convenient Room for those Musicians. Major Flagg will attend them at such Times as he may think proper; and instruct them in Musick. The Commissary will supply them with Provisions, and One Jill of West India Rum per Day and more when he may find it Necessary. The Quarter Master will immediately furnish the necessary cooking Utentils for the Bands.[20]

The inclusion of the fifes and drums, as well as the statement that they were to have equipment for staying one week, would indicate that Sullivan was planning celebrations for the Christmas season and that this order for the band was not related to his correspondence with Washington, who had implied permanent removal. Major Ebenezer Flagg was from the 1st Rhode Island regiment, formerly General Varnum's regiment, and may have been the project officer for the festivities. Major Huntington was not pleased about the order, as Colonel Angell noted in his diary: "22d Dec. 1778. A Cold and uncomfortable Morning It cleared off in the night with Snow about over Shoe it continued an Exceeding Cold day and Nothing remarkable happened Genl Sullivan Sent an order for all the Musicians to attend at Providence as the Band belong'd to Col. Webbs Regt Major Huntington put himself in a most violent passion on the matter Swore the order was a dam'd rascally one if the Genl did give it.''[21] Huntington either struck a bargain with Sullivan, or the band performed exceedingly well at Providence—or a combination of both—for on 30 December 1778, Huntington submitted a request for special uniforms for the band:

A Return for a Suit of Clothing for the Band of Musick belonging to the Officers of Col Sam B Webbs Battalion.

Timothy Olmstead	[opposite each man's name,
Epaphras Jones	requisition for: 1 coat,
Solomon Goodrich	1 vest, 1 breeches, 2 shirts,
John Steel	1 shoes, 2 stockings, 1 hat,
Stephen Moulton	2 rollers]
Prosper Hosmer	
William Hooker	
Jared Bunce	

It is desir'd that the Uniform may be Yellow if to be had if not then White, but be it White or Yellow, wish it may be fac'd with Scarlet, Lin'd with White, & White Underdress White Buttons. Warren, 30th Dec'r 1778.

E Huntington, Maj'r Command'r Col Sam B Webbs Battalion

One week later Huntington was authorized by General Varnum to procure the items, which would be paid for "by the public."[22]

Sullivan did not reply to Washington's letter until 14 January when he wrote:

I have the honor to acknowledge the Receipt of your Excellency's esteem'd Favor of the 20th of December, and in answer to it, beg leave to inform your Excellency that Col. Jackson's Band is by no means compleat. He has four Musicians & but two Instruments of Music which were procur'd by his officers without any expense to the Public. His principal Musician does the duty of Fife Major, and has the Charge of some Lads whose Progress in Musick will not qualify them to do the Duties of the Camp. His Loss therefore will be severely felt, and much regretted. For this Reason I wou'd beg leave to recommend to your Excellency the Band of Colo Webbs, now at Warren. It is compleat, and compos'd of promising Youths, and, as it is independent of the Musick necessary for the duty of the Regiment, Its removal will not be so injurious to the Corps to which it is annex'd. I think it my duty to inform Your Excellency of these Circumstances and shall esteem it equally my duty to comply with any Instructions your Excellency may think proper to give in consequence of the Information. . . .

P.S. Your Excellency will please to intimate in your next which Band you'd prefer, and it shall be immediately sent forward to Hd Quarters.[23]

Washington had been in Philadelphia with the Congress since 22 December and did not return to Middlebrook until 5 February. When he replied to Sullivan's letter, he must have thought that the whole situation was not worth the trouble involved, stating, "I have since been fav'd with yours of the 14 ulto. If Jackson's Band consists of only three performers it will be of no use here, and was Webbs to be ordered it would create as much uneasiness as the sending for Jacksons did."[24]

One month later Sullivan again requested a band from Varnum's brigade, which could only have meant Webb's band. Because of a storm, the band was late in arriving at its destination, and Huntington seems to have received a written rebuke from Sullivan. In his reply, Huntington explained the reason for the band's delay and then told Sullivan about the status of the band:

> Your excellency Observes that we mistake our Privileges as to our Musick, and that all Bands drawing pay from the Publick & eating the Publick Bread are Subject to the Orders of the Commander in Chief, and altho' the Instruments are the property of the officers, 'twould be very Impolite to decline sending them with their Instruments, as they are Subject to be draughted, & do privates duty, should you direct it—I observe the Band of Musick draw Soldiers pay & Provision (& have ever been returned as Present fit for duty, which extra duty has been done by the Regt & not allowed in the Details for the Regt), besides which they receive an Additional pay from the Officers who have already been at a very great Expense for a Master to teach them, & with this Expectation: that they alone would have the right to Command them *as Musick*, altho' Subject, as Soldiers, to the Command of every their Superiors, nor Could it be Esteemed Impolite to decline sending them with their Instruments, as the Matter might be Circumstanced, but which could be determined only on the Reception of such an Order—
>
> Your Excellency's Order for the Extra Cloathing for the Band of Music, I am sensible hath been Sufficient to Convince me you wished to forward the Musick by Encouraging them as you did, with so Generous a Reward, & that it was with the expectation it would be highly Agreeable to them, & Encourage them to Excell in their Respective parts.[25]

In other words, Sullivan, as the commander, could order the band to serve as soldiers any time he wished, but to function as a band was the prerogative of the regimental officers, at whose expense the musical skills were maintained. Just four days later Sullivan left for Washington's headquarters at Middlebrook to take command of the expedition against the Six Nations, and Huntington's command remained at Providence. Generals John Glover and James Varnum, as well as other officers, civilians, and a band of music, escorted Sullivan as far as Johnston, where, after an elegant dinner, "he took a most affectionate Leave of them, and pursued his Journey." Huntington must have been restored to good favor, for the uniforms for his band were finally received on 29 April 1779 and were counted as "a Gratuity to the Band of Musick, over and above the Continental Allowance of clothing."[26]

The eight musicians of the band listed on the clothing return quoted above were all in Captain Charles Whiting's or the "Colonel's Company" of Webb's regiment and had been enlisted by June 1777 for three years. Each was carried on the rolls as a private, not as a musician. Huntington had stated to Sullivan that the musicians were carried as rank and file and that the extra duty was borne by the regiment. Washington pointed out this fact to the brigade commander: "In a circular letter of the 22nd of January [1780], I transmitted the Inspector's reports of December delineating several defects and abuses and exhorting to effectual measures for remedying them. I observe some further matters in the reports of January which require notice. . . . How happens it that there are musicians returned as rank and file in Colonel Webbs Regiment who do no duty in the line? This seems to be an abuse and to require a remedy." On 16 February, Huntington wrote to Webb, still on parole as a prisoner of war, and commented in a postscript, "Money nor promises will reinlist the band." The first of the enlistments was to expire on 20 Februrary, with the others following shortly thereafter. Apparently General John Stark had given the order to Huntington that the musicians were to do duty as soldiers, or were not to be carried on the rolls as such. Accordingly, Olmstead, Jones, Goodrich, Steel, and Moulton were all discharged in early 1780. Hosmer, Hooker, and Bunce were promoted to the rank of sergeant in May 1780 and remained in the regiment until February 1781, though in different companies. Some agreement seems to have been made with the musicians, either by the promotion of the three to sergeant and their attempt to continue the band with other men, or the complete support of the band as civilians not carried on the rolls, for Huntington wrote to Webb in March that "when you call the Band will attend agreeable to your desire."[27]

Nothing further has been located of the band Jackson attempted to form. Perhaps he gave up after the correspondence with Sullivan and Washington, for in July 1780, Dr. Thacher, surgeon of the regiment, wrote that at an entertainment of the officers, "our drums and fifes afforded us with a favorite music till evening, when we were delighted with the song composed by Mr. Hopkinson, called the 'Battle of the Kegs', sung in the best style by a number of Gentlemen."[28] On such an occasion, particularly with singing and entertaining, a band would have been used, if one were available, instead of the drums and fifes. Presumably there was no band in the regiment, so the field music served for the occasion.

Febiger's 2d Virginia Continental Infantry Band

Christian Febiger, a Danish immigrant, began his American military career in May 1775 by serving as adjutant to a Massachusetts regiment. He distinguished himself by his actions at the Battle of Bunker Hill and served as brigade major to General Arnold in the Canadian expedition. He was taken prisoner at Quebec, exchanged a year later, and appointed lieutenant colonel to the 11th Virginia Infantry. He commanded the first regiment of light infantry under General Wayne at the storming of Stony Point and on 14 September 1778 was appointed colonel to the 2d Virginia Continental Infantry.

The 2d Virginia served as part of the main army under Washington, and it was not long before the new colonel began to improve the music of his command. Twenty-one "out-of-key" fifes were turned in at Pluckemin, and a short while later he appointed Thomas Sheldon as fife major with the additional duties of teaching a band of music. Febiger's varied military experience, both in Denmark and in the Continental forces, would have brought him into contact with a number of military bands, and he provided the same for his own unit. On 7 March 1780 he petitioned the Board of War for reimbursement for some of the expenses he had incurred in forming this band, and his letter gives an insight into one of the practices of the period with regard to military musicians:

Being perfectly sensible of the use and Necessity of good Music in an Army, I have allways been very desirous to have a good Band in my Regiment and have twice tried it and been as often disappointed, as no Musicians were to be had in this Country except prisoners or Deserters from the British Army, who as soon as I had two or three of them engagd one would desert me before I could get another in his place, I soon discovered that no Faith was to be put in these people and desisted till last Fall, when the Time of Service of three of my best Fifers expird, I proposd to them to reinlist and I would make a Band of them, but to try them first and engagd a Mr. Schuetz a German Musician to teach them. in the Course of Januay I was so much encouragd by their rapid Progress, that I determind to compleat the Band on the following principles that they should reinlist and serve as long as I livd or Servd in the Army whether in War or peace as Musicians in my Regiment and to do all Dutys belonging to their Station as Musicians and Fifers, and as a Bounty for so doing, I would have them taught Instrumental Music Viz, 4 to learn Clarinetts and Violins, two Bassoons and Bass Viol, two French horns and that they should be entitled to all other Emoluments Such as Cloathing etc as was allowed other Noncommissioned Officers in the Army.—I soon engagd the Number of men I wanted purchasd the Instruments provided a Master to teach the horns, not doubting but if I succeeded the necessary Expenses incurrd would be reimbursd either by the honorable Board in behalf of the United

States or by the State of Virginia. . . . for this nominal Sum of 2382 $\frac{1}{3}$ Dollars or its real Value at 50 for one is forty Seven Dollars four Shillings and ten pence the Contineat [?] would have a Compleat Band of Music with the Instruments ready taught and able to teach others all Natives of this Country and of reputable Parentage to which I have strictly adherd—[29]

These fifers were to be taught both a wind and a string instrument or the equivalent of a fully professional double-handed musician. No further information has been located on "Mr. Schuetz," and the service records at the National Archives do not list him in the colonial forces. Febiger was refused the request for full reimbursement and continued to support the band from his own personal funds. He was successful in obtaining one set of bounty clothing for his eight musicians. The coats were red faced with blue, the reverse of the colors stipulated for the Virginia line, even though the regiment was uniformed mainly in brown because of a shortage of cloth.[30]

There may have been a tradition in the regiment for a band of music, or possibly Febiger's example caused emulation in other units. The former commander of the regiment, Colonel Alexander Spotswood, had resigned almost a year before Febiger was appointed. He returned to Virginia and became a brigadier general in the state militia. In June 1781, as Washington and Rochambeau were moving south toward Yorktown, Spotswood successfully petitioned the Virginia state legislature for the command of two legions of militia. Among the supplies and equipment requested for this command, "the General [Spotswood] also wants two hundred pair of boots—two French horns first and second, four clarionets, one Bassoon and one 'Houtboy' as necessary to the 'harmony and discipline' of the corps." It is not known whether the instruments were ever issued, for the legions were never fully organized. In any case, the request indicates the high priority given to the music of the army and the desire of the commanding officers to include it as an integral part of military organization.[31]

Lee's Partisan Corps Band

In 1776, Henry Lee commanded a company of light dragoons, which was later attached to the 1st Continental Dragoons. For his heroic deeds and meritorious actions, Congress awarded him the rank of major-commandant and authorized him to form a separate corps of three troops. This battalion of Light Dragoons, as it was called, was later designated as Lee's Partisan Corps, and Lee was promoted to lieutenant colonel.

The light dragoon companies, like the infantry, were patterned on

British models. One trumpeter per company was also required to sound the bugle horn. In addition, in the British army, the combined trumpeters were expected to form a band of music consisting of two clarinets, two horns, and a bassoon when serving on foot.

On 1 February 1779 the corps enlisted Philip Roth to serve as "Music-Master." Roth had participated in a concert given in Philadelphia in 1771 for which he had composed an overture for full band. He was at that time the "Master of the Band belonging to his Majesty's Royal Regiment of North British Fusileers" (21st Foot). The presence of such a musician in Lee's corps, in addition to the authorized trumpet major, could only mean that a band existed. No contemporary references have been located specifically identifying this band, but the corps participated in the funeral ceremonies for Brigadier General Enoch Poor in 1780. Dr Thacher described his impressions: "A band of music, with a number of drums and fifes, played a funeral dirge, the drums were muffled with black crape, and the officers in the procession wore crape around the left arm. . . . No scene can exceed in grandeur and solemnity a military funeral. The weapons of war reversed, and embellished with the badges of mourning, the slow and regular step of the procession, the mournful sound of the unbraced drum and the deep-toned instruments, playing the melancholy dirge." General Poor had commanded the New Hampshire brigade, and the corpse was followed by the brigade officers and those of Lee's Corps. It is very possible that Dr. Thacher referred to Lee's band, but since Jackson's regiment was also a part of the New Hampshire brigade at that time, positive identification cannot be made.

After the Revolution, Roth returned to Philadelphia, where he gave private lessons in music. Advertisements in the *Pennsylvania Journal* from 10 September through 7 January 1789 carried the notice that he "TEACHES all kinds of Instrumental Music in the shortest manner, viz. Harpsichord, Piano Forte, Guitar, Flute, Hautboy, Clarinet, Bassoon, French horn, Harp and Thorough-Bass, which is the Ground of Music, &c." In other words, he was a fully professional musician.[32]

Additional Bands of Music

Other Continental units also seem to have had bands, but information is insufficient to identify the units. Dr. Thacher, for instance, was present at an entertainment given in his hospital at Fishkill by General Peter Muhlenberg where the guests were "cheered with military music and dancing, which continued till a late hour in the night." Under an entry of several weeks later, Dr. Thacher described his social activities:

As we are stationed at a considerable distance from the enemy at New York, we feel secure from the annoyance of the dogs of war; and military duty not being very urgent, our officers appear disposed to relax in their discipline, and contract a habit approaching to dissipation. They have adopted the practice of giving suppers alternately, with music and dancing through half the night. These are the favorite amusements of the Virginia and Maryland officers, but they do not accord precisely with my own views of time well spent, though I am frequently enticed to a participation in their banqueting revels.[33]

In spite of his views of "time well spent," a bare two days later he was again at dinner with General Muhlenberg and several Virginia officers and recorded that he "as usual, closed the day with music and dancing." Brigadier General Peter Muhlenberg at that time commanded a brigade composed of the 1st and 14th Continental Virginia Infantry, the 4th Maryland Continental Infantry, and the 1st Virginia State (Militia) Infantry Regiments. Thomas Sheldon, Febiger's fife major and teacher for the band, was originally a fifer in the 14th Virginia, where he may have formed, or gained experience in, a band. At the time of Thacher's entry Sheldon was already in the 2d Virginia. With so much entertaining, particularly when described as "military music," it would seem that a band was implied, but no other indication has been discovered that any of these units had a band. The fifes and drums would hardly have been used for dancing or supper music, and one or two musicians that could have performed on those occasions would not have qualified for the term "military music."

Two years later, Chastellux described a visit to the main army under Washington: "We gained, at length, the right of the army, where we saw the Pennsylvania line; it was composed of two brigades, each forming three battalions. . . . Each brigade had a band of music; the march they were then playing was the *Huron*." The brigades may have had their own bands or may have borrowed those of the artillery regiments then with the army. André Gretry's opera *Le Huron* (1768) contains a "Marche" which would have been suitable for a ceremonial parade, and this is one of the rare instances where a piece of music used in a military ceremony is identified by name. Usually, as with the 3d Massachusetts Brigade's celebration of the anniversary of the surrender of Burgoyne a year later, the presence of a band is mentioned in general terms. Colonel John Greaton was the host for this "elegant entertainment, at which were present Major-General Heath and suite, the officers of the brigade, and a number of other gentlemen." It will be remembered that John Hancock had accused Colonel Greaton of taking his personal musical instruments to use for the regiment, so there was apparently a brigade or regimental band in existence. Unfortunately no other information has come to light, and so this can only be an assumption.[34]

Some of the militia units seem to have continued to use private bands, as they had prior to the Revolution. Christopher Marshall described the Independence Day festivities of 1779 in Lancaster, Pennsylvania: "Near two o'clock went down to the Court House, where, after some little time, having joined Col. Jacob Glotz's battalion of militia, placing me at the head of [the] Committee who walked two by two, then the corporation, the Colonels, one and two, with their battalion colors flying, drums, fifes and band of music, [we] went in procession down Queens street." It must have been a busy day for the musicians, for the following morning at one o'clock they serenaded Marshall in front of his house, "purely to show their regard and respect they owed" to him as an official of the borough.[35]

A band of music was also present at the commencement exercises of the University of Pennsylvania in 1780, playing "at proper intervals." The band is not further identified; it may have been a militia band, a band composed of students of the college, or even possibly Proctor's band. The president and members of Congress were present, as well as the French minister to the United States, the Chevalier de la Luzerne, so the trustees presumably would have tried to obtain the best possible musical group. Chevalier de la Luzerne had arrived at Boston on 3 August 1779 and was greatly feted by the townspeople. He was invited to dinner in Washington's quarters at West Point in September while "a few steps away from us musicians played military and tuneful French airs." At this same minister's hotel in Philadelphia, in the presence of Washington and his lady, America's first attempt at "grand opera" was presented. Francis Hopkinson's *The Temple of Minerva* was performed "by a Band of Gentlemen and Ladies" on 11 December 1781.[36]

Boston also had its bands. Ebenezer Fox wrote of many incidents in 1780 when "a recruiting officer, bearing a flag and attended by a band of martial music, paraded the streets to excite a thirst for glory and a spirit of military ambition." Heath noted one occasion in his memoirs that "three deserters, one a Hessian musician with his horn, came in from the enemy." The deserter was not necessarily a bandsman, for horns were used in the light infantry instead of drums as signaling instruments. Thomas Anburey narrated in his volume that the whole band of the British 62d Foot had deserted, except for the master, and was then "playing to an American regiment in Boston." Anburey's work was "for the most part lifted from earlier publications" and cannot be trusted as accurate, but the anecdote may be true, for the 62d

Foot had surrendered with Burgoyne in 1777, and many of the "Convention Army," as they were called, deserted.[37]

In addition to British musicians being available to the American army, musical instruments at times became part of the spoils of war. An estimate of the value of the British ordnance and stores captured at Stony Point, signed by Henry Knox and dated 1 August 1779, included the addition "of '2 French Horns, 2 Bassoons, 2 Clarinets' with the prices of which Knox was 'entirely unaquainted'; but 'I have been assured that the Light Infantry have been offered one thousand dollars for them by some individuals, I do therefore appraise them at one thousand dollars.' "[38] Stony Point was defended by Lieutenant Colonel Henry Johnson and the 17th Foot, so it must have been their instruments that were captured. Some writers have jokingly described Knox's appraisal as "naive," which is highly unfair. Knox was a bookseller prior to the Revolution and did sell some musical instruments. Just a few months earlier he had made the request for instruments for the artillery brigade band which Hiwell was equipping and training. Inflation was also a consideration. Ward, in writing of this period, stated that there was no "shortage of money; there was plenty of that, bushels of it, to be had of the Congress for the asking, plenty of Continental paper money. . . . It had sunk steadily during the past two years in real value, in purchasing power; and it was still sinking, faster and faster, month by month all that winter. By April 1779 [three months prior to Knox's appraisal], it was so depressed that, as Washington wrote, 'a waggon load of money will scarcely purchase a waggon load of provision.' "[39] Finally, the purpose of the appraisal was to determine a sum that could be divided among the troops that had participated in the attack, and any commander would normally tend to overvalue an object that would then be divided to his command's gain. What happened to the instruments after their appraisal is unknown, but they may very well have been added to the Brigade of Artillery band which Knox commanded.

6. DEFEAT, THEN
VICTORY, IN THE SOUTH

U nable to accomplish anything decisive in the north because of the stalemate with Washington, Sir Henry Clinton, commander in chief of the British forces in North America, determined upon a southern campaign. Georgia quickly capitulated, and a combined Franco-American attempt to recapture Savannah in 1779 was repulsed by the British under Major General Augustine Prevost. The American commander, Major General Benjamin Lincoln, was unable to regain Georgia, but did prevent the fall of Charleston. In the spring of 1780, Clinton moved against Charleston in force and overwhelmed the city by massive numbers and formal siege. The surrender of Charleston on 12 May 1780 was a great blow to the American cause, one from which, in spite of some minor successes, it did not fully recover until the victory at Yorktown more than a year later. A major cause of the ultimate reversal was the arrival of the French forces under Rochambeau and the assistance of Admiral de Grasse and a French fleet.

THE SURRENDER OF CHARLESTON

The city of Charleston, South Carolina, was a thriving community of fewer than fourteen thousand people, of whom more than a third were Negro slaves. It was the only city of importance south of Virginia and one of the four principal American seaports. There was a lively musical environment, and concerts were given frequently. The Saint Cecelia Society, in existence since 1771, had a reputation for excellence throughout the colonies. The military also had its musical groups, for at the funeral of Lieutenant Colonel Bernard Elliott on 27 October 1778 the coffin was preceded by a band of music consisting of "Hautboys, Clarinets, French-Horns & Kettledrums playing a dead March composed by Mr. Beck for this mournful Occasion." The band's unit is not identified, but Colonel Elliott was in the South Carolina Artillery Regiment. No military service record has been found for a "Mr. Beck," so he may have been a civilian teacher hired for the military band, a common practice in European armies.[1]

Clinton, with over fourteen thousand regulars, began a traditional siege of the city on 29 March complete with parallel entrenchments. For defense, Lincoln had a force of less than six thousand men, most of them untried militia. By 8 May, Clinton's approaches were so close to the American lines that Lincoln requested a discussion of terms of capitulation.

The Revolutionary War was still fought for the most part in the gentlemanly manner of the previous centuries. The sense of honor and gallantry was important to the officers and men, particularly in the higher ranks, as their actions reflected on the honor of their country. Of extreme importance to personal and national honor were the terms of capitulation at any surrender. Customary procedures had developed through the sixteenth and seventeenth centuries, and terms were drawn carefully regarding the disposition of the town or fortress surrendered, the inhabitants, public and private property, and most important, reflection on the honor of the commander of the garrison and his men. Simes's *Military Guide for Young Officers* gave explicit instructions to commanders who were forced to surrender either by the course of events reducing them to the point of useless defense or upon the order of their superior officers. The first step was to beat the *Parley* or *Chemade*, "for which one or more drummers and fifers are ordered to the rampart that is next to the attack to give notice to the besiegers, that the Governor has some proposals to make them. . . . The chemade being beat, the fire ceases on both sides, and the Governor sends some officers of distinction to the Commander in Chief of the besiegers." The terms should be very specific as to the disposition of the town, its inhabitants, the army's impedimenta, the provision of covered wagons to allow traitors or deserters to leave with the conquered troops so that they would not be required to face reprisals, and many other details. Very important to the question of honor was the procedure of the surrender itself. Simes gave the following example as that most generally practiced: "That the garrison shall march out through the breach, with their arms, baggage, spare carriages, horses, drums beating, fifes playing, matches lighted on both ends, flying colours, some cannons and mortars, with their appurtenances."[2] Wright explains the significance of the various terms as follows:

The garrison marched out through the breach that had been made in their main work by the enemy's artillery. This demonstrated that the defense had held out until a practicable breach had been made, practicable for a hostile storming party to pass through. If such a breach had not as yet been made and the garrison marched out of one of the gates, they would not, as a rule, be considered as meriting the honors of war. As the garrison had acquitted itself with honor, its exit from the fortress was not as a humiliated and conquered force, deprived of all means of self-defense. It marched forth with flags flying, drums beating, trumpets sounding, fully armed and prepared to defend itself against insult. The terms "matches lighted on both ends" were ancient and handed down from the the days of the matchlock musket. The match which lighted the musket was burning on both ends as frequently in firing the musket the lighted end would be extinguished in the pan.[3]

The instructions were known to the Americans, or at least available to them, for the Simes work was reprinted in Philadelphia in 1776 and was used widely as a manual by the Continental officers. The terms described were not new to the colonies, as can be seen from Fernow's description of the surrender of Fort Christina on the Delaware River in 1655: the governor and the garrison of thirty marched out "with beating of drums, playing of fifes, flying banners, burning matches, musketballs in their mouths, hand and side arms." In April 1780, just a few days before the fall of Charleston, the British had permitted the Spanish defenders of Fort St. Juan, Nicaragua, "to march out with colours flying, drums beating, lighted matches, musket, and side arms," in "favour of the gallant defence which the Commandant has made."[4]

Faced with a hopeless situation, and completely surrounded and outnumbered by British forces, Lincoln offered to capitulate. He requested the conventional terms, including the honors of war, allowing the garrison to march out with colors unfurled and the drums beating a British march. The choice of march performed while surrendering had become a matter of honor, for playing a melody of the victor showed that the vanquished were not so humiliated that they could not exchange courtesies in return for the honors of war. Clinton refused and forced Lincoln to accept the following among the articles of capitulation: "Article 7. The whole garrison shall, at an hour to be appointed, march out of town, to the ground between the works of the place and the canal, where they will deposit their arms. The drums are not to beat a British march, or the colors be uncased." Lincoln had no choice but to submit, and on 12 May 1780 the whole force of over fifty-four hundred Continentals and militia marched out with the colors cased, the music playing *The Turk's March*. The choice of march was no doubt Lincoln's attempt to avoid the complete humiliation inherent in performing an American march under these circumstances.[5]

Following the surrender of Charleston, the American cause seemed to hit its lowest point: "In the North, the high patriotic enthusiasms of the early years waned as the war dragged on, and a creeping paralysis in the war effort set in. By 1780 the Continental currency had practically depreciated out of existence, rendering Congress impotent to pay the soldiers or purchase supplies. At Morristown, N.J., in the winter of 1779–80 the Army suffered worse hardships than it had at Valley Forge." Congress turned to the states for help, asking each to provide clothing for its own troops, as well as quotas for supplies. Morale in the ill-fed, ill-supplied, and ill-paid army naturally suffered, and Washington was faced with several mutinies that had to be severely suppressed. Congress made some efforts to remedy the situation by appointing a new quartermaster general and a superintendent of finance and by replacing the old Board of War by a full-time secretary at war. The paper size of the army was brought closer to reality by reducing the number of infantry regiments to fifty and filling them with the men from the disbanded units. Instead of the former three sergeants and three corporals, the noncommissioned staff of each company now consisted of five sergeants. The battalion retained its fife and drum majors and one drummer and fifer per company, but added a recruiting party of one lieutenant, one fifer, and one drummer, to reside in the state to which they belong to enlist. The number of privates per company was raised from fifty-three to sixty-eight. Major General Nathanael Greene was given command of the southern campaign, and two able officers, Brigadier General Daniel Morgan and Lieutenant Colonel Henry Lee, were ordered to assist him in turning the tide. In the meantime, a new element had been introduced into the war, which helped to revitalize the lagging spirits of the Americans: the landing of Rochambeau and his troops at Newport.[6]

THE ARRIVAL OF ROCHAMBEAU

Lieutenant General Jean Baptiste Donatien de Vimeur, Comte de Rochambeau, had arrived at Newport, Rhode Island, in July 1780 with four regiments of French infantry, supporting artillery and engineers, and a legion of infantry and cavalry. The regiments were the Bourbonnais, Soissonais, Saintonge, and the Royal Deux-Ponts, with the legion known by the name of its commander, the Duc de Lauzun. Americans had seen French troops previously when the Comte d' Estaing brought a force to aid Sullivan in the attempt on Newport in 1778. These troops had been disembarked from the ships for the brief campaign and then as quickly returned to sail off for the West Indies. Rochambeau's force was sent to America for the duration of the war and camped at Newport for almost a year before moving into the southern campaign.

The infantry regiments of the line may not have had as great a complement of troops as the royal regiments on duty at Versailles, but they no doubt would have tried to approximate the royal example as closely as their purses would permit. The Regiment des gardes Françaises was authorized in 1777 to have one drum major, responsible for the instruction and discipline of the music of the regiment, fourteen musicians, and two Negro cymbal players, in addition to the fifers and drummers of the companies. The bands, as in the British army, were supported by the officers. Rochambeau's regiments brought with them the latest musical fashion in military bands, the *Harmoniemusik* supplemented with the new Janissary instruments. Sometime before 1780 the one-keyed piccolo was substituted for the fife in the companies. More in tune and musically preferable to the former instrument, the piccolo may have been used so the fifers could play with the band, thereby reinforcing the melodic line over the Janissary accompaniment. The snare drum was made of brass, twelve inches high and fourteen inches in diameter, weighing about seven and a half pounds, and decorated only with the embossed number of the regiment. The drum major, using a baton, marched in front of the musicians, who were followed by the massed drums of the first battalion. The value of music and the importance of the drum major's position are clear because his was the highest paid enlisted rank in the regiment; he received 10 percent more than the sergeant major of grenadiers. The musicians, as in the American and British armies, received the same pay as a corporal.[7]

Lauzun had his band with him on board the *Provence* during the seventy-day trip to America. "When the great armada was becalmed, as it was from time to time for many days, he would arrange a concert and the other ships gathered around so that the men on the transports without bands might enjoy the rare treat of soothing music." The musical entertainments continued at Newport, and the bands played for dances and festivities. It may be assumed that the band's regular duties of providing music for the dining pleasure of the officers and for the ceremonial occasions of the regiment continued unabated, even though infrequently included as newsworthy in contemporary diaries or journals. Chastellux, for example, was pleased to find a regimental band in attendance when he dined with the Comte de Vaudreuil.[8]

Rochambeau left Newport and proceeded with his men to meet Washington's army at King's Bridge, New York, on 6 July 1781. In honor of the occasion Washington "ordered the [American] drums to beat a French march," and a great review was held the following day.[9] This reference to the drums beating a French march may be local legend, however, or a transposition of a later occurrence at Verplanck's Point in 1782, for neither writer quotes his source, and the official general orders for that period do not refer to music. The review is mentioned by Dr. Thacher, but he does not mention the music performed. In any case, Rochambeau placed himself and his forces under the command of Washington, and together they planned an attack on Clinton's forces in New York.

In August, Washington received word that Admiral Comte de Grasse, transporting three regiments and their supporting auxiliaries, would be made available to the combined forces until 15 October, when they would be required to return to the West Indies. As the defensive position around New York was too strongly entrenched, and he was outnumbered by Clinton's forces, Washington determined to entrap Lord Cornwallis and his army at Yorktown, Virginia. The combined French and American armies were immediately ordered to march southward to Baltimore and the Head of Elk where an improvised flotilla carried them down the Chesapeake to Williamsburg.

The French were well received everywhere they passed along the route to the south. A chaplain with the French army, the Abbé Robin, wrote: "The Americans, whom curiosity brings by thousands to our camp, are constantly received with good humour and festivity; and our military music, of which they are extravagantly fond, is then played for their diversion. At such times officers, soldiers, Americans, of both sexes, all intermingle and dance together." The Continental army reached Philadelphia in early September, and Dr. Thacher wrote that they marched "in slow and solemn step, regulated by the drum and fife. The day following, the French troops marched through the city, dressed in complete uniform of white broadcloth, faced with green, and besides the drum and fife, they were furnished with a complete band of music, which operates like enchantment." White coats faced with green was the uniform of the Saintonge regiment, and Thacher's comment proves conclusively that this regiment had a band in addition to the regular field music. (The lure of the New World must have been too great for one of them, however, for the day after the parade, the *Pennsylvania Packet* advertised that a reward was offered for the apprehension of a deserter from the Saintonge regiment, a musician "who plays on the clarinett.") Abbé Robin went into greater detail concerning this march through the American colonial capitol: "The arrival of the French army at Philadelphia was more like a triumph, than simply a passing through the place: the troops made a halt about a quarter of a league from the city, and in an instant were dressed as elegantly as ever the soldiers of a garrison were upon a day of review: they then marched through the town, with the military music playing before them, which is always particularly pleasing to the Americans." Baron von Closen, one of Rochambeau's aides, noted that a number of ladies assembled at the French ambassador's residence "were enchanted to see such handsome men and to hear such good music."[10]

When they reached Baltimore, the French camped in "a charming position in the middle of a wood" where the band played every evening, "people flocking there to hear the music." The band of the regiment of "the Count de Chalour" [Count de Charlus, Saintonge regiment] appeared in the *Humors of Ben the Soldier* and other theatrical productions in Baltimore.[11]

The army finally reached Williamsburg on 26 September, and there joined with Lafayette's American and de Grasse's French troops to begin the siege of Yorktown.

THE WORLD TURNED UPSIDE DOWN AT YORKTOWN

Prior to the arrival of Washington and Rochambeau and their forces at Williamsburg, the tide had in fact begun to turn in the southern campaign. Frontier militia riflemen had destroyed a Tory force at King's Mountain, resulting in the reluctance of other Tories to join the British cause openly. General Greene divided his force, making it possible for them to live off the country and partially solve the supply problem. General Morgan gained a decisive victory at Cowpens, and Greene, while losing at Guilford Court House, made it a Pyrrhic victory thereby reducing Cornwallis's effectiveness and forcing him to return to Yorktown. Similar "victories" at Hobkirk's Hill and Eutaw Springs further weakened the British position in the south.

While never sufficient, supplies of clothing, food, and equipment became more abundant, and Washington attempted to provide everything in his power to make the campaign a successful one. Uniform regulations had been formulated in 1779, and quantities of uniforms had been ordered from French suppliers. The uniform coat was to be dark blue, with white linings and buttons for the infantry, and with scarlet linings, facings and yellow buttons for the artillery. Waistcoats and overalls were to be white. Separate facings for each individual regiment could not be provided, as commonly practiced in the European armies, so the various Continental regiments were divided by four geographical locations, each with a distinctive facing. Those from the New England states were to face their coats with white; those from New York and New Jersey were to be faced with buff. Pennsylvania, Delaware, Maryland, and Virginia were to have red facings, with Georgia and the Carolinas using blue with buttonholes edged with narrow white lace or tape. The uniform of the artillery was to be faced with scarlet, buttonholes edged with yellow lace. Since the company musicans functioned as conveyors of commands, it was important they be recognized easily in the dust of battle, and therefore they were dressed differently from the other soldiers. Washington stated in a letter to the Continental agents for clothing in Boston that "the Cloathing of the Drums and Fifes should also be characteristic of the Regt. to which they belong, that is, the Ground of the Coat of the same Colour as the Regimental facings.'' In other words, Washington followed the standard practice of the time, dressing the musicians in reverse colors of the regimental uniforms. Figure 14, by Donna Neary, a modern artist specializing in military uniforms of the period, illustrates what is meant by reverse colors. The shaded portions of the private's and drummer's coats would be dark blue, according to the uniform regulations. The unshaded portions of the coats (the ground of the drummer's coat, and the collar, cuffs, and lapels of the private's coat) would then be white, buff, red, blue, or scarlet, depending upon the branch and geographical location. Supplies arrived from time to time during 1780 and 1781, and while the army was not completely clothed at any one time, it began to look like a professional army. The difference between this army and the one which fought at Bunker Hill was not merely one of clothing; the army of 1781 had been trained and hardened, and was able to meet the British regulars on equal terms, something the militia never could do.[12]

This was the army that Washington was bringing to Virginia to combine with the forces of Lafayette, Rochambeau, and de Grasse. Lafayette had been in Virginia with twelve hundred Continentals since the previous summer and had been ordered to prevent Cornwallis from leaving Yorktown. On 30 August 1781, de Grasse landed three French regiments under the command of the Marquis de Saint-Simon, who joined with Lafayette. A British naval attempt to defeat the French was successfully thwarted, and de Grasse established a blockade of the Chesapeake. Washington arrived on 14 September, was received with a twenty-one-gun salute, and passed through the lines of the men. At dinner with Saint-Simon, he was entertained by ''an elegant band of music'' which played Grétry's quartet *Ou peut on être mieux qu'au sein de sa famille?*, ''signifying the happiness of the family, when blessed with the presence of their father, and their great dependence upon him.''[13]

Preparations were made for the final siege. With the example of the French always before them, great emphasis was placed on the ceremonial aspects of the camp routines. Ebenezer Denny described the daily guard mount:

The presence of so many general officers, and the arrival of new corps, seem to give additional life to everything; discipline the order of the day. In all directions troops seen exercising and manoeuvring. Baron Steuben, our great military oracle. The guards attend the grand parade at an early hour, where the Baron is always found waiting with one or two aides on horseback. These men are exercised and put through various evolutions and military experiments for two hours—many officers and spectators present; excellent school, this. At length the duty of the parade comes on. The guards are told off; officers take their posts, wheel by platoons to the right; fine corps of music detailed for this duty, which strikes up; the whole march off, saluting the Baron and field officer of the day, as they pass.[14]

By the end of September all was in readiness and the land forces, under Washington and Rochambeau, approached from Williamsburg. De Grasse's squadron blockaded the Chesapeake so that no relief or escape was possible by sea. The actual siege was begun on 6 October and was carried on in the traditional eighteenth-century fashion of parallels and zigzag trenches approaching the enemy redoubts and line of defense. That evening, Dr. Thacher was assigned to remain in the rear of the troops who were ordered to open the entrenchments near the enemy lines. Since the work was to proceed in the strictest silence, about twenty drummers and fifers, not required to perform musically, were put under Thacher's charge to assist him in case there were any wounded. He gave his medical instruments, bandages, and so on, to one of the drummers with orders to remain constantly by his side. Dr. Thacher wrote, "It was not long, however, before I found to my astonishment that he had left me, and gone in pursuit of some rum, carrying off the articles which are indispensable in time of action."[15]

The various traditions of honor and chivalry were followed, and Lieutenant William Feltman wrote that his regiment, when relieved from their duty in the trenches, marched off "with drums beating and colours flying, after a very fatiguing night." After days of bombardment and an unsuccessful attempt at escape across the York River, Cornwallis called for a parley to discuss terms of capitulation. Denny noted the scene in his journal on 17 October:

In the morning, before the relief came, had the pleasure of seeing a drummer mount the enemy's parapet, and beat a parley, and immediately an officer, holding up a white handkerchief, made his appearance outside their works; the drummer accompanied him, beating. Our batteries ceased. An officer from our lines ran and met the other, and tied the handkerchief over his eyes. The drummer sent back, and the British officer conducted to a house in rear of our lines. Firing ceased totally. . . . Had we not seen the drummer in his red coat when he first mounted, he might have beat away till doomsday. The constant firing was too much for the sound of a single drum; but when the firing ceased, I thought I never heard a drum equal to it—the most delightful music to us all.[16]

A twenty-four-hour truce was arranged to allow commissioners to work on the capitulation agreement. Lieutenant Colonel John Laurens and the Viscount de Noailles presented Washington's terms to Cornwallis's aides, Lieutenant Colonel Thomas Dundas and Major Alexander Ross. Article 3 of the agreement stated: "The garrison of York will march out to a place to be appointed in front of the posts, at 2 o'clock precisely; with shouldered arms, colors cased & drums beating a British or German march—they are then to ground their arms, and return to their encampment, where they will remain until they are dispatched to the place of their destination." Colonel Ross protested the harshness of this article, in not allowing the honors of war. Laurens agreed that it was a harsh article, but reminded Ross that he, Laurens, had been

". . . a capitulant at Charleston—where Gen. Lincoln, after a brave defence of six weeks open trenches, by a very inconsiderable garrison, against the British army and fleet, under Sir Henry Clinton and Admiral Arbuthnot, and when your lines of approach were within pistol-shot of our field works, was refused any other terms for his gallant garrison, than marching out with colors cased, and drums *not* beating a British or a German March."

"But," rejoined Col. Ross, "my Lord Cornwallis did not command at Charleston."

"There, Sir," said Col. Laurens, "you extort another declaration. It is not the individual that is here considered—it is the Nation. This remains an article or I cease to be a Commissioner."

Washington supported his commissioner and insisted that the same honors were to be granted to the surrendering army as were granted to the garrison at Charleston.[17]

In the meantime, the armies waited. On the morning of the truce, 18 October 1781, St. George Tucker noted in his journal that "the British gave us a serenade with the Bag pipe, I believe, & were answered by the French with the Band of the Regiment of deux ponts." At retreat beating that evening, the British played the tune of *Welcome Brother Debtor*, and Tucker noted that "to their conquerors the tune was by no means disagreeable." A modern researcher has located a contemporary edition of the complete poem and melody of this composition. In $\frac{3}{4}$ meter, it is perfectly suited to the retreat parade and certainly would have reflected some of the feeling of the garrison. Since it has been specifically named by a witness to the scene, it is included as figure 15, a melody known to have been performed at a military ceremony during the Revolution.[18]

The agreement was signed on the 19th, with the ceremony to be performed the same day. The terms were publicized, and Knox wrote joyfully to his wife that "they will have the same *honors* as the garrison of Charleston; that is, they *will not* be permitted to unfurl their colors, or *play Yankee Doodle*." At two o'clock in the afternoon, as stipulated in the agreement, the garrison marched out for the formal act of surrendering. A German sergeant, John Doehla, described the scene:

> We marched on the road to Williamsburg in platoons, arms shouldered, through the whole army of the enemy, the band playing. . . . On the right wing of each French regiment was gorgeously paraded a rich standard of white silk, with three golden *fleurs de lis* embroidered on it. Beyond these standards stood the drummers and fifers, and in front of them the band, which played delightfully. . . . The left wing of the line through which we had to march was formed of the Americans; . . . They were paraded in three lines, the first composed of the regulars, who had also a band, playing moderately well.[19]

Another German soldier commented on the "fine music, particularly the musicians of the French." Dr. Thacher described the scene from the point of view of a member of the victorious army: "The Americans were drawn up in a line on the right side of the road, and the French occupied the left. . . . The French troops, in complete uniform, displayed a martial and noble appearance, their band of music, of which the timbrel formed a part, is a delightful novelty, and produced while marching to the ground a most enchanting effect."[20] The "delightful novelty" to which Thacher refers is not the band of music itself, as some writers have implied, but the "timbrel," or tambourine. Thacher was familiar with bands, having mentioned them frequently in his journal, but he had not as yet seen the latest fashion from Europe, the Janissary instruments. The inclusion of the tambourine in his comment definitely established that the French bands did have these instruments and, by inference, that the Americans did not.

General Charles O'Hara, commanding the British forces in place of Lord Cornwallis, "was followed by the conquered troops in a slow and solemn step, with shouldered arms, colors cased, and drums beating a British march." The soldiers marched by in new uniforms, for, rather than have his stores captured by the enemy, Cornwallis had opened his warehouse and authorized a complete issue. Other supplies must have been made available as well, for both Feltman and McDowell noted that "the British prisoners all appeared to be much in liquor." The troops were led by General O'Hara, the second in command, who brought word that Lord Cornwallis was indisposed. Washington had his second in command, General Lincoln, accept the surrender. St. George Tucker noted with elation: "General Lincoln with his Aids conducted them—Having passed thro' our whole Army they grounded their Arms & march'd back again thro' the Army a second Time into the Town—The sight was too pleasing to an American to admit of

Description.'' The morale of the surrendering troops was understandably low, and Denny commented that their ''drums beat as if they did
not care how.'' An old American veteran reminisced to Auguste
Levasseur several years later:

> It was evident to us that the English in their misfortune were especially
> mortified to be obliged to lay down their arms before Americans, for the
> officers and soldiers affected to turn their heads towards the French line.
> Lafayette perceived this, and revenged himself in a very pleasant manner. He
> ordered the music of the light infantry to strike up *Yankee Doodle*, an air which
> the British applied to a song composed to ridicule the Americans at the
> beginning of the war, and which they uniformly sung to all their prisoners.
> This pleasantry of Lafayette was so bitter to them, that many of them broke
> their arms in a rage in grounding them on the glacis.[21]

The news spread, and the legends began to grow. A Boston
newspaper carried the announcement, ''We learn that General Lincoln
received the captured Lord Cornwallis; and that the Army played up
Yankee-doodle, when the British Army marched to lay down their
arms.'' Alexander Garden wrote in 1828 that ''the British army
marched out with colours cased, and the drums beating a British or
German march. The march they chose was—*The World Turned Upside
Down*.'' Many writers have since referred to this tune, skillfully
embroidering the legend. The fact is, however, that the song was not
recognized by the majority, if any, of the witnesses, for none of the
contemporary journals located to date deemed it worthy of mention.
The diaries, letters, or journals of Knox, Rochambeau, John Doehla,
Stephan Popp, Thacher, Feltman, Tilden, Shute, Denny, Richard
Butler, Tallmadge, Davis, Graham, Lee, and the Abbé Robin, all of
whom were present at the ceremonies, make no reference to any
specific music performed. The sole source of the legend seems to be
the anecdote written by Garden in 1828. Aedanus Burke came closest
to describing the music: ''They marched thro' both Armies in a Slow
pace, and to the Sound of Music, not Military Marches, but of certain
Airs, which had in them so peculiar a strain of melancholy, and which
together with the appearance before me excited sentiments far different
from those I expected to enjoy.'' St. George Tucker also mentioned
that ''the whole British Army march'd their Drums in Front beating a
slow March.''[22]

The regiments that surrendered under Cornwallis's command
were the 17th, 23d, 33d, 43d, 71st, 76th, and 80th British regiments of
foot, and the Bose, Ansbach, and Bayreuth German regiments. Appendix A indicates that each of the British regiments may have had a

band in addition to its field music, and the three German regiments, as verified by Doehla above, had theirs. The listing of military stores captured included 81 drums, 1 trumpet, 28 buglehorns, and 5 french horns, but these were all instruments used by the field music. The instruments used by the regimental bands belonged to the regiment and not the crown and would not be included in any captured stores, remaining the property of the regimental officers' mess. With so many bands performing, it seems very unlikely that any one particular melody or march would have been played by all. Garden's anecdote may be correct in that one or more unnamed witnesses recognized the melody performed by one of the bands as *The World Turned Upside Down*. Since many melodies have been associated with that title, it is still impossible to determine which actual melody the spectators heard. Frank Luther included one of the melodies of *Derry Down* in his volume on American songs, and this has served as a basis for many later writers. *Derry Down* was unquestionably very popular at the time, and a "New Song occasioned by the Surrender of Earl *Cornwallis* and his whole army to General Washington," set to that melody, was printed in the Boston *Independent Chronicle* at the same time as the announcement of the victory. This melody is in $\frac{6}{8}$ meter, however, which would have been used for a quick march. The normal cadence was the ordinary, or slow step, and under the circumstances the troops would not have been likely to march to the faster and livelier quickstep used only for maneuvering. Burke, Thacher, and St. George Tucker all specified that the troops marched to the slow step, so the identification of *Derry Down* with the Yorktown surrender is very doubtful.[23]

Another eighteenth-century melody has been associated with this title. Chappell gave the following as the tune of a song variously known as *The World Turned Upside Down*, or *When the King Enjoys His Own Again*:[24]

EXAMPLE 17: *The World Turned Upside Down*

This was an extremely popular Jacobite song and would have been known by the fifers and men of the Highland regiments, if not by the whole British army. The sentiments expressed in either version of the title, whether recognized by the Americans and their French allies or not, certainly reflected the feeling of the despondent men. The meter is appropriate for the cadence of a slow march. Marching out of York-town to this melody or some other familiar tune on that October day, the soliders knew that the world had indeed turned upside down, when a group of armed, rebellious colonists could cause the surrender of British regulars.

7. THE LAST CAMPAIGN

Lieutenant Colonel Tench Tilghman was dispatched directly to Congress with the news of the capture of Cornwallis. The news spread quickly. At every point there was rejoicing and a general belief that the war soon would be over. Congress set 15 December as a general day of thanksgiving and celebration throughout the country. The French army encamped at Williamsburg participated in a *Te Deum*, three volleys of musket fire, and cries of "Long Live the King!" Rochambeau gave a large dinner for the leading residents of the city, followed by a ball "to which all the ladies were invited." The American forces had begun to move north toward New York, and there must certainly have been many lively occasions such as that described by Tilden: "The troops halted yesterday an hour to play a number of tunes on ye drum and fife, for some country girls, a dancing same evening." Some of the troops remained with General Greene to continue the southern campaign, and even there life was more joyous and relaxed than before. Feltman noted in his journal that there were "balls almost every evening" in a number of "very elegant buildings" close to the encampment and that the inhabitants were "very polite and genteel." On another occasion, Generals Greene, Wayne, Mordecai Gist, and "a number of other gentlemen officers went about fifteen miles into the country from camp to an elegant entertainment." Baron von Closen observed that in Williamsburg "there are endless balls; the women love dancing with as much passion as the men hunting and horse-racing." Tallmadge noted: "The campaign having again opened [1782], the general opinion was that the toils and perils of the war would soon close, and that peace might soon be looked for to terminate the struggle. The country seemed already to feel as if our independence was sure, and as if little effort was now needed to consummate the work."[1]

The optimism was not universal, however. A large British force had surrendered once before, at Saratoga in 1777, and the enemy had pressed the war even more vigorously. Britain still ruled the seas, and the French navy that had helped Washington at Yorktown had sailed back to the West Indies, leaving the complete American coastline open to attack. A force of over seventeen thousand men, almost three times that captured with Cornwallis, was stationed at New York and capable of actively continuing the conflict. Tallmadge remembered some fifty years later that Washington "impressed upon the army the necessity of strict discipline, that the troops might be prepared for any emergency." The commander in chief continued to press the Congress and the governors for supplies, equipment, and most of all, for men to fill the ranks. Within a week of the victory at Yorktown, Washington confided to the governor of Virginia: "I will candidly confess to Your Excellency, that my only apprehension (which I wish may be groundless) is, lest the late important success, instead of exciting our exertions, as it ought to do, should produce such a relaxation in the prosecution of the War, as will prolong the calamities of it." After a brief rest at Mount Vernon, Washington went to Philadelphia "to stimulate Congress to the best Improvement of our late Success, by takg. the most vigorous and effectual Measures, to be ready for an early and decisive Campaign the next year." The Continentals were ordered to the vicinity of New York for the winter encampment, while Rochambeau's force was to remain near Yorktown and Williamsburg, joining the Americans the following spring.[2]

Militia units took advantage of the stores of military equipment captured at Yorktown, and Lieutenant Hiwell continued to supervise and inspect the army's music. The various bands of music continued to perform their mission, and preparations were made for what all hoped would be the last campaign of the war.

LIEUTENANT HIWELL, INSPECTOR

The 3d Regiment of Artillery had not participated in the Yorktown campaign, but had remained on duty near West Point, watching the movements of General Clinton in New York. John Hiwell, serving as lieutenant in the regiment with the additional duties of inspector and superintendent of music, continued in this position in the northern area. The long period of garrison duty must have loosened discipline and resulted in an apathy on the part of the soldiers, particularly the company musicians, for an order of December 1781 attempted to bring these men back into the routine of camp duties: "The drummers & Fifers have the easiest duty in garrison. All those of the 2d Brigade who have drums & Fifes will parade & beat off from the Comm[and]er['s] Quarters, Reveille, Troop, Retreat & Tattoo, the latter precisely at eight at night, the defaulters will be confined & on conviction before a garrison Court Martial, shall be sentenced to draw stone two days for every non-appearance or neglect of either of the above duties, unless the delinquent shall have a statement from the Comm[andin]g officer of his Regt. of his being unwell, or so illy clothed as to be rendered unfit for duty."[3] Major General William Heath was in command of the northern sector, and his troops had received new clothing, but the musicians had not been included "as there was a probability of an alteration." Writing to Washington, Heath wanted to know if the matter had been determined, "as many of them [the musicians] are very naked." The "alteration" that Heath referred to was criticism of the method of recruiting musicians for the army that had been submitted by the secretary at war to the Congress in December 1781:

> The method hitherto practiced in the Army of inlisting men to serve as fifers and drummers and paying them additional pay is attended with manifest injury to the service for nothing is more common than to see men employed in that duty who are in every respect fit for soldiers, whilst boys hardly able to bear arms are put into the ranks, and the Commanding officers of Corps have not the power of remedying this evil without violating the engagement of the men enlisted as *drummers* or *fifers*.
>
> I therefore wish Congress would be pleased to order, that for the future no recruit should be *engaged* as drummer or fifer; but that the commanding officers of Corps should be authorized to employ such of their men on that duty from time to time as shall be most proper and that the additional pay to such who shall be so employed hereafter shall be appropriated to the repair of their drums and fifes. Also that the number of men employed on that duty in any Corps, shall not exceed the proportion allowed the respective Corps in the establishment.[4]

Major General Benjamin Lincoln, who had been appointed secretary at war shortly after his participation in the victory at Yorktown, submitted a resolution to that intent for consideration. This resolution was adopted by the Congress on 24 December and published in the general orders of 22 January 1782:

> Resolved, that in future no recruit shall be inlisted to serve as a drummer or fifer. When such are wanted, they shall be taken from the soldiers of the corps in such numbers and of such description as the Commander in Chief or commanding officer of a separate army shall direct, and be returned back and others drawn out as often as the good of the service shall make necessary.
>
> That all drummers and fifers, after being supplied each with a good drum and fife, shall keep the same in repair by stoppages from his pay, in such manner as the commanding officer of the corps shall direct.[5]

Lincoln had informed Washington on the day previous to the general order that Congress had authorized the commander in chief to determine the number of fifers and drummers for each regiment and suggested that orders be issued to have them clothed. This matter settled, Washington was able to reply to Heath's inquiry. Forwarding the resolution that had been published, Washington qualified the information by stating that the order "prohibits enlisting any More under that Denomination [fifer or drummer], but does not affect those already in service." Heath was therefore permitted to order the necessary clothing.[6]

The question of the musicians having been resolved, there still remained the problem of suitable equipment for them. The commissary general of military stores, Samuel Hodgdon, had on hand 150 new drum shells, but only 20 fifes in preparation for the coming campaign. A rush order was given to a local drum maker, Henry Frailey, for 63 complete drums, additional accessories, and extra heads.[7]

The extent of Hiwell's influence in these actions is unknown, for his name does not appear in any of the correspondence. It would seem logical, however, that Washington, particularly while he was away from the army, would have relied upon the actions and reports of the music specialist. The sole mention of the inspector throughout the winter appears in Heath's memoirs, where he remarked that Hiwell had fallen through the ice while crossing the Hudson River, "but fortunately got out again."[8]

There is no question about the extent of Hiwell's involvement once Washington returned to the main army. As no equipment had arrived, the inspector was sent directly to the secretary at war in Philadelphia with a letter from Washington:

Mr. Hiwell, Inspector of Music, who is charged with these Dispatches, will lay before you the state of the Drums and Fifes of the several Regts in this Army; the duty can scarcely be done for want of them; it is therefore of importance the deficiency should be made up immediately; if Mr. Hiwell can be of any service in selecting or procuring the instruments, he may be detained until the business can be effected, if you think his services will compensate the expence to the public, if not he will return after furnishing you with all the information necessary to put it in a speedy train of execution. . . .

P.S. Mr. Hiwell is furnished with twenty five dollars for his Expences; all the Money that could be raised.[9]

Hiwell received the twenty-five dollars on 5 May, with instructions that it "be used oeconomically, regular vouchers taken for all the expenditures, & the accounts settled with the Paymaster General." Some idea of the state of the army's finances may be gained by the great attention to accounting for his sum, representing "all the Money that could be raised."[10]

The trip may not have been necessary, for the day after Hiwell left for Philadelphia, Hodgdon forwarded "a number of drums & other Musical apparatus" to the deputy commissary at Fishkill, with instructions to refer to Hiwell's own inspection returns. The remainder of the needed items were promised to be sent as soon as possible after that time.[11]

Perhaps the commissary general had been overly optimistic or the army had increased in strength greater than expected, for in August,

Washington again wrote to the secretary at war that there was "a Deficiency of about 30 Drums and 20 Fifes (as you will perceive by the Inspection Returns) which should likewise be supplied."[12]

In preparation for the meeting of the American army with Rochambeau's regiments, which were marching northward from their winter encampment, Washington repeated his orders of previous years in regard to the position of the inspector of music: "The Inspector of Music will see that exact uniformity in the different beats prevail throughout the army. The signals of the drum as pointed out in the regulations are to be continually made use of and pointedly attended to; the Drum and fife majors of the several corps comprising this army will every day assemble to receive the instructions of the inspector of music at such convenient time and place as he shall point out. This order to continue in force until the inspector of music shall report them perfect in their duties."[13] As the meeting with the French drew near, the army moved down the Hudson River by boat from its position at Newburgh to Verplanck's Point. The movement was conducted as if it were a normal foot march, with "the Musick of different regiments playing alternately, if the situation of the boats will admit of it; the Inspector of Musick will regulate the beats." Shortly after, Hiwell was again reminded of his responsibility to standardize the beats, and off-duty drummers and fifers were required to assemble on the grand parade "to receive the instructions of the Inspector of Music." Wishing to see the state of readiness of his army, Washington ordered a full review of all units, less those necessary for camp security. The review pleased Washington, and he publicly thanked the Officers in orders "for their unremitted care and attention to their respective duties." The drummers and fifers were required to practice two hours daily each morning, while Colonel John Lamb of the 2d Artillery required his musicians to practice an additional three hours each afternoon. The emphasis on ceremony extended to details smaller than company size, and specific orders were given regarding the placing of the musicians: "When Guards march by Platoons it is to be observed as a General rule, that the Drummers and fifers, if there be any, dress with the front rank of the first platoon, the Drumr. on the right of the Serjeant, and the fifer on the right of the Drummer."[14]

The meeting of the French and American armies took place at Verplanck's Point on 21 September 1782. A French officer wrote a friend that "a band of American music which played during the dinner, added to the gaiety of the company." The band is not further identified, but it may have been Crane's band, since Hiwell had been instrumental in preparing the arrangements.[15]

A grand review was held the next day, which Rochambeau recalled in his memoirs:

The general [Washington] wishing to give evidence of his respect for France and his gratitude for her benefits, had us pass between two lines of his troops, who were clothed, equipped, and armed for the first time since the beginning of the revolution, partly with cloth and arms that had come from France, and partly from the English stores captured from Cornwallis's army, which the French army had generously relinquished to the American army. General Washington had his drummers beat the French march throughout this review, and the two armies met here again with the most evident marks of mutual satisfaction.[16]

An eighteen-year-old French ensign in the Deux Ponts regiment, Jean-Baptiste-Antoine de Verger, noted in his diary that "the Whole American Army paraded before M. de Rochambeau. . . . The regiment from the province of New York had a good band, as did another from Massachusetts."[17] Again the bands are not identified, but Crane's band was from Massachusetts, and the New York band may have been that of Van Cortlandt's 2d New York Continental Infantry.

While these events were taking place in the allied camp, significant changes had been made in that of the British. In May of that year Sir Guy Carleton had relieved Clinton of command of the British forces in North America and had begun to offer hints at settlement of the dispute. In July the British were withdrawn from Savannah, and in August, Carleton notified Washington that he had suspended hostilities and that a peace conference was being held in Paris.

The two armies settled down to wait the result of the negotiations. In New York the British officers organized a subscription series of concerts, as well as performances in benefit of "distressed refugee families." Rivington's music store had available a "fresh assortment of Violins and Violin Bows, Guitars of various prices, Clarinets, Hautboys, Bassoons, German Flutes, French Horns," and many other items.[18]

The French headed north once again, as if preparing to go into winter quarters around Boston. Social activities continued on the march, and one writer narrated that on at least one occasion "the most elegant and handsome young ladies of the neighborhood danced with the officers on the turf, in the middle of the camp, to the sound of military music."[19]

The waiting continued, and the army carried on as usual. Lieutenant Colonel Ebenezer Stevens of the 2d Artillery requested one of the large Hessian brass drums, "completely equipt and ornamented," and the fifers and drummers were shortly afterward inspected by

Hiwell. The commissary general of military stores, Samuel Hodgdon, gathered supplies of drums and fifes, with their accessories, ready to be distributed to the army that was continually being reduced in size. Provisional articles of peace were signed in November, but the final treaty was dependent upon peace being concluded with America's allies, France and Spain. In December, Charleston was returned to the Americans, and only the city of New York remained in British possession.[20]

Hodgdon issued his musical equipment to the army in February, and Washington reminded the officers and musicians of their responsibility:

> In whatever Regiments or Corps the full compliment of Drums and Fifes have been furnished by the public since the Resolve of Congress of the 22d January 1782 that supply must be made good and kept compleat by regular stoppages from the weekly allowances of the pay of such Drummers and fifers as may be deficient. Colonels and Commandants of those corps are responsible for the execution of this order, and in all other regiments or Corps the most efficacious measures should be taken to obtain a sufficient number of the articles without a moments delay, which are to be kept compleat in the same manner.

To ensure obedience, the inspector of music was instructed to be present at the general inspection of each regiment scheduled for the following month and to make a report directly to the commander in chief on "the state of the Music, and the number of Instruments in each." Hiwell's reports have not been located, but they must have been favorable, for no further comments appeared in the orders while the army waited for the final cessation of hostilities.[21]

THE BANDS OF MUSIC

The musicians of Webb's 3d Connecticut Infantry band had been discharged by the end of 1781, as were those of Jackson's 16th Massachusetts Infantry. No references have been located regarding Lee's Partisan Corps band, but those of Crane, Proctor, and Febiger continued to perform. In addition, references appear to Van Cortlandt's 2d New York Continental Infantry band.

On 31 May 1782 the army celebrated the birth of a son to the king of France with an elegant dinner, complete with *feu de joi* and fireworks. Crane's regiment formed a line of escort for the more than five hundred gentlemen and ladies who were invited, and "a martial band charmed our senses with music, while we feasted our appetites and gazed with admiration on the illustrious guests and the novel spectacle exhibited to our view. The cloth being removed, thirteen appropriate toasts were drank, each one being announced by the discharge of thirteen cannon and accompanied by music.'' Since Crane's regiment formed the escort, it would seem logical to assume that the regimental band provided the music. Less than a month later, a band performed at an entertainment prepared by the officers of the 9th Massachusetts Infantry at West Point. Colonel Jackson's 16th Massachusetts had been reorganized and consolidated with the 9th Massachusetts, which he now commanded. The music may have been provided by his band, if it still existed, or again by Crane's band, stationed in that garrison.[22]

Not wishing to disband his army completely prior to the formal acceptance of the peace treaty, Washington decided to grant furloughs, thereby maintaining the theoretical organization of the army. Having functioned as a unit for so many years, the members of Crane's band remained together even while home on leave. The *Salem Gazette* of 16 January 1783 carried the following announcement: ''The *Massachusetts* Band of Musick being home a few days on furlough, propose, with permission, to perform at Concert Hall, in Salem, to-morrow evening. This band belongs to Col. Crane's Artillery, is complete, and will have the assistance of two or three capital performers. The Musick will consist of Overtures, Symphonies, Harmony and Military Musick, Solos, Duets on the Horns, and some favourite SONGS by the Band; to begin at six o'clock and end at half past nine.'' The concert was performed ''at so great acceptance'' that the band was engaged to assist in a concert for the poor a week later. Less than a month after that the band performed a similar concert at Portsmouth, which Pichierri noted as being the ''first real public concert recorded in New Hampshire.''[23]

A regimental order dated 7 January 1783, while the band was on leave, stated that ''all the Drums & Fifes are to draw provisions by a Return from the Fife Major.'' As members of the individual companies, the fifers and drummers always shared their rations and cooking equipment with their tentmates in the unit. This is the first instance noted of the field music being consolidated into one unit for other than musical purposes.

The band returned in time for the announcement of the cessation of hostilities on 19 April, and finally the day arrived for which the men had been waiting so patiently: ''Regimental Orders, 9th June 83. . . . The Men engaged during the war are to parade tomorrow morning 10 o'Clock before Col[onel's] Quarters—prepared to march to their respective homes—. . . . The Non Commissioned Staff and Band are to [be] furnished with Musketts and Accoutrements from the 3 years men.''[24]

Colonel Thomas Proctor, who had commanded the 4th Regiment of Artillery since its entry into Continental service, resigned his commission in April 1781 and returned to private life in Philadelphia. Major Andrew Porter assumed command of the regiment in October of that year and served until the reorganization of the artillery on 17 June 1783.

March 1782 found the regiment scattered, with the headquarters serving at Lancaster and Carlisle, Pennsylvania, and the remainder apportioned to Fort Pitt and the southern army. The regimental drum and fife majors were serving with the headquarters, as were seven drummers and fifers and four musicians. While not as large as the band had been in previous years under Proctor's command, they nevertheless functioned musically. A memorandum book, probably kept by the commissary general of military stores, has a notation for that same month of the prices of a bassoon, clarinets, concert french horns, and trumpets, all "wanted for the use of Major Porter's Regt Artilly."[25]

On 1 January 1783 the 4th Artillery was reduced to a battalion of four companies, but retained the regimental band. Shortly after, a Corps of Artillery was formed of the remaining companies, and the members of the regimental band were permitted to return to their homes.[26]

The band of music that Colonel Christian Febiger had begun in 1779 was still performing well in 1782 when he wrote to Washington to justify his actions and to petition for the reimbursement of expenses which he had paid from his own funds. The letter reviewed the history of the band and asked for the annual bounty uniform for his nine musicians. Febiger and his band must have been under some criticism, for the letter went to some length to justify its continuance:

The Detachment [of Virginia troops ordered to proceed to the southern campaign] was order'd to march on Wednesday, but, for want of Waggons, it was detained till Thursday the 14th. The men [were] very uneasy about Pay and other necessarys, [and], when ordered to [by?] Colo Posey to strike their tents, refused, saying they could not march without money. I was on the Spott; with a little Threatening, some Persuasion, and an excellent Band of Music to play them off, all was quieted; and, from Colo Poseys Letters to me, as per Letter A, they march on cheerfully. . . .

[After reviewing the history of the formation of the band in 1779, Febiger continued] I drew the recruiting money—exclusive of which I have incurr'd a very considerable private Expence in finishing [furnishing?] their Instruction and purchasing new Instruments, which, however, reverts to the Right on the Death of [or?] Discharge of either of the men—on the 7th of March 1780. I Sollicited the Board of War on the Subject; they would not grant me a Warrant for the Expence incurred, under the name of a *Band*, as every regt might claim the same though they would not take the same Pains.

The men are enlisted to serve as Musicians & Fifers & to do duty as such. Their Music had more Influence on the minds and Motions of the Militia last Summer in this State than would the Oratory of a Cicero; and, in the recruiting Business, they are at least as usefull as a well spoken recruiting Serjt.

All I wish is, that the usual Bounty, given at the Time I engaged them, may be allow'd me (as I actually made Use of that Sum) in the Settlement of My Publick Accounts. Any extra Expence incurr'd I must pay myself.

I engaged a Master and eight. One is dead, & one, from a hurt he receiv'd, is invalided. I have put Soldiers Fifers in their places, and still continue my Number. Seven are equal to any Band in this country; the other two improving. My Reasons for being prolix on this Subject is that I may not be thought to have made improper Use of Publick Money.

Febiger attached to this letter the one he had received from Lieutenant Colonel Thomas Posey of the 7th Virginia which stated, "Your Band has been of infinite Service. I don't know that I have ever seen men more delighted with it, than on the march. I esteem Sheldon [the fife major and master musician] much."[27]

In a brief autobiographical sketch written after the war, Colonel Philip Van Cortlandt noted, "All my regiment having joined at and near Schenectady, I marched and encamped on the Patroons Flats. I had then the largest and most healthy regiment in America, not excepting French, English, or Germans, and a fine band of music." Van Cortlandt assumed command of the regiment in November 1776. Because the regiment lacked the bare essentials of weapons, clothing, and equipment, it is doubtful that the band existed at that time. An inspection of the regiment in 1780 showed that there were nine drummers and fifers, a drum major, and only 114 enlisted men present for duty. The inspector added the comment that "the Music [is] equal to that of any Regt in the [New York] Brigade." The inspector may have been referring to a band of music or to the field music. Except for the comment of the French officer Verger, quoted previously, no indication has been located for the existence of a band in any other New York regiment. A bill for musical instruments given to the governor of New York in 1783 by the paymaster of this regiment, however, proves that the band at that time, besides the drums and fife, had two french horns, two bassoons, and four clarinets. This does not limit the band's existence to that year, for Van Cortlandt noted in his autobiography that in June 1783, "it was resolved by the officers of the New York brigade to present Governor George Clinton with the stand of colors and instruments of music belonging to the Brigade." In the first instance Van Cortlandt wrote of his band, and yet in the second the instruments belonged to the brigade rather than to the regiment. It is possible, therefore, that the paymaster's bill was to reimburse the officers, or Van Cortlandt himself, if the instruments were to be used by the musicians functioning as a brigade rather than a regimental band.[28]

THE ARMY DISBANDS

On 19 April 1783 the men were informed that the war had been concluded. Heath recounted the event in his memoirs: "19th.—At noon, the Proclamation of Congress for a cessation of hostilities was published at the door of the New Building [at Newburgh, New York], followed by three huzzas; after which a prayer was made by the Rev. Mr. Gano, and an anthem (*Independence*, from Billings) was performed by vocal and instrumental music." Preparations may have been made as early as two weeks prior, for at that time the general orders had required all off-duty drummers and fifers in the cantonment to report to Hiwell's tent "for inspection and further instruction." Heath does not mention a band specifically, and it is possible that the anthem was performed with combined bands, drummers, and fifers, or any combination of the musical resources of the army.[29]

Naturally, with the end of the war, the men wished to leave army life and return to their homes. Congress was fearful, however, since this was only a preliminary treaty. Full ratification would not come until the settlement between Britain and the American allies, France and Spain. On 1 May, Washington published the congressional resolve in the general orders for the day: "Resolved, that in the opinion of Congress, the time of the men engaged to serve during the war, does not expire until the ratification of the definitive treaty of peace. That such of the non-commissioned officers and private soldiers of the above description, as continue in service to that period, shall be allowed their fire arms and accoutrements, as an extra reward for their long and faithful services."[30] The resolution was broadened so that all soldiers who were being discharged and who had served their full period of enlistment honorably were permitted to retain their arms. The resolution was not specific in regard to the company musicians, the fifers and drummers. The secretary at war wrote to Washington to obtain clarification: "The commanding officers are applying for arms for the Musick—The donation of arms to the troops was in consequence of your Excellency's recommendation. Should you be of opinion, all circumstances considered, they have a right to arms, I think no difficulty will arise in Congress from the measure." The Continental generals must have advised that the musicians should be allowed to retain only their fifes or drums, for on the same date as the above letter a dozen regimental commanders petitioned Washington in this regard:

We have been informed, that the General officers are of opinion that Drummers and Fifers instead of having arms should be allowed to retain their Drums and Fifes.—As the arms, are by Congress bestowed on the Soldiers as a Gratuity for their services, and the Drums and Fifes, be as but a small proportion to them, in value, we are constrained (tho' reluctantly) to address Your Excellency, on the subject; and to request that you will be pleased to order arms to be furnished them.

It is extremely painful to us, to be under the disagreeable necessity of troubling Your Excellency on so trivial a matter; but, a regard to justice, and an attention to the feelings of those we have long had the Honor to Commmand will we hope apologize to you for our Conduct.

Washington did not think it "so trivial a matter" and replied immediately:

Having before this Time given my opinion that it was not the Intention of Congress by their Resolution of 23d Apl. that the Music should have Arms delivered to them at being discharged; but that they should take with them their Drums and fifes; and this Determination having been carried into Effect by the Regiments which are gone. It is now too late to make any alteration. But was not this the case, reasons may be adduced which would operate against the Request made in your joint letter of the 7th Instant; the Music hav[in]g had but an easy share of Duty compared with the other Soldiers, an additional Pay, with their Music found by the Public, It is supposed that their Circumstances will fully Ballance the Gratuity intended by Congress.

The matter seems to have been settled at that point, for no further correspondence has been located. The men of Crane's band were given arms at the time of their discharge, but this was because they were carried as soldiers and noncommissioned officers, not as company musicians.[31]

Not until September 1783 was the definitive treaty acknowledging the independence of the United States of America formally signed. At the end of that month the British evacuated New York, and Washington entered in a triumphant procession. The newspaper accounts did not mention any musical group in the parade; it is possible that the army's bands had all been discharged by that time. General Knox commanded the troops preparing the way for Washington's entry, and were a band available he certainly would have had them present for the parade. On the other hand, possibly the reporters did not consider it newsworthy to mention a band, since one normally would have expected to find such in this type of ceremonial procession.

Shortly afterward, Washington bade farewell to his officers at Fraunces Tavern in New York, tendered his resignation to Congress, and returned to Mount Vernon in the hope of resuming his private life after so many hard years of struggle.

Congress had voted the officers five years' full pay in recompense for their services, and the inspector of music drew certificates amounting to over thirty-three hundred dollars including back pay. At the same time, Hiwell joined the Society of the Cincinnati that had been formed the previous May and paid his dues of one month's salary, or thirty-three and one-third dollars. With the remaining money he moved to Providence, where he opened "a school of instrumental music [where he taught] the German flute, clarinet, basson, French horn, etc.," and advertised "a Concert of Instrumental Music (consisting of Clarinetts, Flutes, French-Horns, Bassoons, etc.)" to be given at the State House.[32]

After Washington's resignation, the senior officer in the Continental army was Major General Henry Knox. In January 1784 he commanded but seven hundred rank and file. Remembering the threats of mutiny and rebellion in the dissatisfied army near the close of the war, Congress decided that standing armies in time of peace were "inconsistent with the principles of republican Governments, dangerous to the liberties of a free people," and might be "converted into destructive engines for establishing despotism." Consequently, on 2 June 1784, Knox was directed to discharge all except fifty-five men at West Point and twenty-five at Fort Pitt needed to guard the nation's remaining military stores. With a proper complement of officers to command these men, this was for a short time the full extent of the nation's armed forces, and the Continental army passed into history.[33]

APPENDIXES

APPENDIX A

Bands of Music in British Regiments of Foot, 1755–1783

Regiment of Foot	Service in America[1]	Documentation[2]
1	1758–64	1767: "This regiment hath fifers and a band of Music"
		1777: "8 private soldiers acting as musicians"[3]
2		
3	1781–82	1749: Band concert at Lewes, England[4]
		1754: "The Regiment has a band of music"[5]
		1774: "nine musicians, all enlisted men"
		1784: "Band of Music uncommonly good"
4	1774–80	1768: "Band of Music good"
		1774: "six musicians"
		1774: Funeral procession in Boston
5	1775–80	1770: "fourteen men as musicians"
6	1775–78	1771: "no band of music"
		1784: "very good band"
7	1774–76	1769: "Music but indifferent"
	1781–82	1772: "Band of Music"
8	1769–82	1768: "had no music"
		1787: "a full band"
9	1766–69	1772: "Band of Music"
	1777–82	1777: Surrendered with Burgoyne
10	1768–78	1770: Drum major's and 8 musicians' coats made
		1784: "Very good band"
11		1774: "8 musicians"
12		1783: Victory parade, Gibraltar
13		1767: Concert horns, clarinets, bassoon reeds purchased
		1777: "12 music"
14	1768–77	

APPENDIX A *(continued)*

Regiment of Foot	Service in America[1]	Documentation[2]
15	1758–67 1776–82	1772: "Band of Music" 1773: "Band of Music good & genteely dressed" 1774: Clarinets purchased 1785: "This Regiment have a good band of Musick"
16	1768–82	
17	1758–67 1776–82	1762: Regimental march includes clarinet 1772: "Band of music good & handsomely dressed" 1779: Instruments captured at Stony Point 1781: Surrendered with Cornwallis
18	1767–75	1767: "An excellent band of music" 1767: Performed at Philadelphia 1773: Performed at Philadelphia 1777: "7 music"
19	1781–82	1774: "Band of Music newly formed"
20	1777–82	1769: "Band of Music" 1769: 10 suits of musicians' clothing made 1774: "8 musicians" 1777: Surrendered with Burgoyne
21	1766–73 1777–82	1771: Music Master Roth's concert in Philadelphia 1777: Surrendered with Burgoyne
22	1758–65 1776–82	1767: Brass cymbals purchased 1768: "Band of Music" 1770: Nine suits of clothing made 1773: "making clothes for a Band of Music"
23	1773–82	1768: "Band of Music very fine" 1773: Music performed in theater in New York 1781: Surrendered with Cornwallis
24	1777–81	1777: Had cymbals[6] 1777: Surrendered with Burgoyne 1785: "Very good band"
25		1768: "have a bag-piper in the Band of Music" 1777: "the Drum Major plays on the cymbal; 15 music"
26	1768–81	1781: Returned home after over 13 years' service in America

APPENDIX A *(continued)*

Regiment of Foot	Service in America[1]	Documentation[2]
		1785: "no band" (possibly implying that there had been one previously)
27	1758–67 1776–82	1769: "Band of Music" 1775: "8 music" 1788: Regimental band in funeral procession, Dublin[7]
28	1758–67 1776–82	1775: "8 music" 1784: "a good Band of Music"?
29	1766–73 1777–82	1769: Concert for fife major, Boston 1771: Concert in New York 1774: "only 2 musicians enlisted as soldiers" 1777: Surrendered with Burgoyne 1785: Band performing at Fort Niagara
30	1781–82	
31	1766–73 1776–82	1777: Surrendered with Burgoyne
32		
33	1776–82	1769: "Band of Music" 1774: "9 musicians" 1781: Surrendered with Cornwallis
34	1764–69	1770: Musical instruments purchased 1771: "have a Band of Music" 1777: Surrendered with Burgoyne
35	1758–64 1775–82	1766: Band played for the 12th Foot 1768: "Has a Band of Music"
36		1770: French horns and bassoons purchased 1772: "Allowance to the Band of Music"
37	1776–82	1772: "Band of Music"
38	1775–82	1768: "Hath a Band of Music" 1771: "Have a good band of Music"[8] 1787: "Good Band; have tambourines and cymbals"
39		
40	1758–65 1775–82	1771: "Band of Music"

APPENDIX A *(continued)*

Regiment of Foot	Service in America[1]	Documentation[2]
41	(Invalids Regiment)	
42	1758–67 1776–82	1760: "1 piper to the Grenadier Co." 1773: "2 Pipers and a very good Band of Music" 1775: "10 Music"
43	1758–63 1775–82	1768: "Band of Music" 1773: Trumpet for light infantry company 1781: Surrendered with Cornwallis
44	1758–65 1776–82	1772: "Band of Music"
45	1758–65 1776–78	1781: "No Band" 1784: "Band"
46	1758–67 1776–82	1769: "Band of Music"
47	1758–63 1774–82	1767: "Fifers and a Band of Music" 1777: Surrendered with Burgoyne
48	1758–63	
49	1775–81	1769: "Band of Music"
50		1777: "10 music in all, but one was a sergeant and five drums"
51		
52	1766–78	
53	1777–82	1777: Surrendered with Burgoyne
54	1776–82	1773: "5 Fifers are more than the King's Regulations"
55	1758–63 1776–82	1768: "Band of Music"
56		1783: Victory parade, Gibraltar
57	1776–82	1768: Musical instruments purchased 1771: "Band of Music"
58	1758–63	1767: "Fifers and a Band of Music" 1777: Clarinet purchased 1783: Victory parade, Gibraltar
59	1766–75	1768: Masonic parade, Boston

APPENDIX A *(continued)*

Regiment of Foot	Service in America[1]	Documentation[2]
60	1756–72	1767: Concert in New York
61		
62	1756–57 1777–82	1777: Surrendered with Burgoyne 1778: Anburey's comment re band deserting
63	1776–82	1773: "Good Band of Music"
64	1768–82	1768: Masonic parade, Boston 1771 –75: Concerts in Boston
65	1769–78	1784: "Band of Music"
66		
67		1772: "Band of Music" 1784: "Very good band"
68		
69	1768–69 1782	
70	1779–82	1777: "An handsome Band of Music genteely dressed"
71	1777–82	1775: Regiment raised 1781: Surrendered with Cornwallis
72		1778: Regiment raised 1783: Regiment disbanded
73		1778: Regiment raised 1783: Regiment disbanded
74	1779–82	1778: Regiment raised 1783: Regiment disbanded
75		1778: Regiment raised 1783: Regiment disbanded
76	1779–82	1778: Regiment raised 1781: Surrendered with Cornwallis 1783: Regiment disbanded
77	1758–63	1764: Regiment disbanded 1778: Regiment raised 1783: Regiment disbanded

APPENDIX A *(continued)*

Regiment of Foot	Service in America[1]	Documentation[2]
78	1758–63	1778: Regiment raised 1783: Regiment disbanded
79		1778: Regiment raised 1783: Regiment disbanded
80	1758–63 1779–82	1764: Regiment disbanded 1778: Regiment raised 1781: Surrendered with Cornwallis 1783: Regiment disbanded
81		1778: Regiment raised 1783: Regiment disbanded
82	1779–82	1778: Regiment raised 1783: Regiment disbanded
83		1778: Regiment raised 1783: Regiment disbanded
84	1779–82	1779: Regiment raised 1783: Regiment disbanded

APPENDIX B

Chronological Listing of Fife Tutors

ca. 1756   *The Compleat Tutor for the Fife* . . . London: Rutherford, 21 pp. (Thomas E. Warner, *An Annotated Bibliography of Woodwind Instruction Books, 1600–1830*, no. 91).

ca. 1760   *The Compleat Tutor for the Fife* . . . London: Thompson & Son, 24 pp. (Warner, *Bibliography*, no. 94).

ca. 1767   *The Compleat Tutor for the Fife* . . . London: Thos. Bennett, 24 pp. (Warner, *Bibliography*, no. 112a).

ca. 1770   *Compleat Instructions for the Fife* . . . London: Longman Lukey & Co., 36 pp. (Warner, *Bibliography*, no. 116).

ca. 1770   *The Compleat Tutor for the Fife* . . . London: C. & S. Thompson, 34 pp. (Warner, *Bibliography*, no. 117).

APPENDIX B *(continued)*

ca. 1776   *A Compleate Tutor for the Fife*. Philadelphia: Michael Hillegas. (Warner, *Bibliography*, no. 131), unlocated.

ca. 1780   *Compleat Instructions for the Fife* . . . London: T. Skillern, 36 pp. (Warner, *Bibliography*, no. 136).

ca. 1780   *Entire New & Compleat Instructions for the Fife* . . . London: Longman and Broderip, 36 pp. (Warner, *Bibliography*, no. 140).

ca. 1790   *New and Complete Instructions for the Fife* . . . London: G. Goulding, 32 pp. (Warner, *Bibliography*, no. 168).

ca. 1796   *Entire New and Compleat Instructions for the Fife* . . . London: John Preston, 32 pp. (Warner, *Bibliography*, no. 185).

1803   Hulbert, James, Jr. *A Variety of Marches* . . . Northampton: James Hulbert, Jun., 12 pp. (Warner, *Bibliography*, no. 269; Richard J. Wolfe, *Secular Music in America, 1801–1825*, no. 4390).

ca. 1805   *The Compleat Tutor for the Fife* . . . Philadelphia: George Willig, 30 pp. (Warner, *Bibliography*, no. 273; Wolfe, *Secular Music*, no. 9425).

1805   *The Fifer's Companion* . . . Salem: Joshua Cushing, 76 pp. (Warner, *Bibliography*, no. 275; Wolfe, *Secular Music*, no. 2790).

ca. 1807   Hulbert, James, Jr. *The Complete Fifer's Museum* . . . Northampton: Simeon Butler, 24 pp. (Warner, *Bibliography*, no. 290; Wolfe, *Secular Music*, no. 4387).

ca. 1808   *Complete Instructions for the Fife* . . . London: H. Andrews, 32 pp. (Warner, *Bibliography*, no. 293).

1808   *The Village Fifer*. Exeter: Norris & Sawyer, 72 pp. (Warner, *Bibliography*, no. 295; Wolfe, *Secular Music*, no. 9491).

1810   Hazeltine, Daniel. *Instructor in Martial Music* . . . Exeter: C. Norris and Co., 48 pp. (Wolfe, *Secular Music*, no. 3575).

1812   Narramore, William W., and Jewitt, A. *The Fifer's Assistant*. (Warner, *Bibliography*, no. 328; Wolfe, *Secular Music*, no. 6456), unlocated.

1812   Robbins, Charles. *The Drum and Fife Instructor*. Exeter: C. Norris and Co., 64 pp. (Wolfe, *Secular Music*, no. 7506).

1812   Ashworth, Charles S. [See drum manuals]

ca. 1815   *Entire New and Compleat Instructions for the Fife* . . . London: Muzio Clementi & Co., 36 pp. (Warner, *Bibliography*, no. 336).

ca. 1815   *A New and Complete Preceptor for the Fife* . . . Albany: Daniel

Steele, 26 pp. (Warner, *Bibliography*, no. 338; Wolfe, *Secular Music*, no. 7211).

ca. 1815   Potter, Samuel. *The Art of Playing the Fife* . . . London: Samuel Potter, 23 pp. (Warner, *Bibliography*, no. 344).

1815   *The Martial Musician's Companion* . . . [District of] Maine: Rufus Porter. (Wolfe, *Secular Music*, no. 7201), unlocated.

1817   Rumrille, J. L., and Holton, H. [See drum manuals]

1818   Robinson, Alvan, Jr. *Massachusetts Collection of Martial Musick*. Hallowell: E. Goodale, 56 pp. (Warner, *Bibliography*, no. 360; Wolfe, *Secular Music*, no. 7520).

1819   *A New and Complete Preceptor for the Fiff* [sic] . . . Utica: William Williams, 48 pp. (Warner, *Bibliography*, no. 363; Wolfe, *Secular Music*, no. 7212).

1820   Robinson, Alvan, Jr., *Massachusetts Collection of Martial Musick*. 2d ed. Exeter: Robinson, 72 pp. (Warner, *Bibliography*, no. 360; Wolfe, *Secular Music*, no. 7521).

ca. 1820   Blake, G. E. *Fife Instructor*. (Warner, *Bibliography*, no. 368), unlocated.

1826   Robinson, Alvan, Jr. *Massachusetts Collection of Martial Musick*. 3d ed. Hallowell: E. Goodale, 72 pp. (Warner, *Bibliography*, no. 360).

ca. 1830   *Fife Instructer* [sic] . . . Hallowell: Glazier, Masters & Smith, 36 pp. (Warner, *Bibliography*, no. 435).

1861   Keach, Burdill, and Cassidy, *The Army Drum and Fife Book*. Boston: Oliver Ditson and Co., 64 pp.

1870   Strube, Gardiner A. *Strube's Drum & Fife Instructor*. New York: D. Appleton & Co., 61 pp.

ca. 1905   *Drum-Major's Manual*. London: Henry Potter & Co., 65 pp.

APPENDIX C
Chronological Listing of Drum Manuals

ca. 1760   *The Drummer's Instructor* . . . London: R. Spencer. Unlocated.

1777   Winters, George L. *Kurze Anweisung das Trommel-Spielen* . . . Berlin: George Ludwig Winters Wittwe, 19 pp. Library of Congress.

ca. 1785   *The Young Drummer's Assistant.* London: Longman & Broderip. Unlocated.

1810   Hazeltine, Daniel. [See fife tutors]

1811   Mann, Herman. *The Drummer's Assistant* . . . Dedham: H. Mann & Co. (Richard J. Wolfe, *Secular Music in America, 1801–1825*, no. 5537), unlocated.

1812   Ashworth, Charles S. *A New, Useful and Complete System of Drum-Beating* . . . Washington, D.C.: n.p., 40 pp. (Wolfe, *Secular Music*, no. 310).

1812   Robbins, Charles. [See fife tutors]

1815   Porter, Rufus. [See fife tutors]

1815   Potter, Samuel. *The Art of Beating the Drum* . . . London: Samuel Potter, 28 pp. The British Library.

1815   *The Young Drummer's Assistant* . . . New York: Nathan Weston, Jun. (Wolfe, *Secular Music*, no. 9757), unlocated.

1817   Rumrille, J. L., and Holton, H. *The Drummer's Instructor; or Martial Musician*. Albany: Packard & Van Benthuysen, 40 pp. (Wolfe, *Secular Music*, no. 7694).

1818   Robinson, Alvan, Jr. [See fife tutors]

ca. 1819   Lovering, Levi. *The Drummer's Assistant* . . . Philadelphia: Bacon & Co., 24 pp. (Wolfe, *Secular Music*, no. 5466).

ca. 1830   Glazier, Masters & Smith. [See fife tutors]

1861   Keach, Burdill, and Cassidy. [See fife tutors]

1870   Strube, Gardiner A. [See fife tutors]

ca. 1905   *Drum-Major's Manual.* London: Henry Potter & Co., 65 pp.

APPENDIX D

Sources for Musical Examples

Concordance of page number references used in developing the musical examples contained in chapter 4.

Example	Rutherford (ca. 1756)	Thompson (ca. 1760)	Bennett (ca. 1767)	Preston (ca. 1796)	Willig (ca. 1805)	Hazeltine (1810)	Robbins (1812)	Ashworth (1812)	Potter (1815)	Rumrille & Holton (1817)
2 The General	12	7	10	8	10	—	58	10/32	21	18/35
3 The March	—	—	—	—	—	7	10	23	—	13
4 The Reveille	12	7	10	7	10	—	58	12/28	26	26/39
5 The Troop or Assembling	9	7	10	8	10	—	59	6-7	19	20
6 The Retreat	17	11	—	11	—	—	62	7	20	25
7 The Tattoo	18	12	9	11	9	—	—	8	20	19
8 To Arms	13	7	10	8	10	—	61	9/31	21	25/39
9 The Parley, or Church Call	—	—	—	—	—	—	—	22/34	25	17/34
10 Roast Beef	—	—	—	—	—	—	—	11/33	24	17/34
11 The Drummers Call	8	14	11	13	11	8/23	58	6/30	18	16/34
12 The Pioneers March	10	24	21	—	23	10/25	59	10/32	21	19/35
13 The Three Cheers	—	—	—	—	—	11/25	—	6	—	16
14 The Grenadiers March	11	10	23	10	25	—	—	20/34	23	24/37
15 The Rogues March	10	14	—	13	—	10/32	24	11/33	22	25/39
16 Roslin Castle	—	—	—	—	22	26	34	—	—	—

APPENDIX E

Some Published Collections Suitable for Military Bands

1695   *The Sprightly Companion: Being a Collection of the Best Foreign Marches, Now Play'd in all Camps.* London: Henry Playford, 16 pp. (Thomas E. Warner, *An Annotated Bibliography of Woodwind Instruction Books, 1600–1830*, no. 21; Edith B. Schnapper, *The British Union-Catalogue of Early Music*, 2:969, hereafter cited as BUCEM).

1697   *Military Musick; Or the Art of Playing on the Haut-Bois . . .* London: Thomas Crosse. (Warner, *Bibliography*, no. 23), unlocated.

APPENDIX E *(continued)*

1733   *Musica Bellicosa; Or, Warlike Music*. London: I. Walsh, 2 vols. (BUCEM 2:718).

1758   *Forty Airs for Two Violins German Flutes or Guittars. Consisting of Tattoo's Night Pieces & Marches as They Are Perform'd in the Hessian and Prussian Armies*. London: J. Oswald, 20 pp. (BUCEM 1:13).

1758   *Warlike Musick*. London: I. Walsh, 4 vols. (BUCEM 2:718).

1759   *Fifty-five Marches for the Militia*. London. J. Oswald, 28 pp. (BUCEM 2:748).

ca. 1759   *Thirty Favourite Marches which Are Now in Vogue*. London: C. & A. Thompson, 10 pp. (BUCEM 2:648).

1761   *A Collection of Airs and Marches for Two Violins or German Flutes, Some of Which Have Basses*. London: R. Bremner, 96 pp. (BUCEM 1:13).

ca. 1770   *XXIV Favourite Marches in Five Parts, as They Are Perform'd by His Majesty's Foot and Horse Guards*. London: C. & S. Thompson. [parts] (BUCEM 2:648).

ca. 1770   *A Collection of Quick Marches as Performed by the Guards Light Horse*. London: C. & S. Thompson, 16 pp. (BUCEM 1:483).

1771   *A Second Collection of XXIV Favourite Marches in 7 Parts as They Are Perform'd by His Majesty's Foot and Horse Guards*. London: C. & S. Thompson. [parts] (BUCEM 2:648).

ca. 1772   *A Second Collection of Quick Marches with Basses . . . collected by Capn Robt Hinde*. London: C. & S. Thompson, 20 pp. (BUCEM 1:483).

ca. 1775   *A Third Collection of Twenty-four Quick Marches with Basses . . . collected by Capn R. Hinde*. London: Longman Lukey & Co., 13 pp. (BUCEM 1:483).

ca. 1775   Valentine, John. *A Collection of Marches in Four Parts*. London: C. & S. Thompson. [parts] (BUCEM 2:1031).

ca. 1777   *A Second Collection of Airs and Marches for Two Violins, German Flutes and [or] Hautboys, all of Which Have Basses for the Violoncello or Harpsichord*. Edinburgh: N. Stewart, 96 pp. (BUCEM 1:13).

1778   [Reed, John.] *A Set of Marches*. London: R. Bremner, 33 pp. (BUCEM 2:870).

ca. 1780   *An Evening's Amusement being Twelve Favorite Minuets Six*

APPENDIX E *(continued)*

Duetts Six New Marches and Seven Solo-minuets with an Accompanyment. London: Longman and Broderip, 40 pp. (BUCEM 2:585).

ca. 1780 *Six Military Divertimentos for Two Clarinetts, Two Horns and a Bassoon. Composed by Rathgen and other Eminent Authors Residing in England*. London: J. Betz. [parts] (BUCEM 2:874).

ca. 1781 [Reed, John.] *A Sett of Minuets and Marches*. London: R. Bremner, 30 pp. (BUCEM 2:870).

ca. 1785 *Military Amusement, Being a Collection of Favourite Marches . . . Adapted for Two German Flutes*. London: T. Skillern, 96 pp. (BUCEM 2:675).

ca. 1785 Raimondi, Ignazio. *Six Grand Marches for a Military Band*. London: Ignazio Raimondi, 25 pp. (BUCEM 2:871).

1796 *Military Amusement*. Philadelphia: B. Carr's Musical Repository, 24 pp. (Charles Evans, *American Bibliography*, no. 30795).

1800 Holyoke, Samuel. *The Instrumental Assistant*. Vol. 1. Exeter, N.H.: H. Ranlet. (Warner, *Bibliography*, no. 234; Evans, *Bibliography*, no. 37643).

1803 Hulbert, James, Jr. *A Variety of Marches, Consisting of Common Times, Quick Steps, Double Drags, and Trio's*. Northampton: James Hulbert, Jr., 12 pp. (Warner, *Bibliography*, no. 269; Richard J. Wolfe, *Secular Music in America, 1801–1825*, no. 4390).

1807 Holyoke, Samuel. *The Instrumental Assistant*. Vol. 2. Exeter, N.H.: Ranlet and Norris, 102 pp. (Warner, *Bibliography*, no. 289; Wolfe, *Secular Music*, no. 3935).

1807 Olmstead, Timothy. *Martial Music*. Albany: Daniel Steele, 44 pp. (Wolfe, *Secular Music*, no. 6660).

1807 Shaw, Oliver. *For the Gentlemen*. Dedham, Mass.: H. Mann, 52 pp. (Warner, *Bibliography*, no. 291; Wolfe, *Secular Music*, no. 7940).

ca. 1816 Taylor, Raynor, arr. *The Martial Music of Camp Dupont*. Philadelphia: G. E. Blake, 24 pp. (Wolfe, *Secular Music*, no. 9266).

1819 Goodale, Ezekiel. *The Instrumental Director*. 1st ed., unlocated.

1829 Goodale, Ezekiel. *The Instrumental Director*. 3d ed. Hallowell: Glazier, Masters & Co., 104 pp. (Wolfe, *Secular Music*, no. 3168).

NOTES

PREFACE
    1. Richard F. Goldman, *The Wind Band* (Boston: Allyn & Bacon, 1961), p. 7.
    2. Victor Herbert, as quoted in ibid., p. 66.
    3. Oscar G. Sonneck, *Early Concert-Life in America*, p. 151.

CHAPTER I
    1. Leo Tolstoy, *War and Peace*, trans. Constance Garnett, as quoted in Samuel A. Stouffer et al., *The American Soldier* (Princeton: Princeton University Press, 1949), p. 3.
    2. Alfred Vagts, *History of Militarism* (New York: W. W. Norton, 1937), p. 79.
    3. Bell I. Wiley, *The Common Soldier in the Civil War* (New York: Grosset and Dunlap, 1951), p. 157.
    4. Henry G. Farmer, *Military Music*, p. 52.
    5. Jacob A. Kappey, "Wind-Band," *Grove's Dictionary of Music and Musicians*, 1st ed., 4:467.
    6. Department of the Army, "Army Band," *Table of Organization and Equipment No. 12–107G* (Washington, D.C.: Government Printing Office, 1968), p. 2.
    7. Farmer, *Military Music*, pp. 15–16.
    8. Henry G. Farmer, "16th–17th Century Military Marches," *Journal of the Society for Army Historical Research* 28 (1959): 49.
    9. Henry G. Farmer, "March," *Grove's Dictionary of Music and Musicians*, 5th ed., 5:564–65.
    10. William Windham, *A Plan of Discipline Composed for the Use of the Militia of the County of Norfolk*, p. 23; Great Britain, *General Regulations and Orders for His Majesty's Forces*, p. 5; Great Britain, *Rules and Regulations for the Formation, Field Exercise, and Movements of His Majesty's Forces*, pp. 7, 16–17.
    11. France, *Instruction que le roi a fait expédier pour régler provisoirment l'exercice de ses troupes d'infanterie*, pp. 20, 22; Georg Kandler, *Deutsche Armeemärsche* (Bad Godesberg: Hohwacht-Verlag, 1962), p. 13; Georg Pausch, *Journal of Captain Pausch, Chief of the Hanau Artillery during the Burgoyne Campaign* (Albany: Joel Munsell's Sons, 1886), pp. 106–7.
    12. Great Britain, *Rules and Regulations*, p. 17.
    13. Bennett Cuthbertson, *A System for the Complete Interior Management and Oeconomy of a Battalion of Infantry* (Dublin: Boultier Grierson, 1768), pp. 14–16.
    14. J. H. Leslie, "The Colours of the British Marching Regiments of Foot in 1751," *Journal of the Society for Army Historical Research* 7 (1928): 2; Sir John W. Fortescue, *A History of the British Army*, 2:268; R. Money Barnes, *A History of the Regiments & Uniforms of the British Army* (London: Seeley Service & Co., 1962), p. 318.
    15. Charles James, *A New and Enlarged Military Dictionary* (London: T. Egerton, 1802), s.v. "Musicians."
    16. Kenneth S. Rutherford, "Drum," *Grove's Dictionary of Music and Musicians*, 5th ed., 2:774; Charles R. Day, *A Descriptive Catalogue of the Musical Instruments Recently Exhibited at the Royal Military Exhibition* (London: Eyre & Spottiswoode, 1891), p. 231; Jehan Tabourot [Thoinot Arbeau], *Orchésographie*, ed. Mary Stewart Evans (1948; reprint ed., New York: Dover Publications, 1967), pp. 18–19; Marie Bobillier [Michel Brenet], *La Musique militaire* (Paris: Henri Laurens, 1917), p. 70.
    17. Charles Ffoulkes, "Notes on Early Military Bands," *Journal of the Society for Army Historical Research* 17 (1938): 195; H. Malibran, *Guide à l'usage des artistes et des costumiers contennant la description des uniformes de l'armée française de 1780 à 1848*, p. 172.
    18. Day, *Catalogue*, pp. 231–32; Nicholas Bessaraboff, *Ancient European Musical Instruments* (Cambridge: Harvard University Press, 1941), p. 32.
    19. Henry G. Farmer, *Memoirs of the Royal Artillery Band*, p. 27n.
    20. Francis Grose, *Military Antiquities*, 1:315.

21. Charles James, *The Regimental Companion* (London: T. Egerton, 1811), p. 262; Francis Grose, *Advice to the Officers of the British Army* (1783; reprint ed., New York: Agathynian Club, 1867), p. 121.

22. James Wolfe, *General Wolfe's Instructions to Young Officers* (London: J. Millan, 1768), p. 48; Thomas Simes, *Military Guide for Young Officers*, 1:239.

23. Henry G. Farmer, "Drum-Major," *Grove's Dictionary of Music and Musicians*, 5th ed., 2:776–77.

24. Thomas Simes, *A Military Course for the Government and Conduct of a Battalion*, p.221; similar instructions or outlines of duties are also contained in Prussia, *Regulations for the Prussian Infantry*, p. 419, James Turner, *Pallas Armata* (London: Richard Chiswell, 1683), p. 224, and Etienne Binet, *Essay de merveilles de nature et des plus nobles artifices* (Paris: Jacq. Dugast, 1646), p. 138.

25. Thomas Simes, *The Military Medley* (London: n.p., 1768), p. 30; James, *Regimental Companion*, p. 255; Jacques François de Chastenet, Marquis de Puysegur, *Art de la guerre* (Paris: n.p., 1749), vol. 1, pl. I, V, VI; A. E. Haswell Miller and N. P. Dawnay, *Military Drawings and Paintings in the Collection of Her Majesty the Queen* (London: Phaidon Press, 1966), pl. 128; Bobillier, *Musique militaire*, p. 59; Charles Ffoulkes and E. C. Hopkins, *Sword, Lance and Bayonet* (New York: Arco Publishing Co., 1966), p. 116.

26. Great Britain, *The Manual Exercise as Ordered by His Majesty in 1764*, p. 17; Prussia, *Regulations*, pp. 27, 95; Cuthbertson, *System*, p. 124; Percy Sumner, "Army Inspection Returns—1753 to 1804," *Journal of the Society for Army Historical Research* 4 (1925): 112; United States, *Regulations for the Order and Discipline of the Troops of the United States*, pl. I.

27. Cuthbertson, *System*, pp. 11–12; Henry G. Farmer, *History of the Royal Artillery Band*, p. 56n; Simes, *Medley*, p. 30.

28. Grose, *Antiquities*, 2:43; Cuthbertson, *System*, p. 12.

29. Henry G. Farmer, *The Rise and Development of Military Music*, p. 29; "Notes and Queries," *Journal of the Society for Army Historical Research* 1 (1922): 224; Binet, *Essay*, p. 148; Grose, *Antiquities*, 2:43.

30. Adam Carse, *Musical Wind Instruments* (New York: Da Capo Press, 1965), p. 82; William Shakespeare, *The Merchant of Venice*, 1596, act 2, sc. 5, line 30, and *Othello*, 1604, act 3, sc. 3, lines 348–50.

31. Tabourot [Arbeau] *Orchésographie*, p. 39; Henry G. Farmer, *Handel's Kettledrums and Other Papers on Military Music*, p. 12; the musical notation of the fife tunes is contained in Farmer's *Rise*, p. 32; William B. Squire, as rev. Henry G. Farmer, "Military Calls," *Grove's Dictionary of Music and Musicians*, 5th ed., 5:775; *Oxford Universal Dictionary*, s.v. "sounds."

32. Grose, *Antiquities*, 2:248; Farmer, *Handel's Kettledrums*, pp. 11–16; Cuthbertson, *System*, p. 15.

33. George Smith, *An Universal Military Dictionary* (London: J. Millan, 1779), p. 117; Prussia, *Regulations*, pp. 2–3; Henry G. Farmer, "Drums and Fifes," *Grove's Dictionary of Music and Musicians*, 5th ed., 2:781.

34. Henry R. Knight, *Historical Records of the Buffs* (London: Medici Society, 1905–51), 1:202–3; Harold C. Wylly, *History of the Manchester Regiment* (London: F. Groom, 1923), 1:47–48; Stephen Kemble, "Kemble Papers," *Collections of the New York Historical Society* 16 (1883): 258; "Raising of a Regiment in the War of American Independence," *Journal of the Society for Army Historical Research* 27 (1949): 107.

35. Turner, *Pallas Armata*, p. 219; R. H. Wallace, ed., "Regimental Routine and Army Administration in North America in 1759: Extracts from Company Order Books of the 42d Royal Highland Regiment," *Journal of the Society for Army Historical Research* 30 (1952): 11.

36. William A. Cocks, "Bagpipe," *Grove's Dictionary of Music and Musicians*, 5th ed., 1:345–46; Anthony Baines, *Woodwind Instruments and Their History* (New York: W. W. Norton & Co., 1957), pp. 214–17.

37. Baines, *Woodwind Instruments*, p. 215; Cocks, "Bagpipe," p. 352.

38. Carse, *Musical Wind Instruments*, p. 229.

39. Henry G. Farmer, "Crusading Martial Music," *Music & Letters* 30 (1949): 245.

40. Jean Froissart, *Chronicles*, 1:533, as quoted in Sir Sibbald D. Scott, *The British Army* (London: Cassell, Potter, and Galpin, 1868), 2:392.

41. Sumner, "Inspection Returns," 3:244; Charles M. Lefferts, *Uniforms of the American, British, French, and German Armies in the American Revolution*, p. 176.

42. Lyndesay G. Langwill, "The Waits," *Hinrichsen's Year Book* 7 (1952): 173–75; an abridged version appears in *Grove's Dictionary of Music and Musicians*, 5th ed., s.v. "Waits"; Adam Carse, *The Orchestra in the Eighteenth Century* (Cambridge: W. Heffer & Sons, 1940), pp. 33, 112–13; Peter Panov, *Militärmusik in Geschichte und Gegenwart* (Berlin: Karl Siegismund, 1938), pl. 174; *Metronome Magazine* 37 (1921) passim.

43. (Cited) Farmer, *History*, p. 30; similar ceremonies in France were described by Georges Kastner, *Manuel général de musique militaire à l'usage des armées françaises*, p. 163.

44. Fortescue, *History*, 2:592; *Morning Advertiser* (London), 29 March 1749, as cited in ibid.; Ffoulkes, *Sword*, p. 77.

45. Farmer, *History, p.* 25; Fortescue, *History*, 2:582, 2:589, 3:519, 3:520n; *Journal of the Society for Army Historical Research* 21 (1942): 154; Kemble, "Papers," 16:217–18.

46. The full text of the "Articles of Agreement" may be found in Farmer, *History*, pp. 9–10; ibid., p. 12.

47. (Cited) Cecil C. P. Lawson, *A History of the Uniforms of the British Army*, 3:126; Ffoulkes, *Sword*, p. 78; Prussia, *Regulations*, p. 412; Malibran, *Guide*, p. 185.

48. Farmer, *Handel's Kettledrums*, p. ix; Simes, *Medley*, pp. 255–56; (cited) Farmer, *History*, p. 34.

49. Fortescue, *History*, 1:14.

50. British Museum, Harleian MS, 4690, as quoted by Joseph Strutt, *Horda Angel-Cynnan* (London: T. Jones, 1774–76), 2:45, and Grose, *Antiquities*, 2:41.

51. Harold C. Hind, "Military Band," *Grove's Dictionary of Music and Musicians*, 5th ed., 5:766–67.

52. Farmer, *Military Music*, pp. 20–21; Farmer, *Rise*, pp. 46–48; many of these marches are preserved in the Philidor manuscripts in Paris, and several are to be found in Kastner, *Manuel*; brief examples are also to be found in Kappey, "Wind Band," Hind, "Military Band," and Farmer, *Rise*, pp. 46–47.

53. (Cited) Farmer, *Rise*, pp. 47–48; Hector Adkins, *Treatise on the Military Band* (London: Boosey & Co., 1931), p. 5; Eric Halfpenny, "The English Debut of the French Hautboy," *Monthly Musical Record* 79 (1949): 153.

54. (Cited) *Journal of the Society for Army Historical Research* 7 (1928): 259–60; Great Britain, *An Abridgement of the English Military Discipline*, pp. 7, 127, 183; Farmer, *Handel's Kettledrums*, p. 43.

55. Thomas E. Warner, "Indications of Performance Practice in Woodwind Instruction Books of the 17th & 18th Centuries" (Ph.D. diss., New York University, 1964), p. 268; Eric Halfpenny, "A 17th Century Tutor for Hautboy," *Music & Letters* 30 (1949): 355–63.

56. *Journal of the Society for Army Historical Research* 29 (1951): 135; Hind, "Military Band," p. 767; Great Britain, *Rules and Regulations*, p. 313, and *Manual*, p. 17; Prussia, *Regulations*, p. 94; Carse, *Orchestra*, p. 135.

57. Henry Chamberlain, *A New and Compleat History and Survey of the Cities of London and Westminster* (London: J. Cooke, 1770), p. 330.

58. Farmer, *Rise*, p. 55n; Carse, *Musical Wind Instruments*, p. 65; Kandler, *Deutsche Armeemärsche*, p. 7; *Journal of the Society for Army Historical Research* 7 (1928): 259; Panov, *Militärmusik*, p. 61; Sir John W. Fortescue, *The Last Post* (London: W. Blackwood & Sons, 1934), p. 252.

59. Bobillier, *Musique militaire*, p. 62.

60. Humphrey Bland, *A Treatise of Military Discipline* (London: D. Midwinter, 1743), p. 60; ibid. (London: W. Johnston, 1762), p. 67; Bobillier, *Musique militaire*, p. 59; Hind, "Military Band," p. 768; Farmer, *Rise*, p. 56; Robert Hinde, *Discipline of the Light Horse*, pp. 206–7; Hinde used the date 1764, but Farmer, *Handel's Kettledrums*, p. 60, cited 23 July 1766 as the date of the Horse Guards order; Farmer, *Military Music*, p. 28.

61. Clarence E. Wiggins, "Editions for Modern Band of Selected Works from Early Nineteenth Century English Band Music" (DMA diss., University of Southern California, 1966), p. 100; Wolfgang A. Mozart, *Don Giovanni*, K. 527, 1787, act 2, sc. 13; George Cucuel, *Etudes sur un orchestre au XVIIIème siècle* (Paris: Librarie Fischbacher, 1913), p. 22; Stanley Sadie,

"The Wind Music of J. C. Bach," *Music and Letters* 37 (1956): 107–8; Charles Burney, *An Eighteenth-Century Musical Tour in Central Europe and the Netherlands* (London: Oxford University Press, 1959), 2:30, passim; Kastner, *Manuel*, p. 124; Bobillier, *Musique militaire*, p. 63; Warwick Wroth, *The London Pleasure Gardens of the Eighteenth Century* (London: Macmillan and Co., 1896), pp. 243–44, 296–98; Karl F. Pohl, *Mozart und Haydn in London* (Vienna: C. Gerold, 1867), 1:72n; Baines, *Woodwind Instruments*, pp. 298–99.

62. Thurston Dart, *The Interpretation of Music*. (London: Hutchinson's University Library, 1954), pp. 68–70; W. T. Parke, *Musical Memoirs* (London: Henry Colburn and Richard Bentley, 1830), 2:241; Oscar G. Sonneck and William T. Upton, *A Bibliography of Early Secular American Music*, p. 507; Carse, *Orchestra*, pp. 121–22, 124, 165.

63. Alfred Einstein, *Mozart, His Character, His Work* (London: Oxford University Press, 1945), p. 202.

64. Karl Geiringer, *Haydn, A Creative Life in Music* (New York: W. W. Norton & Co., 1946), pp. 257, 286.

65. Grose, *Antiquities*, 1:416–22.

66. Farmer, *History*, p. 52.

67. Burney, *Musical Tour*, 2:6.

68. Wolfgang A. Mozart, *Così Fan Tutte*, K. 588, 1790, act 2, sc. 4; Hugh E. Everard, *History of Thos. Farrington's Regiment, Subsequently Designated the 29th (Worcestershire) Foot* (Worcestershire: Littlebury & Co., 1891), p. 339.

69. Department of the Army. *Field Manual No. 12–50*, 1946, p. 86; ibid., 1957, p. 86.

70. Great Britain, *Rules and Regulations*, p. 96; a similar restriction to the use of music is found in the *General Regulations* of 1786.

71. Rutherford, "Drum," p. 773; Curt Sachs, *The History of Musical Instruments* (New York: W. W. Norton & Co., 1940), p. 435.

72. Day, *Catalogue*, p. 233.

73. Sachs, *Musical Instruments*, p. 437.

74. Farmer, *Handel's Kettledrums*, p. 45.

75. Ibid.; Sachs, *Musical Instruments*, pp. 437–38; Farmer noted that the British Coldstream Guards had a Turkish crescent in 1785, but such instances are quite rare before 1800, and this reference may be spurious; a beautiful example of a crescent may be found in Alexander Buchner, *Musical Instruments through the Ages* (London: Batchworth Press, 1961), no. 262.

76. Farmer, *Handel's Kettledrums*, p. 46.

77. Burney, *Musical Tour*, 2:2, 23; Sumner, "Inspection Returns," 4:112; idem, "Cox & Co., Army Agents. Uniform Items from their Ledgers," 17:147; Farmer, *Military Music*, p. 35, and *History*, pp. 52, 54; this is a correction of his earlier date of 1782 found in his *Handel's Kettledrums*, p. 45, and *Rise*, p. 73.

78. A photograph of an actual horn of the shape depicted can be seen in R. Morley-Pegge, *The French Horn* (London: Ernest Benn, 1960), pl. III, no. 1; according to the note accompanying the photograph, it is the earliest known type of crook used on the horn, but no more specific date is given than "eighteenth century"; Hinde, *Discipline*, p. 556.

CHAPTER 2

1. Russell F. Weigley, *History of the United States Army*, pp. 3–4.

2. E. Z. Massicotte, "La Musique militaire sous le régime français," *Recherches historique* 39 (1933): 387–88; "Minutes of the Council and General Court," *Virginia Magazine of History and Biography* 19 (1911): 374–76; William W. Hening, comp., *The Statutes at Large*, 1:222; payment in tobacco was continued until 1756, when one shilling twopence per day was authorized; Charles W. Brewster, *Rambles about Portsmouth*, 2 vols. (Portsmouth, N.H.: Lewis W. Brewster, 1873), 1:20; Louis Pichierri, *Music in New Hampshire 1623–1800* (New York: Columbia University Press, 1960), pp. 14–15; I. N. P. Stokes, *The Iconography of Manhattan Island, 1489–1909*, 6 vols. (New York: Robert H. Dodd, 1915–28), 1:70; *Virginia Magazine of History and Biography* 4 (1897):140, 143; 8 (1900):206; 2 (1895):264; 12 (1904):190–91; 38 (1930):81; *William and Mary Quarterly* 7 (1899):306.

3. "Journal of John Barnwell," *Virginia Magazine of History and Biography* 6 (1898):50, 54; (cited) *Virginia Gazette*, 9 Dec. 1737, 14 Dec. 1739; Pichierri, *Music*, p. 17.

4. Hening, *Statutes*, 5:17.

5. Weigley, *History*, p. 8.

6. *Pennsylvania Gazette*, 26 June 1755; "Extracts from the Diary of Daniel Fischer, 1755," *Pennsylvania Magazine of History and Biography* 17 (1893):273.

7. *Pennsylvania Gazette*, 25 March 1756; *Pennsylvania Journal*, 25 March 1756.

8. Weigley, *History*, p. 17.

9. Stanley M. Pargellis, *Lord Loudon in North America* (New Haven: Yale University Press, 1933), p. 106; Weigley, *History*, pp. 18–19.

10. Oscar G. Sonneck, *Early Concert-Life in America*, p. 9n; (cited) *Boston News-Letter*, 16–23 April 1716.

11. (Cited) *Boston Gazette*, 3–10 Feb. 1729, 28 June 1764; Annie H. Thwing, *The Crooked & Narrow Streets of the Town of Boston* (Boston: Marshall Jones Co., 1920), p. 86.

12. William A. Fischer, *Notes on Music in Old Boston* (Boston: Oliver Ditson Co., 1918), p. 180.

13. (Cited) *Gentleman's Magazine* 38 (1768):511–12; *New York Journal*, 13 Oct. 1768; John Rowe, *Letters and Diary of John Rowe, Boston Merchant* (Boston: W. B. Clarke Co., 1903), p. 180.

14. *Boston Evening Post*, 20 March 1769.

15. Ibid., 10 April 1769; Thomas Walter, *The Grounds and Rules of Musick Explained*, MI29.124S, Boston Public Library, Boston, Massachusetts.

16. *Boston Gazette*, 13 March 1769; *Boston Chronicle*, 9–13 March 1769, 26–29 June 1769; Rowe, *Letters*, pp. 184, 204–5; Sonneck, *Early Concert-Life*, pp. 260–61; *Boston Evening Post*, 11 and 18 Oct. 1773: the newspaper advertisements did not specify the performers or group, but Frederick W. Coburn, in "Flagg, Josiah," *Dictionary of American Biography*, 6:449–50, claimed that it was Flagg's military band that performed, but the entry is not documented; Oliver A. Roberts, *History of the Military Company of Massachusetts*, 3 vols. (Boston: Alfred Mudge & Son, 1898), 2:66.

17. *Boston News-Letter*, 9 May 1771; *Massachusetts Gazette*, 9 May 1771, supplement 16 May 1771; Sonneck, *Early Concert-Life*, pp. 257, 262; *Boston Evening Post*, 26 Oct. 1772, 13 Sept. 1773, 4 April and 9 May 1774; Rowe, *Letters*, p. 240.

18. Thomas E. Warner, "Indications of Performance Practice in Woodwind Instruction Books of the 17th & 18th Centuries" (Ph.D. diss., New York University, 1964), pp. 307–8; *Boston Evening Post*, 29 March, 23 Aug., and 13 Sept. 1773; *Boston News-Letter*, 9 Sept. 1773.

19. "Letters of John Andrews, Esq., of Boston, 1772–1776," *Proceedings of the Massachusetts Historical Society* 8 (1866):323–24; *Boston Evening Post*, 7 June, 27 Sept. 1773; *Boston News-Letter*, 10 June 1773; Roberts, *History*, 2:178.

20. "Letters of John Andrews," p. 342.

21. Rowe, *Letters*, p. 288; *Boston Evening Post*, 5 Sept. 1774.

22. "Letters of John Andrews," p. 400; *New York Journal*, 30 March 1775.

23. (Cited) Esther Singleton, *Social New York under the Georges 1714–1776* (New York: D. Appleton & Co., 1902), pp. 288, 293–95; *New York Mercury*, 18 March 1765, as quoted in Rita S. Gottesman, "The Arts & Crafts in New York," *Collections of the New York Historical Society* 49 (1938):204; (cited) *New York Journal*, 15 June 1775.

24. Julian Mates, *The American Musical Stage before 1800* (New Brunswick: Rutgers University Press, 1962), p. 29; *New York Gazette*, 6 Nov. 1769; *New York Mercury*, 6 Nov. 1769, 9 Jan. 1770; *New York Journal*, 14 Feb. 1771; Sonneck, *Early Concert-Life*, p. 12.

25. Singleton, *Social New York*, p. 309; *New York Gazette*, 13 April 1767; *New York Journal*, 16 April 1767.

26. *Virginia Gazette*, 21 April 1768.

27. *New York Mercury*, 7, 14, and 21 Jan. 1771; *New York Journal*, 17 and 24 Jan. 1771; *New York Gazette*, 21 June and 5 July 1773.

28. *Pennsylvania Gazette*, 21 March 1749, 20 Jan. 1757, 27 Dec. 1759; see also Oscar G. Sonneck, *Francis Hopkinson, the First American Poet Composer, and James Lyons, Patriot, Preacher, Psalmodist* (Washington, D.C.: H. L. McQueen, 1905), pp. 23–24; Sonneck, *Early Concert-Life*, pp. 17, 22, 50; *Pennsylvania Journal*, 24 Sept. 1767.

29. *Pennsylvania Journal*, 19 Nov. 1767; *Pennsylvania Gazette*, 19 Nov. 1767; *Boston*

Evening Post, 13 Sept. 1773; (cited) Beata Francis and Eliza Keary, eds., *The Francis Letters*, 2 vols. (London: Hutchinson & Co., n.d.), 1:91.

30. Philip Bate, *The Oboe* (London: Ernest Benn, 1962), p. 40.

31. *Pennsylvania Gazette*, 28 Nov. 1771.

32. *Virginia Gazette*, 23 May 1771, 19 Nov. 1772; Maurer Maurer, "The 'Professor of Musick' in Colonial America," *Musical Quarterly* 36 (1950):511–24; *Virginia Gazette*, 11 Dec. 1766; Philip V. Fithian, *Journal & Letters of Philip Vickers Fithian, 1773–1774*, ed. Robert G. Albion and Leonidas Dodson (Williamsburg: Colonial Williamsburg, 1943), p. 76.

33. *Virginia Gazette*, 4 June and 3 Dec. 1767, 29 Sept. 1768, 11 April and 29 Aug. 1771, 17 Sept. 1772, 14 Nov. 1777.

34. *Virginia Gazette*, 28 March 1766; similar advertisements may be found in the editions of 30 July 1767, 1 April and 25 Nov. 1773, 22 Dec. 1768, and *South Carolina Gazette*, 19 April 1770.

35. Julian P. Boyd, ed., *The Papers of Thomas Jefferson*, 13 vols. (Princeton: Princeton University Press, 1950), 2:195–96.

36. Hans T. David, "Background for Bethlehem: Moravian Music in Pennsylvania," *Magazine of Art* 32 (1939):224–25; Adelaide L. Fries, ed., *Records of the Moravians in North Carolina*, 8 vols. (Raleigh: Edwards & Broughton Printing Co., 1922–43), 1:80, 122, 148; Harry H. Hall, *The Moravian Wind Ensemble* (Ann Arbor: University Microfilms, 1967), passim; *Virginia Gazette*, 25 July 1766, 18 July 1771; Hennig Cohen, *South Carolina Gazette* (Columbia: University of South Carolina Press, 1953), passim; *South Carolina Gazette*, 22 March 1773, as quoted in Sonneck, *Early Concert-Life*, p. 22; (cited) *Maryland Gazette*, 13 Aug. 1752, as quoted in George O. Seilhamer, *History of the American Theatre* (Philadelphia: Globe Printing House, 1888–90), 1:33.

37. William C. White, *A History of Military Music in America* (New York: Exposition Press, 1944), p. 20.

CHAPTER 3

1. Charles Evans, *American Bibliography*, no. 10330; Virginia, *Journal of the Proceedings of the Convention Held at Richmond, March 20, 1775* (Williamsburg: J. Dixon & W. Hunter, 1775), pp. 16–17; *Virginia Gazette*, 29 July 1775.

2. *Virginia Gazette*, 1 April 1775; (cited) William Hening, *The Statutes at Large*, 9:9–10, 31, 76; "Resolutions of the Mansfield Militia, January 16, 1775," *Military Collector and Historian* 19 (1967):27; (cited) Pennsylvania, *An Act to Regulate the Militia of the Commonwealth of Pennsylvania* (Philadelphia: John Dunlap, 1777), p. 19.

3. Christopher Ward, *The War of the Revolution*, 1:50; Arthur B. Tourtellot, *William Diamond's Drum* (Garden City: Doubleday & Co., 1959).

4. Massachusetts, *The Journals of Each Provincial Congress of Massachusetts in 1774 and 1775, and of the Committee of Safety* (Boston: Dutton and Wentworth, 1838), p. 520; John W. Wright, *Some Notes on the Continental Army*, p. 20.

5. (Cited) *Virginia Gazette*, 27 May 1775; Detmar Finke, "The Army's Birthday," *Army Digest* 22 (1967):6; Russell F. Weigley, *History of the United States Army*, p. 29.

6. James M. Webb, *Reminiscences of Gen'l Samuel B. Webb of the Revolutionary Army* (New York: Globe Stationery and Printing Co., 1882), p. 16; (cited) *Virginia Gazette*, 17 June, 29 July, and 30 Sept. 1775; *Pennsylvania Packet*, 31 July 1775; (cited) *New York Mercury*, 17 April 1775; Peter Force, ed., *American Archives*, 4:468; Philip V. Fithian, *Journal and Letters of Philip Vickers Fithian, 1773–1774*, ed. Robert G. Albion and Leonidas Dodson (Williamsburg: Colonial Williamsburg, 1943), p. 24.

7. George Washington, *The Writings of George Washington from the Original Manuscript Sources, 1745–1799*, 3:335, 339, 357, 362, 378, 497, 514, 516.

8. Oliver L. Spaulding, *United States Army in War and Peace* (New York: G. P. Putnam's Sons, 1937), p. 20; Record Group 93, Orderly Book of William Farrington, 195:72–73, National Archives.

9. Harold L. Peterson, *The Book of the Continental Soldier*, p. 256; Weigley, *History*, pp. 33–34; Washington, *Writings*, 4:136, 205.

10. Israel Hutchinson, "Orderly Book," *Proceedings of the Massachusetts Historical Society* 16 (1878):347–48.

11. "Orderly Book, Fourth Pennsylvania Battalion, Col. Anthony Wayne, 1776," *Pennsylvania Magazine of History and Biography* 30 (1906):211.

12. Washington, *Writings*, 5:156; Worthington C. Ford, ed., *Journals of the Continental Congress, 1774–1789*, 2:220.

13. Delaware, *The Militia Law* (Wilmington: n.p., 1776), p. 14; Force, *Archives*, 6:1504; Weigley, *History*, p. 46; Washington, *Writings*, 1:234, 5:238, 337, 12:30–32; Board of War to Washington, 6 July 1776, Heath to Washington, 13 Aug. 1777, Washington Papers, Library of Congress.

14. Henry R. Knight, *Historical Records of the Buffs*, 4 vols. (London: Medici Society, 1905–51), 1:202–3; Percy Sumner, "Cox & Co., Army Agents. Uniform Items from Their Ledgers," *Journal of the Society for Army Historical Research* 17 (1938):150; idem, "Army Inspection Returns—1753 to 1804," *Journal of the Society for Army Historical Research* 4 (1925):33, 108; John G. Simcoe, *Simcoe's Military Journal* (New York: Bartlett & Welford, 1844), pp. 132–33.

15. *Pennsylvania Evening Post*, 11 July 1776; William B. Reed, *Life and Correspondence of Joseph Reed* 2 vols. (Philadelphia: Lindsay and Blackiston, 1847), 1:237; (cited) Henry P. Johnston, *The Battle of Harlem Heights* (New York: Macmillan Co., 1897), p. 173.

16. Hancock to Schuyler, 13 July 1776, Schuyler to Gates, 19 July 1776, Schuyler to Hancock, 20 July 1776, Hancock to Schuyler, 30 Dec. 1776, Schuyler Papers, New York Public Library.

17. Andrew Lewis, *Orderly Book* (Richmond: n.p., 1860), pp. 7, 46.

18. (Cited) *Virginia Gazette*, 19 April 1776; Hening, *Statutes*, 9:143.

19. Weigley, *History*, p. 35; (cited) Force, *Archives*. 3:147; *Virginia Gazette*, 6 May 1775.

20. "The Diary of Lt. John Barker," *Journal of the Society for Army Historical Research* 7 (1928):155.

21. Ward, *War*, 1:24; *Journal of the Society for Army Historical Research* 16 (1937):5.

22. *Freeman's Journal* (Portsmouth, N.H.), 21 Jan. 1777.

23. Ward, *War*, 1:350; *Pennsylvania Ledger*, 6 Dec. 1777.

24. *Pennsylvania Ledger*, 23 May 1778; Winthrop Sargent, *The Life and Career of John André* (Boston: Ticknor and Fields, 1861), pp. 167–77.

25. Ward, *War*, 1:209.

26. Great Britain, *The Parliamentary Register* 3 (1776):287–95, 504–8; 7 (1777):44–49; George O. Trevelyan, *The American Revolution*, 6 vols. (London: Longmans, Green and Co., 1903), 1:303; *New York Gazette*, 28 Oct. 1776.

27. Andreas Wiederhold, "Colonel Rall at Trenton," *Pennsylvania Magazine of History and Biography* 22 (1898):462–63; *Pennsylvania Evening Post*, 14 Jan. and 5 July 1777; "Extracts from the Rev. Dr. Muhlenberg's Journals of 1776 and 1777," *Collections of the Historical Society of Pennsylvania* 1 (1853):158; Lynn Montross, *Rag, Tag and Bobtail*, p. 170; (cited) Edmund C. Burnett, ed., *Letters of Members of the Continental Congress*, 2:399.

28. Ward, *War*, 1:422; (cited) Stephan Popp, *A Hessian Soldier in the American Revolution* (n.p., 1953), p. 9.

29. Charles M. Lefferts, *Uniforms of the American, British, French, and German Armies in the American Revolution*, pp. 220, 231; *New York Royal Gazette*, 25 July–12 Sept. 1778; *New York Gazette*, 22 March 1779.

30. Washington, *Writings*, 8:181–82.

31. "Orderly Book of Capt. Sharp Delaney," *Pennsylvania Magazine of History and Biography* 32 (1908):303; (cited) Israel Putnam, *General Orders* (Brooklyn: Historical Printing Club, 1893), p. 79; "Orderly Book of the Pennsylvania State Regiment of Foot, May 10 to August 16, 1777," *Pennsylvania Magazine of History and Biography* 22 (1899):308; "The Journal & Orderly Book of Captain Robert Kirkwood of the Delaware Regiment of the Continental Line," *Papers of the Historical Society of Delaware* 56 (1910):62; (cited) "Sergeant John Smith's Diary of 1776," *Mississippi Valley Historical Review* 20 (1933):256.

32. Ford, *Journals*, 8:670; James Thacher, *Military Journal of the American Revolution*,

p.83; Ammi R. Robbins, *Journal of the Rev. Ammi R. Robbins* (New Haven: B. L. Hamlen, 1850), p. 43; Thomas Balch, *Papers Relating Chiefly to the Maryland Line during the Revolution* (Philadelphia: Seventy-Six Society, 1857), pp. 84–85.

33. Campbell Dalrymple, *A Military Essay* (London: D. Wilson, 1761), p. 229; Robert Hinde, *Discipline of the Light Horse*, pp. 206–7; Simcoe, *Journal*, pp. 166–67; (cited) Marko Zlatich, "Uniforming the 1st Regiment of the Continental Light Dragoons," *Military Collector & Historian* 20 (1968):35–36; idem, "Pulaski's Independent Legion," *Military Collector & Historian* 16 (1964):101.

34. Peterson, *Book*, p. 262; William Heath, *General Orders Issued by Major General William Heath When in Command of the Eastern Department 23 May 1777–3 October 1777*, pp. 6–7.

35. Record Group 93, MSS 18791 (cited) 20152 National Archives; Francis B. Heitman, *Historical Register of the Officers of the Continental Army during the War of the Revolution*, p. 222; *Massachusetts Soldiers and Sailors of the Revolutionary War*, 7:972; Weigley, *History*, p. 40.

36. Heitman, *Register*, p. 337; *Pennsylvania Archives*, 2d ser., 11:129, 180; 5th ser., 3:950; *Pennsylvania Magazine of History and Biography* 6 (1882):375.

37. Peterson, *Book*, p. 262; *Pennsylvania Archives*, 5th ser., 3:961.

38. William E. Birkheimer, *Historical Sketch of the Organization, Administration, Materiel, and Tactics of the Artillery, United States Army*, p. 8.

39. Compiled Military Service Records, Revolutionary War, National Archives; Timothy Olmstead, *Martial Music* (Albany: Daniel Steele, 1807); Samuel B. Webb, *Correspondence and Journals*, 3 vols. (New York: Wickersham Press, 1893–94), 1:233, 237, 239.

40. Washington, *Writings*, 10:524, 11:132, 366; (cited) Henry Bicker, "Orderly Book of the 2d Pennsylvania Continental Line," *Pennsylvania Magazine of History and Biography* 36 (1912):39, 240.

41. Simon V. Anderson, *American Music during the War for Independence, 1775–1783*, pp. 114–115; (cited) George Ewing, *George Ewing, Gentleman, a Soldier of Valley Forge*, (Yonkers, N.Y.: Thomas Ewing, 1928), pp. 44–45, 48–51; (cited) Elias Boudinot, *Journal of Historical Recollections of American Events during the Revolutionary War* (Philadelphia: F. Bourquin, 1894), p. 78; Elijah Fisher, *The Journal of Elijah Fisher while in the War for Independence, and Continued after He Came to Maine* (Augusta: Badger and Manley, 1880), pp. 7, 11–12; Washington, *Writings*, 11:354–56; *Pennsylvania Evening Post*, 20 May 1778; *Pennsylvania Packet*, 13 May 1778.

42. John C. Fitzpatrick, ed., *George Washington's Accounts of Expenses While Commander-in-Chief of the Continental Army 1775–1783* (Boston: Houghton-Mifflin Co., 1917), p. 53; idem, "The Bands of the Continental Army," *Daughters of the American Revolution Magazine* 57 (1923):190.

43. "A General Return of the Continental Army under the Command of His Excellency George Washington Esquire at the Valley Forge in Pennsylvania Jany 19th 1778," Record Group 93, National Archives.

CHAPTER 4

1. United States, *Regulations for the Order and Discipline of the Troops of the United States*, as reprinted in facsimile in Joseph R. Riling. *Baron Von Steuben and His Regulaions*, pp. 71, 152.

2. General orders, 22 Jan. 1782, as quoted in George Washington, *The Writings of George Washington from the Original Manuscript Sources, 1745–1799*, 23:458.

3. Captions are taken from United States, *Regulations*, pp. 91–92; see Appendix B for a listing of fife tutors, and Appendix C for a listing of drum manuals; see Appendix D for a concordance of page number references used in developing the musical examples.

4. William Windham, *A Plan of Discipline Composed for the Use of the Militia of the County of Norfolk*, 3:91; Washington, *Writings*, 9:79–80. That the British used this beat in the same manner can be seen from the *Orderly Book of Lieut. Gen. John Burgoyne* (Albany: J. Munsell, 1860), pp. 71, 97, and passim; Charles K. Bolton, *The Private Soldier under Washington* (New York; C. Scribner's Sons, 1902), p. 196.

5. United States, *Regulations*, p. 68; Windham, *Plan*, 3:91.

6. Washington, *Writings*, 9:79–80; United States, *Regulations*, p. 68.

7. Humphrey Bland, *A Treatise of Military Discipline*, p. 156; the 1762 edition is identical in this regard; Windham, *Plan*, 3:92.

8. George Ewing, *George Ewing, Gentleman, a Soldier of Valley Forge* (Yonkers, N.Y.: Thomas Ewing, 1928), p. 34.

9. John P. Muhlenberg, "Orderly Book, 26 March–20 December 1777," *Pennsylvania Magazine of History and Biography* 34 (1910): 32, 34.

10. Washington, *Writings*, 9:127.

11. Windham, *Plan*, 3:90; (cited) Bernard Elliott, "Diary of Captain Bernard Elliott," *Charleston Year Book*, 1889, p. 241; Prussia, *Regulations for the Prussian Infantry*, p. 182; Washington, *Writings*, 3:352.

12. James McMichael, "Diary of Lieutenant James McMichael of the Pennsylvania Line, 1776–1778," *Pennsylvania Magazine of History and Biography* 16 (1892): 130.

13. Robert Kirkwood, "The Journal & Orderly Book of Captain Robert Kirkwood of the Delaware Regiment of the Continental Line," *Papers of the Historical Society of Delaware* 56 (1910): 57–58; United States, *Regulations*, pp. 77–79.

14. Windham, *Plan*, 3:3.

15. William Heath, *General Orders Issued by Major General William Heath When in Command of the Eastern Department 23 May 1777–3 October 1777*, p. 81; John F. Grimké, "Order Book of John Faucheraud Grimké," *South Carolina Historical and Genealogical Magazine* 13 (1912): 109; Washington, *Writings*, 8:181–82, 10:433–34.

16. Windham, *Plan*, 3:92; Prussia, *Regulations*, p. 291; France, *Ordonnance du roy, portant reglement sur le service de l'infanterie en campagne*, pp. 46–47; Washington, *Writings*, 6:231.

17. Windham, *Plan*, 3:92; (cited) Andrew Lewis, *Orderly Book* (Richmond: n.p., 1860), p. 76; Thomas Simes, *Military Guide for Young Officers*, p. 18.

18. (Cited) William Henshaw, "The Orderly Books of Colonel William Henshaw," *Proceedings of the American Antiquarian Society* 57 (1947): 72–73; (cited) Elliott, "Diary," pp. 236–7; Heath, *General Orders*, p. 107; Lewis, *Orderly Book*, p. 47.

19. Charles S. Ashworth, *A New, Useful and Complete System of Drum-Beating*, p. 8.

20. Elliott, "Diary," pp. 217, 219, 245; Anthony Wayne, *Orderly Book of the Northern Army* (Albany: J.Munsell, 1859), pp. 52, 131.

21. Kirkwood, "Journal," p. 61; Lewis, *Orderly Book*, pp. 43, 74.

22. Washington, *Writings*, 3:317, 6:233.

23. United States, *Regulations*, p. 71; John Tudor, *Deacon Tudor's Diary* (Boston: Wallace Spooner, 1896), pp. 54–55; George L. Winters, *Kurze Anweisung das Trommel-Spielen*, p. 17; William Heath, *Memoirs of Major-General William Heath*, p. 24; (cited) Philip V. Fithian, *Letters to His Wife* (Vineland, N.J.: Smith Printing House, 1932), p. 34.

24. Christopher Ward, *The War of the Revolution*, 1:430, but not documented.

25. Winthrop Sargent, *The Life and Career of John André* (Boston: Ticknor and Fields, 1861), p. 112, but also not documented.

26. François, Marquis de Chastellux, *Travels in North America in the Years 1780, 1781 and 1782*, 1:213; for an understanding of the eighteenth-century use of the *Parley* or *Chamade* and the rules of warfare, see Simes, *Military Guide*, p. 18; Ebenezer Denny, *Military Journal of Maj. Ebenezer Denny*, (Philadelphia: J.B. Lippincott & Co., 1859), p. 44.

27. Windham, *Plan*, 3:93–94, 103–4.

28. Thomas Simes, *A Military Course for the Government and Conduct of a Batalion*, p. 177; Samuel Elbert, "The Order Book of Samuel Elbert, Colonel and Brigadier General in the Continental Army, October, 1776, to November, 1778," *Collections of the Georgia Historical Society* 5 (1902): 5; Walter Stewart, "Orderly Book of the Pennsylvania State Regiment of Foot," *Pennsylvania Magazine of History and Biography* 22 (1899): 210; orders, 16 March 1779, orderly books of the 2d Regiment of Continental Artillery, New York Historical Society.

29. Claude M. Simpson, *The British Broadside Ballad and Its Music* (New Brunswick: Rutgers University Press, 1966), pp. 604–5; William Chappell, *Popular Music of the Olden Time*,

2 vols. (1859; reprint ed. New York: Dover Publications, 1965), 2:636; *Drum-Major's Manual*, pp. 44, 46.

30. Brigade orders, 19 Aug. 1777, Christian Febiger Papers, Virginia State Library.

31. Washington, *Writings*, 8:308; Thomas Balch, *Papers Relating Chiefly to the Maryland Line during the Revolution* (Philadelphia: Seventy-Six Society, 1857), p. 16.

32. Georg Pausch, *Journal of Captain Pausch, Chief of the Hanau Artillery during the Burgoyne Campaign* (Albany: Joel Munsell's Sons, 1886), p. 148; Washington, *Writings*, 8:181–82.

33. Washington, *Writings*, 10:433–34.

34. Richard Kane, *A New System of Military Discipline* (London: J. Millan, 1745), p. 116; United States, *Field Manual No. 12–50* (Washington, D.C.: Department of the Army, 1969), pp. 42, 82.

35. Windham, *Plan*, 3:11, 92; Percy Sumner, "Army Inspection Returns—1753 to 1804," *Journal of the Society for Army Historical Research* 4 (1925); 110: adjutant general to Boscawen, 13 Aug. 1772, Royal Welch Fusiliers Regimental Museum.

36. Orders, 16 March 1779, orderly books of the 2d Regiment of Continental Artillery, New York Historical Society; Charles Robbins, *The Drum and Fife Instructor*, p. 17; Potter, *Drum-Major's Manual*, p. 50.

37. Washington, *Writings*, 3:497, 514, 516, and passim; instances of drumming out can be found in almost every one of the orderly books listed in the Notes, as this was a very common and widespread practice; James Stevens, "The Revolutionary Journal of James Stevens of Andover, Mass.," *Historical Collections of the Essex Institute* 48 (1912): 47.

38. George Weedon, *Valley Forge Orderly Book* (New York: Dodd, Mead & Co., 1902), p. 215; Washington, *Writings*, 4:268.

39. (Cited) Balch, *Papers*, pp. 20–21; Nathaniel Morgan, "Journal of Ensign Nathaniel Morgan at the Siege of Boston, 1775," *Collections of the Connecticut Historical Society* 7 (1899): 108.

40. Washington, *Writings*, 10:265–66, 11:83–84; McMichael, "Diary," pp. 157–58.

41. Cecil C.P. Lawson, *A History of the Uniforms of the British Army*, 3:106–7.

42. H. Oakes-Jones, "Lodging the Colour," *Journal of the Society for Army Historical Research* 5 (1926): 188.

43. William Duane, *The System of Infantry Discipline* (n.p., 1814), p. 107; Bland, *Treatise*, pp. 7–11; United States, *Rules and Regulations for the Field Exercise and Manoevres of Infantry* (New York: T. & W. Mercein, 1815), pp. 228–29.

44. United States, *Regulations*, pp. 115, 117, 123–26; Heath, *General Orders*, p. 361.

45. Benjamin Boardman, "Diary of Rev. Benjamin Boardman," *Proceedings of the Massachusetts Historical Society* 7 (1892): 412.

46. A.R. Robbins, *The Journal of the Rev. Ammi R. Robbins* (New Haven: B.L. Hamlen, 1850), pp. 37–38.

47. Simes, *Military Guide*, pp. 358–59; Prussia, *Regulations*, p. 324.

48. Henry G. Farmer, *History of the Royal Artillery Band*, p. 82; James Hulbert, *The Complete Fifer's Museum*, p. 10; Oscar G. Sonneck and William T. Upton, *A Bibliography of Early Secular American Music*, p. 261; Charles Evans, *American Bibliography*, no. 36111; John Bemrose, *Reminiscences of the Second Seminole War* (Gainesville: University of Florida Press, 1966), p. 11.

49. John Boyer, "A Journal of Wayne's Campaign," *Collections of the Michigan Pioneer and Historical Society* 34 (1904):552; Carl Engel, *Music from the Days of George Washington* (Washington, D.C.: George Washington Bicentennial Commission, 1931), p. 17; Rocellus S. Guernsey, *New York City and Vicinity during the War of 1812-15*, 2 vols. (New York: C.L. Woodward, 1889–95), 2:143.

CHAPTER 5

1. George Washington, *The Writings of George Washington from the Original Manuscript Sources, 1745–1799*, 12:30–32, 287, 331, 337, 393, 429; 14:431; 15:163; Record Group 93, 131, National Archives; Board of War to Washington, 10 May 1779, Washington Papers, Library of Congress.

2. Washington, *Writings*, 17:425; 18:46, 75; 19:479; 20:186; Board of War to Washington, 28 Feb. 1780, Washington Papers, Library of Congress; Record Group 93, 133:126, 151:168, 21206, National Archives.

3. Record Group 93, 31534, 28626:19, 92:8, 36–37, 84, National Archives.

4. Record Group 93, 162:36–37, National Archives; Washington , *Writings*, 22:398, 424.

5. Record Group 93, 56:6, National Archives.

6. James Thacher, *Military Journal of the American Revolution*, p. 159.

7. *Pennsylvania Packet*, 6 March 1779; Francis S. Drake, *Life & Correspondence of Henry Knox*, pp. 60–61.

8. Record Group 93, 111:191, National Archives.

9. Bremner to Peters, 22 June 1779, Peters Papers, Historical Society of Pennsylvania; Record Group 93, 111:48, 223, 120:31, National Archives.

10. Diary of Samuel Adams, 9 July 1779, New York Public Library.

11. (Cited) Washington, *Writings*, 18:22–23, 261n, 22:424; John J. Smith and John F. Watson, *American Historical and Literary Curiosities* 2 vols. (Philadelphia: Lloyd P. Smith, 1847), 1:22; François, Marquis de Chastellux, *Travels in North America in the Years 1780, 1781 and 1782*, p. 147.

12. "Journal of Samuel Holton, M.D., while in the Continental Congress, May 1778 to August 1780," *Historical Collections of the Essex Institute* 55 (1919): 166; "Diary of the Hon. William Ellery of Rhode Island," *Pennsylvania Magazine of History and Biography* 11 (1888): 477.

13. Holton, "Journal," p. 168.

14. *Pennsylvania Packet*, 2 Jan. 1779.

15. *Pennsylvania Archives*, 5th ser., 3:991, 994; Record Group 93, Revolutionary War Rolls, National Archives.

16. Frederick Cook, ed., *Journals of the Military Expedition of Major General J. Sullivan Against the Six Nations in 1779* (Auburn, N.Y.: Knapp, Peck & Thomson, 1887), pp. 5, 248, 254.

17. Cook, *Journals*, pp. 25–26, 71, 230, 263; "Adam Hubley, Jr., Colo. Comdt 11th Penna Regt. His Journal, Commencing at Wyoming, July 30th, 1779," *Pennsylvania Magazine of History and Biography* 33 (1909): 282, 419.

18. John C. Fitzpatrick, ed., *George Washington's Accounts of Expenses while Commander-in-Chief of the Continental Army 1775–1783* (Boston: Houghton-Mifflin Co., 1917), p. 65; *Pennsylvania Archives*, 5th ser., 3:999, 1002–5.

19. Washington, *Writings*, 13:440.

20. Thacher, *Journal*, p. 157; Edward Field, ed., *Diary of Colonel Israel Angell* (Providence: Preston & Rounds Co., 1899), p. 31n.

21. Field, *Angell*, p. 31.

22. Ebenezer Huntington, *Letters Written by Ebenezer Huntington during the American Revolution* (New York: Fred Heartman, 1915), p. 109.

23. "Letters and Papers of Major General John Sullivan," *Collections of the New Hampshire Historical Society* 14 (1931): 491.

24. Washington, *Writings*, 13:452n; 14:110.

25. Sullivan, "Letters," pp. 542–44; the original letter of Sullivan, to which this letter is a reply, is not included in the published correspondence.

26. *Providence Gazette*, 3 April 1779; Huntingon, *Letters*. p. 110.

27. Washington, *Writings*, 18:62–63; James Webb, *Reminiscences of Gen'l Samuel B. Webb of the Revolutionary Army* (New York: Globe Stationery and Printing Co., 1882, pp. 206–7; Compiled Military Service Records, National Archives.

28. Thacher, *Journal*, p. 204.

29. Francis Heitman, *Historical Register of the Officers of the Continental Army during the War of the Revolution*, p. 173; Record Group 93, 118:36, National Archives; Compiled Military Service Records, National Archives; Febiger to Board of War, 7 March 1780, letter book, Febiger Papers, Virginia State Library.

30. Peter F. Copeland and Marko Zlatich, "2nd Virginia Regiment of the Continental Line, 1779–1781," *Military Collector & Historian* 17 (1965): 86.

31. (Cited) *Calendar of Virginia State Papers*, 2:175; Marko Zlatich, "The 1st and 2nd Virginia State Legions, 1781–1783," *Military Collector & Historian* 17 (1965): 35–37.

32. Heitman, *Register*, p. 260; Robert Hinde, *Discipline of the Light Horse*, p. 206; *Pennsylvania Archives*, 5th ser., 3:892; *Pennsylvania Gazette*, 28 November 1771; Compiled Military Service Records, National Archives; Thacher, *Journal*, pp. 212–13.

33. Thacher, *Journal*, pp. 154–55.

34. Chastellux, *Travels*, 1:120; *New York Packet*, 25 Oct. 1781, as quoted in Frank Moore, *Diary of the Revolution* 2 vols. (New York: n.p., 1865), 2:506.

35. Christopher Marshall, *Extracts from the Diary of Christopher Marshall* (Albany: Joel Munsell, 1877), pp. 223–24.

36. *Pennsylvania Journal*, 12 July 1780; (cited) François, Marquis de Barbé-Marbois, *Our Revolutionary Forefathers* (New York: Duffield & Co., 1929), p. 115; Oscar G. Sonneck, *Francis Hopkinson, the First American Poet Composer and James Lyons, Patriot, Preacher, Psalmodist* (Washington, D.C.: H.L. McQueen, 1905), pp. 106, 111.

37. Ebenezer Fox, *Adventures of Ebenezer Fox in the Revolutionary War* (Boston: Charles Fox, 1838), pp. 57, 79, and passim; Thomas Anburey, *Travels Through the Interior Parts of America in a Series of Letters* (London: William Lane, 1789), 2:228; Whitfield J. Bell, "Thomas Anburey's 'Travels Through America': A Note on Eighteenth-Century Plagiarism," *Papers of the Bibliographical Society of America* 37 (1943): 23–26; William Heath, *Memoirs of Major-General William Heath*, p. 189.

38. Washington, *Writings*, 16:63, footnote by the editor, John C. Fitzpatrick.

39. Christopher Ward, *The War of the Revolution*, 2:595.

CHAPTER 6

1. Christopher Ward, *The War of the Revolution*, 2:656; (cited) John F. Grimké, "Order Book of John Faucheraud Grimké," *South Carolina Historical and Genealogical Magazine* 13 (1912):99–100.

2. Thomas Simes, *Military Guide for Young Officers*, 1:158–60.

3. John W. Wright, *Some Notes on the Continental Army*, p. 47.

4. Berthold Fernow, trans. and comp., *Documents Relating to the History of the Dutch and Swedish Settlements on the Delaware River* (Albany: Argus Co., 1877), p. 104; Stephen Kemble, "Kemble Papers," *Collections of the New York Historical Society* 17 (1884): 212–13.

5. *Pennsylvania Journal*, 14 June 1780; *Pennsylvania Gazette*, 14 June 1780; William Moultrie, *Memoir of the American Revolution* (New York: D. Longworth, 1802), 2:101.

6. Department of the Army, *American Military History* (Washington, D.C.: Government Printing Office, 1956), p. 89; Worthington C. Ford, ed., *Journals of the Continental Congress, 1774–1789*, 18:959; George Washington, *The Writings of George Washington from the Original Manuscript Sources, 1745–1799*, 20:277–81.

7. Baron Dunoyer de Noirmont and Alfred de Marbot, *Costumes militaires français*; Georges Kastner, *Manuel général de musique militaire à l'usage des Armées françaises*, p. 117; Charles M. Lefferts, *Uniforms of the American, British, French, and German Armies in the American Revolution*, pp. 238, 244; France, *Ordonnance du roi, pour régler l'exercice de ses troupes d'infanterie*, pp. 280–81.

8. (Cited) Stephen Bonsal, *When the French Were Here* (Garden City: Doubleday Doran & Co., 1945), pp. 10, 58, 71; François, Marquis de Chastellux, *Travels in North America in the Years 1780, 1781, and 1782*, 2:234.

9. Lynn Montross, *Rag, Tag and Bobtail*, p. 422; Allan Forbes, "Marches and Camp Sites of the French Army," *Proceedings of the Massachusetts Historical Society* 58 (1924–25): 277; James Thacher, *Military Journal of the American Revolution*, p. 265.

10. Claude C. Robin, *New Travels Through North-America* (Philadelphia: Robert Bell, 1783), pp. 24, 44; Thacher, *Journal*, p. 272; *Pennsylvania Packet*, 8 and 13 Sept. 1781; Ludwig, Baron von Closen, *The Revolutionary Journal of Baron Ludwig von Closen, 1780–1783* (Chapel Hill: University of North Carolina Press, 1958), p. 120.

11. Forbes, "Marches and Camp Sites," pp. 160, 164; Lubov Keefer, *Baltimore's Music* (Baltimore: J.H. Furst Co., 1962), p. 28.

12. Washington, *Writings*, 12:451, 16:387; Detmar H. Finke and H. Charles McBarron, Jr., "Continental Army Uniform Specifications, 1779–1781," *Military Collector & Historian* 14 (1962): 35–41.

13. Richard Butler, "General Richard Butler's Journal of the Siege of Yorktown," *Historical Magazine* 8 (1864): 105–6.

14. Ebenezer Denny, *Military Journal of Maj. Ebenezer Denny*, (Philadelphia: J.B. Lippincott & Co., 1859), pp. 39–40.

15. Thacher, *Journal*, p. 282

16. William Feltman, *The Journal of Lt. William Feltman of the 1st Pennsylvania Regiment* (Philadelphia: H.C. Baird, 1853), p. 321; Denny, *Military Journal*, p. 44.

17. John J. Smith and John F. Watson, *American Historical and Literary Curiosities*, 2 vols. (Philadelphia: Lloyd P. Smith, 1847), 2:1; Alexander Garden, *Anecdotes of the American Revolution*, 3 vols. (Charleston: A.E. Miller, 1822–28), 3:17; Washington, *Writings*, 23:237.

18. "St. George Tucker's Journal of the Siege of Yorktown, 1781," *William and Mary Quarterly* 5 (1948): 391–92; Edmund P. Gibson, "Trivia," *William and Mary Quarterly* 7 (1950): 593–95.

19. Francis S. Drake, *Life & Correspondence of Henry Knox, Major General in the American Revolutionary Army*, p. 70; the diary of John C. Doehla, as quoted in Friedrich Kapp, *The Life of Frederick William von Steuben* (New York: Mason Bros., 1859), pp. 459–64.

20. Stephan Popp, *A Hessian Soldier in the American Revolution* (n.p., 1953), p. 28; Thacher, *Journal*, pp. 288–89.

21. Thacher, *Journal*, p. 289; Feltman, *Journal*, p. 322; McDowell quoted in *Pennsylvania Archives*, 2nd ser., 15:303; Tucker, "Journal," pp. 392–93; Denny, *Military Journal*, p. 44; Auguste Levasseur, *Lafayette in America in 1824 and 1825*, 2 vols. (Philadelphia: Carey and Lea, 1829), 1:191.

22. *Boston Independent Chronicle*, 8 Nov. 1781; Garden, *Anecdotes*, 3:17; Benjamin Tallmadge, *Memoir of Colonel Benjamin Tallmadge* (New York: Gilliss Press, 1904), p. 67; Samuel Graham, "An English Officer's Account of His Services in America—1779–1781," *Historical Magazine* 9 (1865): 273; Henry Lee, *Memoirs of the War in the Southern Department of the United States*, 2 vols. (Philadelphia: Bradford and Inskeep, 1812), 2:360; John B. Tilden, "Extracts from the Journal of John Bell Tilden, Second Pennsylvania Line, 1781–1782," *Pennsylvania Magazine of History and Biography* 19 (1895): 63; Daniel Shute, "The Journal of Dr. Daniel Shute, Surgeon in the Revolution, 1781–1782," *New England Historical and Genealogical Register* 84 (1930): 386; Jean, Comte de Rochambeau, *Mémoires militaires*, 2 vols. (Paris: Chez Fain, 1809), 1:295; John Davis, "Journal of Captain John Davis of the Pennsylvania Line," *Pennsylvania Magazine of History and Biography* 5 (1881): 305; Burke to Middleton, "Correspondence of Hon. Arthur Middleton, Signer of the Declaration of Independence," *South Carolina Historical and Genealogical Magazine* 26 (1925): 187.

23. Tucker, "Journal," pp. 392–93; Record Group 93, 151:195, National Archives; *Magazine of American History* 7 (1881): 451:53; Frank Luther, *Americans and Their Songs* (New York: Harper & Bros., 1942); *Independent Chronicle* (Boston), 8 Nov. 1781.

24. William Chappell, *Popular Music of the Olden Time*, 2 vols. (1859; reprint ed., New York: Dover Publications, 1965), 2:437; transposed to D major as more suitable for the fife.

CHAPTER 7

1. Ludwig, Baron von Closen, *The Revolutionary Journal of Baron Ludwig von Closen* (Chapel Hill: University of North Carolina Press, 1958), pp. 168–69, 176; John B. Tilden, "Extracts from the Journal of Lieutenant John Bell Tilden, Second Pennsylvania Line, 1781–1782," *Pennsylvania Magazine of History and Biography* 19 (1895): 212; William Feltman, *The Journal of Lt. William Feltman of the 1st Pennsylvania Regiment* (Philadelphia: H.C. Baird, 1853), pp. 34, 36; Benjamin Tallmadge, *Memoir of Colonel Benjamin Tallmadge* (New York: Gilliss Press, 1904), pp. 69–70.

2. Tallmadge, *Memoir*, p. 70; George Washington, *The Writings of George Washington from the Original Manuscript Sources, 1745–1799*, 23:271, 347.

3. Garrison orders, 29 Dec. 1781, orderly books of the 3d Regiment of Continental Artillery, New York Historical Society.

4. Heath to Washington, 10 Jan. 1782, Washington Papers, Library of Congress; Worthington C. Ford, ed., *Journals of the Continental Congress, 1774–1789*, 21: 1182–83.

5. Washington, *Writings*, 23: 458.

6. Secretary at war to Washington, 21 Jan. 1782, Washington Papers, Library of Congress; Washington, *Writings*, 23:457.

7. Record Group 93, 92:158–59, 164, National Archives.

8. William Heath, *Memoirs of Major-General William Heath*, p. 302.

9. Washington, *Writings*, 24:219.

10. Record Group 93, 187:85, 191:22, National Archives; Humphreys to Hiwell, 5 May 1782, Washington Papers, Library of Congress.

11. Record Group 93, 92:193, National Archives.

12. Washington, *Writings*, 24:454.

13. Ibid., p. 489.

14. Ibid., 25:94, 103, 105, 130–31, 134–35, 169, 203; regimental orders, 17 Sept. 1782, orderly books of the 2d Regiment of Continental Artillery, New York Historical Society.

15. *Pennsylvania Packet*, 24 Oct. 1782.

16. Jean, Comte de Rochambeau, *Mémoires militaires* (Paris: Chez Fain, 1809), 1:309.

17. Anne S.K. Brown and Howard C. Rice, *The American Campaigns of Rochambeau's Army*, 2 vols. (Princeton: Princeton University Press, 1972), 1:166.

18. *New York Royal Gazette*, 9 Jan., 27 April, and 27 Nov. 1782.

19. François, Marquis de Chastellux, *Travels in North America in the Years 1780, 1781 and 1782*, 2:212n.

20. Record Group 93, 28626:68,151:238, National Archives; garrison orders, 7 Nov. 1782, orderly books of the 2d Regiment of Continental Artillery, New York Historical Society.

21. Washington, *Writings*, 26:138.

22. Heath, *Memoirs*, pp. 319–20; (cited) James Thacher, *Military Journal of the American Revolution*, pp. 311–12.

23. *Salem Gazette*, 16 and 23 Jan. 1783; *New Hampshire Gazette*, 15 Feb. 1783; Louis Pichierri, *Music in New Hampshire* (New York: Columbia University Press, 1960), p. 112.

24. Regimental orders, 7 Jan. and 9 June 1783, orderly book of the 3d Regiment of Artillery, New York Historical Society.

25. *Pennsylvania Archives*, 5th ser., 3:1038; Record Group 93, 28626:52, National Archives.

26. William E. Birkhimer, *Historical Sketch of the Organization, Administration, Materiel, and Tactics of the Artillery, United States Army*, p. 346.

27. Febiger to Washington, 14 March 1782, Washington Papers, Library of Congress; Posey to Febiger, 16 Feb. 1782, enclosed with above letter.

28. Philip Van Cortlandt, "Autobiography of Philip Van Cortlandt," *Magazine of American History* 2 (1878): 292, 297–98; Christopher Ward, *The War of the Revolution*, 1:146; review, 5 July 1780, Revolutionary War Muster Rolls, New York Public Library; Clinton manuscript no. 4, 477, State Library, Albany, as cited in Asa B. Gardiner, "Uniforms of the American Army," *Magazine of American History* 1 (1877): 484; this manuscript did not survive the fire of 1911.

29. Heath, *Memoirs*, p. 341; Washington, *Writings*, 26:282.

30. Washington, *Writings*, 26:372.

31. Secretary at war to Washington, 7 June 1783; Colonels Swift, S.B. Webb, Lamb, Crane, Butler et al. to Washington, 7 June 1783, Washington Papers, Library of Congress; Washington, *Writings*, 26:482–83.

32. Record Group 93, 144:22, 147:54, 29741, National Archives; *Providence Gazette*, 24 April and 26 June 1784.

33. Ford, *Journals*, 27:518, 524.

APPENDIX A

1. Compiled from Worthington C. Ford, *British Officers Serving in America 1754-1774*, and *British Officers Serving in the American Revolution 1774–1783*.

2. Items not otherwise documented are from this study or from Percy Sumner, "Army Inspection Returns—1753 to 1804," and "Cox & Co., Army Agents. Uniform Items from Their Ledgers," *Journal of the Society for Army Historical Research*.

3. J.C. Leask and H.M. McCance, *The Regimental Records of the Royal Scots (1st Foot) or Royal Regiment of Foot* (Dublin: A. Thom, 1915), p. 200.

4. *Lewes Journal*, 25 Dec. 1749, as quoted in the *Journal of the Society for Army Historical Research* 32 (1954): 182; the full program is included in the advertisement, showing four symphonies, four concertos, and two solos.

5. Henry R. Knight, *Historical Records of the Buffs (3d Foot)*, 4 vols. (London: Medici Society, 1905–51), 1:217.

6. Cecil C.P. Lawson, *A History of the Uniforms of the British Army*, 3:127.

7. *Walker's Hibernian Magazine*, 1788, p. 445.

8. H.C.B. Cook, "The 38th Foot: A Line Regiment in 1769 to 1722," *Journal of the Society for Army Historical Research* 46 (1968): 96.

SELECTED BIBLIOGRAPHY

Fife tutors, drum manuals, and collections published primarily for military bands have been omitted from this listing and are to be found in Appendixes B, C, and E respectively.

MANUSCRIPT MATERIALS

New York. New York Historical Society. Orderly books of the 2d Regiment of Continental Artillery, 1778–83. [John Lamb, colonel]
————. New York Historical Society. Orderly books of the 3d Regiment of Continental Artillery, 1781–83. [John Crane, colonel]
————. New York Public Library. Diary of Samuel Adams, 1776–80.
————. New York Public Library. Philip Schuyler papers.
Philadelphia. Historical Society of Pennsylvania. Christian Febiger letter books.
Richmond. Virginia State Library. Christian Febiger papers.
Washington, D.C. Library of Congress. George Washington papers.
————. National Archives. Record Group 93. War Department Collection of Revolutionary War Records.
————. National Archives. Compiled Military Service Records.

PUBLISHED WORKS

Anderson, Simon V. *American Music during the War for Independence, 1775–1783*. Ann Arbor: University Microfilms, 1965.
Birkheimer, William E. *Historical Sketch of the Organization, Administration, Materiel, and Tactics of the Artillery, United States Army*. Washington, D.C.: J. J. Chapman, 1884.
Bland, Humphrey. *A Treatise of Military Discipline: In Which is Laid Down and Explained the Duty of the Officer and Soldier through the Several Branches of the Service*. London: D. Midwinter, 1743. Rev. ed. London: W. Johnston, 1762.
Burnett, Edmund C., ed. *Letters of Members of the Continental Congress*. 8 vols. Washington, D.C.: Carnegie Institution of Washington, 1921–36.
Camus, Raoul F. *The Military Band in the United States Army Prior to 1834*. Ann Arbor: University Microfilms, 1969.
Chastellux, François, Marquis de. *Travels in North America in the Years 1780, 1781 and 1782*. 2 vols. London: G. G. J. and J. Robinson, 1787.
Curtis, Edward E. *The Organization of the British Army in the American Revolution*. New Haven: Yale University Press, 1926.
Drake, Francis S. *Life & Correspondence of Henry Knox, Major General in the American Revolutionary Army*. Boston: S. G. Drake, 1873.

Dunoyer de Noirmont, Baron, and Marbot, Alfred de. *Costumes militaires français*. 2 vols. Paris: Clement, 1845.

Evans, Charles. *American Bibliography*. 13 vols. Chicago: Blakely Press, 1903–55.

Farmer, Henry G. *Handel's Kettledrums and Other Papers on Military Music*. London: Hinrichsen, 1950.

———. *History of the Royal Artillery Band*. London: Royal Artillery Institution, 1954.

———. *Memoirs of the Royal Artillery Band*. London: Boosey & Co., 1904.

———. *Military Music*. New York: Chanticleer Press, 1950.

———. *The Rise and Development of Military Music*. London: Wm. Reeves, 1912.

Force, Peter, ed. *American Archives*. 9 vols. Washington, D.C.: M. St. Clair Clarke and Peter Force, 1848.

Ford, Worthington C. *British Officers Serving in America 1754–1774*. Boston: David Clapp & Son, 1894.

———. *British Officers Serving in the American Revolution 1774–83*. Brooklyn, N.Y.: Historical Printing Club, 1897.

———, ed. *Journals of the Continental Congress, 1774–1789*. 34 vols. Washington, D.C.: Government Printing Office, 1904–37.

Fortescue, Sir John W. *A History of the British Army*. 13 vols. London: Macmillan Co., 1899–1930.

France, Ministère de la Guerre. *Instruction que le roi a fait expédier pour régler provisoirment l'exercice de ses troupes d'infanterie*. Versailles: l'Imprimerie du Roi, 1775.

———. *Ordonnance du roy, portant reglement sur le service de l'infanterie en campagne*. Strasbourg: Chez Jean-François Le Roux, 1753.

———. *Ordonnance du roi, pour régler l'exercice de ses troupes d'infanterie*. Metz: Chez Jean-Baptiste Collignon, 1776.

Great Britain. Adjutant General's Office. *An Abridgment of the English Military Discipline*. London: John Bill, 1685.

———. *General Regulations and Orders for His Majesty's Forces*. London: War Office, 1786.

———. *The Manual Exercise as Ordered by His Majesty in 1764*. Boston: T. & J. Fleet, 1774.

———. *Rules and Regulations for the Formation, Field Exercise, and Movements of His Majesty's Forces*. London: War Office, 1794.

Grose, Francis. *Advice to the Officers of the British Army*. New York: Agathynian Club, 1867.

———. *Military Antiquities*. 2 vols. London: T. Egerton, 1801.

Heath, William. *General Orders Issued by Major General William Heath When in Command of the Eastern Department 23 May 1777–3 October 1777*. Brooklyn, N.Y.: Historical Printing Club, 1890.

———. *Memoirs of Major-General William Heath*. New York: William Abbatt, 1901.

Heitman, Francis B. *Historical Register of the Officers of the Continental*

Army during the War of the Revolution. Washington, D.C.: W. H. Lowdermilk & Co., 1893.

Henning, William W., ed. *The Statutes at Large: Being a Collection of All the Laws of Virginia from the First Session of the Legislature in the Year 1619.* 13 vols. Philadelphia: Thomas DeSilver, 1808–23.

Hinde, Robert. *Discipline of the Light Horse*. London: W. Owen, 1778.

Kastner, Georges. *Manuel général de musique militaire à l'usage des armées françaises*. Paris: Didot Frères, 1846.

Lawson, Cecil C. P. *A History of the Uniforms of the British Army*. 4 vols. London: P. Davies, 1940–66.

Lefferts, Charles M. *Uniforms of the American, British, French, and German Armies in the American Revolution*. New York: New York Historical Society, 1926.

Malibran, H. *Guide à l'usage des artistes et des costumiers contennant la description des uniformes de l'armée française de 1780 à 1848*. Paris: Boivin & Cie., 1907.

Massachusetts. *Massachusetts Soldiers and Sailors of the Revolutionary War*. 7 vols. Boston: Wright & Potter Printing Co., 1896–1908.

Miller, A. E. Haswell, and Dawnay, N. P. *Military Drawings and Paintings in the Collection of Her Majesty the Queen*. London: Phaidon Press, 1966.

Montross, Lynn. *Rag, Tag and Bobtail: The Story of the Continental Army, 1775–1783*. New York: Harper, 1952.

Peterson, Harold L. *The Book of the Continental Soldier*. Harrisburg: Stackpole Co., 1968.

Prussia. Kriegsministerium. *Regulations for the Prussian Infantry*. London: J. Nourse, 1759.

Riling, Joseph R. *Baron Von Steuben and His Regulations*. Philadelphia: Ray Riling Arms Books Co., 1966.

Schnapper, Edith B. *The British Union-Catalogue of Early Music*. 2 vols. London: Butterworths Scientific Publications, 1957.

Simes, Thomas. *A Military Course for the Government and Conduct of a Battalion: Designed for Their Regulations in Quarters, Camp, or Garrison*. London: Thomas Simes, 1777.

———. *Military Guide for Young Officers*. 2 vols. Philadelphia: J. Humphreys, R. Bell, and R. Aitken, 1776.

Sonneck, Oscar G. *Early Concert-Life in America*. New York: Musurgia Publishers, 1949.

———, and Upton, William T. *A Bibliography of Early Secular American Music*. New York: Da Capo Press, 1964.

Steuben, Friedrich, Baron von. *See*: United States. Inspector General's Office.

Sumner, Percy. "Army Inspection Returns—1753 to 1804." *Journal of the Society for Army Historical Research* 3 (1924):227–60; 4 (1925):23–27, 91–95, 104–16, 168–76; 5 (1926):25–33, 66–74, 126–31; 6 (1927): 159–64.

———. "Cox & Co., Army Agents. Uniform Items from Their Ledgers."

Journal of the Society for Army Historical Research 17 (1938):92–101, 135–57.

Thacher, James. *Military Journal of the American Revolution*. Hartford: Hurlbut, Williams & Co., 1862.

United States. Inspector General's Office. *Regulations for the Order and Discipline of the Troops of the United States*. Philadelphia: Styner and Cist, 1779, reprinted by Ray Riling Arms Books Co., 1966.

Ward, Christopher. *The War of the Revolution*. 2 vols. New York: Macmillan Co., 1952.

Warner, Thomas E. *An Annotated Bibliography of Woodwind Instruction Books, 1600–1830*. Detroit: Information Coordinators, 1967.

Washington, George. *The Writings of George Washington from the Original Manuscript Sources, 1745–1799*. Edited by John C. Fitzpatrick. 39 vols. Washington, D.C.: Government Printing Office, 1931–44.

Weigley, Russell F. *History of the United States Army*. New York: Macmillan Co., 1967.

Windham, William. *A Plan of Discipline Composed for the Use of the Militia of the County of Norfolk*. London: J. Shuckburgh, 1759.

Wolfe, Richard J. *Secular Music in America, 1801–1825*. 3 vols. New York: New York Public Library, 1964.

Wright, John W. *Some Notes on the Continental Army*. Vails Gate, N.Y.: National Temple Hill Association, 1963.

INDEX